a/long prairie lines:

AN ANTHOLOGY OF LONG PRAIRIE POEMS

a/long prairie lines:

AN ANTHOLOGY OF LONG PRAIRIE POEMS

DANIEL S. LENOSKI, EDITOR

TURNSTONE PRESS

Turnstone Press
607-100 Arthur Street
Winnipeg, Manitoba
Canada R3B 1H3

Turnstone Press gratefully acknowledges financial assistance from the following in the publication of this book:
Canada Council
Manitoba Arts Council
Saskatchewan Arts Board

This book was printed by Hignell Printing Limited.
Printed and bound in Canada.

Cover illustration by Dennis Burton, from his *Henry Kelsey Series I*, Chin-Chin and Pelikan India Ink and concentrated transparent water colour on cartridge paper, 18" x 24", 1981. Photography by Edward Cavell. This is one of nine illustrations from Burton's *Henry Kelsey Series* which were reproduced in Jon Whyte's *Homage, Henry Kelsey* (Winnipeg: Turnstone Press, 1981).

Dennis Burton describes himself as a "second-generation Toronto abstract expressionist 1956-65, a garterbelt-erotic-'pop' painter 1965-89." In 1970 he created a 6¢ stamp honouring Henry Kelsey for Canada Post. He has been a Foundation Division Instructor at Vancouver's Emily Carr College of Art and Design since 1980.

Cover design by Bruce Reimer, Lazer-fare Media Services

Canadian Cataloguing in Publication Data

Main entry under title:

A/long prairie lines: an anthology of long prairie poems

Includes bibliographical references.
ISBN: 0-88801-143-1

1. Canadian poetry (English)—Prairie Provinces*.
2. Canadian poetry (English)—20th century*.
I. Lenoski, Daniel S., 1943-

PS8295.5.P7A46 1989 C811/.54/0809712 C89-098171-X
PR9198.2.P68A46 1989

To
Brigitte
Anushka Stéphane
Erin Jason

that together we might see more sky

Acknowledgements and Permissions

HOMAGE, HENRY KELSEY, © Jon Whyte, is reprinted from *Homage, Henry Kelsey* (Winnipeg: Turnstone Press, 1981) by permission of the author.

THE FIRST WOMAN, © Lorna Crozier, is reprinted from *The Weather* (Moose Jaw: Coteau Books, 1983) by permission of the author and Coteau Books.

WILD MAN'S BUTTE, © Anne Szumigalski and Terrence Heath, is reprinted from *Wild Man's Butte* (Moose Jaw: Coteau Books, 1979) by permission of the authors.

THE WIND OUR ENEMY, © Anne Marriott, is reprinted from the Ryerson Poetry Chapbook Series (Toronto: Ryerson, 1939) by permission of the author. "The Wind Our Enemy" was reprinted in *The Circular Coast* (Oakville: Mosaic Press, 1984).

SEED CATALOGUE, © Robert Kroetsch, is reprinted from *Seed Catalogue* (Winnipeg: Turnstone Press, 1977) by permission of the author. "Seed Catalogue" is now part of *Field Notes, The Collected Poetry of Robert Kroetsch* (Toronto: General Publishing Co., 1981).

HOMESTEAD, 1914 (SEC. 32, TP4, RGE2, W3RD, SASK.), © Andrew Suknaski, is reprinted from *Wood Mountain Poems* (Toronto: Macmillan, 1976) by permission of the author.

THE SHUNNING, © Patrick Friesen, is reprinted from *The Shunning* (Winnipeg: Turnstone Press, 1980) by permission of the author.

GRASSHOPPER, © Helen Hawley, is reprinted from *Grasshopper* (Winnipeg: Turnstone Press, 1984) by permission of the author.

FIELDING, © Dennis Cooley, is reprinted from *Fielding* (Saskatoon: Thistledown Press, 1983) by permission of Thistledown Press.

MARSH BURNING, © David Arnason, is reprinted from *Marsh Burning* (Winnipeg: Turnstone Press, 1980) by permission of the author.

CALGARY, THIS GROWING GRAVEYARD, © Aritha van Herk, originally appeared in slightly different form in *NeWest Review*, Vol. 13, No. 4 (Dec. 1987). Reprinted by permission of the author.

"For this relief much thanks . . ."

to

all the authors and to Kate Bitney, Larry Desmond, Manuela Dias, Joe Donatelli, Father Harold Drake, Rosemary Dwyer, Bob Finnegan, Lucia Flynn, Gerry Friesen, Anita Gagnon-Kowalczuk, Eileen Holmes, Jan Horner, Paula Kelly, Claus Lappe, Fern Lewis, Harry Loewen, Mary-Beth Montcalm, Wayne Moodie, Donna Norell, Kathy Pettipas, Brian Philips, Bob Smith, Andris Taskans, Wayne Tefs, Roy Vogt, Bill Wsiaki, the Japanese Consulate in Winnipeg, the reference section of the Winnipeg Centennial Library, and the staff of St. Paul's College and St. John's College Libraries,

especially

Brigitte Lenoski, Marilyn Morton, Patricia Sanders

without whose help this anthology would have been impossible.

Don't break this circle
Before the song is over
Because all of our people
Even the ones long gone
Are holding hands

> Sarain Stump, "Round Dance"
> (1974), epigraph to *Tawow*
> Vol. 4, No. 3 (1974)

. . . at
last we become them

in our desires, our desires
mirages, mirrors, that are theirs, hard-
riding desires, and they
become our true forbears, moulded
by the same wind or rain,
and in this land we
are their people, come
back to life.

> John Newlove, "The Pride" (1968)

Contents

(Pre)face

OLD SONG

far voices
and fretting leaves
this music the
hillside gives

but in the deep
Laurentian river
an elemental song
for ever

a quiet calling
of no mind
out of long aeons
when dust was blind
and ice hid sound

only a moving
with no note
granite lips
a stone throat

LAURENTIAN SHIELD

Hidden in wonder and snow, or sudden with summer,
This land stares at the sun in a huge silence
Endlessly repeating something we cannot hear.
Inarticulate, arctic,
Not written on by history, empty as paper,
It leans away from the world with songs in its lakes
Older than love, and lost in the miles.

This waiting is wanting. . . .

The preceding lines were written by Frank Scott in 1928 and 1927 respectively, but they were constantly in my mind as I researched this anthology. Reading and rereading, pushing the margins of settlement further into the psychic and generic long-unpopulated space, made me increasingly aware of the significance of the long poem as an incarnation of the literary vocation in the prairie provinces. The long poem was clearly an appropriate literary form not only because it encompassed lyric experience on the frontier, but also, like the sprawling geography, it propagated the oral tradition of telling, "[o]ur endless talk,"[1] a tradition that Rudy Wiebe has identified in the "Introduction" to *The Story Makers* (1970) as especially strong in Western Canada.

In the above poems Scott is not speaking specifically about Manitoba, Saskatchewan and Alberta, but his words can be extended to the prairie itself even as the Shield gives way to the Great Plains in all three provinces and therefore in Jon Whyte's "Homage, Henry Kelsey" and David Arnason's "Marsh Burning."

Robert Kroetsch has said that the language of the Canadian space is silence.[2] This seems especially true of the prairies and the north. "Our inherited literature, the literature of the European past and of Eastern North America, is emphatically the literature of a people who have not lived on the prairies."[3] Despite the explosion of western writing since 1970, a large part of the region, Shield and prairie, remains unvoiced, dominated as yet by inanimate lips, a parched throat. And the long pcem itself, as Michael Ondaatje points out in the introduction to *The Long Poem Anthology* (1979), has been neglected by anthologists.

On the other hand, there *have* been a surprising number of attempts to speak in the genre on behalf of the region—many more than I anticipated. Once I began my explorations, my experience matched that of Ondaatje. Longer poetic forms began to pop up everywhere, like mushrooms in Manitoba.

Unfortunately, lost in the long distances of space and time, such voicing was "far," the sound of "fretting leaves" in the fall. It was losing contact with its potential audience; like the Shield in Scott's poem, it too was "wanting." That is, many long poems had fallen out of print, or were in danger of doing so soon. Thus, the *raison d'être* of my long enterprise was confirmed.

Indeed, only two of the poems in *a/long prairie lines* have been endowed with the power of echo and influence. Anne Marriott's modernist poem "The Wind Our Enemy" is a Canadian classic, while Robert Kroetsch's postmodern "Seed Catalogue"—where Marriott's stark prairie style and mosaic structure have been overgrown—has been reprinted several times. Ondaatje clearly honoured the influence of "Seed Catalogue" in *The Long Poem Anthology*. And, when we limit the space and view these works from the closer and flatter vantage point of the prairies, Kroetsch's and Marriott's poems grow even more in stature.

At the same time, like their less accessible counterparts, both possess an anxiety to retrieve the past and name the space. Dorothy Livesay has used the word "documentary" to identify other manifestations of this anxiety in the long poem in Canada[4] and David L. Jeffrey has rationalized such a quality by calling it the result of the Canadian's "felt *need* for history, both in its recollection and in its creation."[5] Continuing, Jeffrey quotes Rudy Wiebe: "The principal task of the Canadian writer, is not simply to explain his contemporary world; it is to create a past, a lived history, a vital mythology."[6] Jeffrey has pushed this approach even further by arguing that such a need is often manifested in Canadian writing in the motif of the search for family. Elsewhere, in the "Introduction" to *Stories from Western Canada* (1972), Wiebe has pointed out that westerners possess a special sensitivity to time and space that is inevitably part of the prairie literary vision as well. It is not surprising, then, that all the poems in this anthology explore the past extensively and seven of them do so by travelling through domestic environs.

At this point, however, it is important to observe that I am not equating poetry and formal history. The history manifested in this anthology and of which Jeffrey speaks is closer to what Robert Kroetsch, following Michel Foucault, has tagged "archeology":

> It . . . makes *this place* with all its implications, available to us for literary purposes. We have not yet grasped the whole story; we have hints and guesses that slowly persuade us toward the recognition of

> larger patterns. Archeology follows the fragmentary nature of the story against the coerced unity of traditional history. Archeology allows for discontinuity. It allows for layering. It allows for imaginative speculation. . . .[7]

Like the archeologist, the poet in the long poems in this volume is a "finding [wo]man who is essentially lost."[8] Many of the following poems approach the condition of documents in their urgency to embody the past. Found material is important to several of the anthologized poets. Jon Whyte prefaces "Homage, Henry Kelsey" with Kelsey's doggerel verse and follows Kelsey's journals in his exploration of Manitoba and Saskatchewan. In "Marsh Burning," David Arnason uses letters from the Manitoba Archives.

Dennis Cooley in "Fielding" and Anne Marriott in "The Wind Our Enemy" are similarly concerned with the *authentic*, providing us with prairie winter and summer at particular times and recording the sounds of the radio and the wind to prairie ears. Rather resembling the clown at the rodeo in *The Words of My Roaring* (1966), Robert Kroetsch not only saves Pete Knight from the dust under the hooves of "Slowdown," but conveys to us "traces"[9] of the design provided by the seed catalogue for the lives of prairie people in the thirties and forties. Arnason and Patrick Friesen in "The Shunning" similarly deal with the traces of the Icelandic and Mennonite experiences in Manitoba.

Kroetsch's reference to the "palimpsest" in "Seed Catalogue" seems, paradoxically enough, especially appropriate to foreground here. All of the writers in this collection—and a good many of the others who were candidates as well—are wrestling with the skeletal remains of a fading past, fading not merely because formal historians are ignoring it, not merely because Canada has been a colonized country, not merely because the west is viewed as politically, socially and fiscally less significant than Central Canada with its meccas—Toronto, Montreal, Hamilton or Ottawa—but also because *that* is the way of the world.

Indeed, especially sensitive to the rhythms of the region's space, the poets in this volume often acknowledge that birth and death are symbols of each other; they help define each other. As Kroetsch has put it in *The Lovely Treachery of Words*, "Even abandonment gives a memory."[10] Andrew Suknaski's "Homestead, 1914" and Dennis Cooley's "Fielding" are poems in which the parent is assessed in very different ways, but both imply that the way forward for the speaker is to explore the relationship with the parent. In neither poem is the father merely killed; instead, his remains are laid to rest within the literary corpus, or perhaps I should say, the *word* of the son. "There is always something left behind."[11] As we have learned from post-structuralism, the world is (re)-(in)vented.

The manifestations of this process on the level of narrative are more deliberate in some poems than in others and often recall Livesay's description of the intercourse between poets and the forbears they have discovered in their "dig(s)." She sees this as a "conscious attempt to create a dialectic between the objective facts and the subjective feelings of the poet."[12] Whyte, Kroetsch, Arnason, van Herk, Suknaski, Cooley and Friesen interpret the past even while they record it. At the same time, a blend of voices, of subject and object, occurs in their writing. Thus, in "Homage, Henry Kelsey" and "The First Woman," both poets play with voice until the reader is no more capable of separating Crozier from Marie Anne Lagimodière or Jon Whyte from his literary ancestor than we are of excising the spirit of Louis Riel from Johnny Canuck or from "the first woman" herself.

Like professional explorers and archeologists, the poets in this volume not only stride through time, moving back and forth along the energy lines between their discoveries and themselves, but they also find naming and travelling through space crucial to their discipline. In fact, Arnason, van Herk, Hawley, Cooley, Kroetsch, Whyte, Kelsey and Crozier seem almost obsessed with both. Arnason travels west on the Trans-Canada Highway from the Maritimes and southwest from Iceland to Gimli, naming as he travels. And an entire section of his poem does almost nothing but name things indigenous to the shores of Lake Winnipeg. Such naming confers existence on the west as a cultural entity of value and dignity. Such naming says: "Hey, here we are! We have something to say! We have sounds and sights and images . . . history and stories and people that are as silly *and* as profound as you Brits, Yanks, Frenchmen and Easterners." It "selves" us.

The footnotes in this volume were meant to augment such selving.

Despite the fact that much of the poetry in *a/long prairie lines* is "writerly"[13] and travels along postmodern frontiers, the notes are designed to provide some hospitality and direction for a voyage through the physical, psychic and verbal geography of Western Canada—even as one does when an outsider or a relative visits one's home. Besides, if more celebrated and well-known poets from other countries can be sanctified by notes, perhaps Canadian poets can too. Finally, one of my major criticisms as a teacher as well as a reader of Canadian poetry has been that often editors in this country haven't dated poems, nor provided information about the history of publication, about words, names, and places not readily accessible.

As implied above, my choices were determined by a literary corpus that operated as explorer, archeologist, namer, traveller and actor in an attempt to retrieve a faded past, a fading present in a place often called "Next Year Country." Not all the poems I encountered operated as such, but a large proportion did. Accordingly, like many of the poets in the tradition, leaping through vast distances of space and time, and from one level of being to another, playing archeologist, explorer, traveller and namer, I tried hard to cover as many western constituencies—genderic, geographical, historical, ethnic, rural, urban and domestic—as possible. For example, "Calgary, this growing graveyard" was included first because it's a good poem, but also because it is one of the few long urban poems I encountered; it is also by an Albertan. *And*, it deals with urban history that is pointed far beyond Calgary itself. Van Herk, like many others, is mythmaking, transforming the bread of history into the eucharist of myth. So are Anne Szumigalski and Terrence Heath. But "Wild Man's Butte" covers slightly different ground. It is not a loosely structured postmodern phenomenon but a Romance engendered by a man and woman that operates on the personal, cultural and archetypal level and manifests both Native and pioneer experience amid the harshness of the Saskatchewan Badlands.

On the other hand, as Lorna Crozier has pointed out in the "Preface" to *A Sudden Radiance* (1987), for many of us the prairie has long ago ceased to be alien as Edward McCourt, Henry Kriesel and Laurence Ricou see it.[14] It is home. Accordingly, I was concerned that this space be represented as attractive as well as dangerous. Despite the fact that Helen Hawley's "Grasshopper" reveals a wanderer encountering a fragmented society, it also manifests a search for a locus beyond the literal, a mythical prairie space . . . home. Similarly, though "Marsh Burning," "Fielding" and "The Shunning," not to mention several of the other poems, deal with the death and suffering that has been part of our tradition, they also reveal the prairie experience as familiar, domestic and ordinary—to coin a phrase, "lightning *and* love," "a winter and warm."[15] Here the magical and the mythical emerge from the mundane and work-a-day rather than the formidable; we are inside as well as outside the house.

Of course, some constituencies were not visited, not adequately represented. Ondaatje's citation of the words of Calvino's Count of Monte Christo is as appropriate here as in his anthology: "In planning a book . . . the first thing to know is what to exclude."[16] Thus, not sufficiently heard is the voice of the early prairie experience implied by such poetry as Douglas Durkin's *The Fighting Men of Canada* (1918) and Robert Wilson's *Dreams of Fort Garry* (1931). There we encounter attempts to glorify the ordinary man and document the western experience during war-time. However, the rhythms of sound and psyche speak of elsewhere as much as the subject matter speaks of here. Though these poems were of historical interest, they were also aesthetically inappropriate.

Similarly omitted were long poems written by Natives or Francophones, though the experience of both is often voiced vicariously in this volume. Both traditions have certainly interacted in a fertile manner with the Anglophone one and early in my deliberations I did search vigorously through Francophone poetry of the west, not to mention Native poetry such as *The Wishing Bone Cycle.*[17] But these are important *parallel* traditions, often written in other Canadian languages, and should be the topic of further consideration by scholars and readers who operate in closer proximity to them than I can, or in closer proximity than translation allows. Thus, I decided to concentrate on the Anglophone manifestation of the long prairie poem. *Here*, especially painful were the exclusion of—among many others—Barry McKinnon's fine poem *I Wanted to Say Something* (1975), Marion R.

Smith's *Prairie Child* (1974), Eli Mandel's "Prologue to Blood Lines" (1977), John Newlove's "The Pride" (1968), Don Gutteridge's *Riel: a poem for voices* (1968), Ed Dyck's *The Mossbank Canon* (1982) and any selection from either Kristjana Gunnars' *Settlement Poems 1* (1980) and *2* (1980) or from Watson Kirkconnell's *The Flying Bull and Other Tales* (1949). The latter in particular I will return to often. It operates in the spirit of the tall tale, full of wild hyperbole, lyricism and humour, and I highly recommend it.

In any case, all anthologies can be blamed for omissions. Indeed, as a reviewer I have done some of the blaming myself—though I bitterly regret it at the moment. Nevertheless, in this anthology I have tried to represent the prairie wing of the Canadian corpus of long poems that seems to be growing rapidly. In doing so I have hoped to honour the poets, the voices they represent, the genre and the reader as well. It is perhaps appropriate, then, that the title of the first poem in the anthology begins with the word "Homage."

Daniel S. Lenoski
St. Paul's College
University of Manitoba
November 7, 1989

---

1. Robert Kroetsch, "The Moment of the Discovery of America Continues," *The Lovely Treachery of Words* (Toronto: Oxford University Press, 1989), p. 17.

2. "Introduction," *Boundary* 2, 3, No. 1 (Fall 1974), 1-2.

3. Robert Kroetsch, "The Moment of the Discovery of America Continues," *The Lovely Treachery of Words*, p. 5.

4. "The Documentary Poem: A Canadian Genre," *Contexts of Canadian Criticism*, ed. Eli Mandel (Chicago and London: University of Chicago Press, 1971).

5. David L. Jeffrey, "Biblical Hermeneutic and Family History in Contemporary Canadian Fiction: Wiebe and Laurence," *Mosaic* XI, 3 (Spring 1978), 88.

6. *Ibid.*

7. "The Moment of the Discovery of America Continues," *The Lovely Treachery of Words*, p. 7.

8. "For Play and Entrance: The Contemporary Canadian Long Poem," *The Lovely Treachery of Words*, p. 129.

9. "Where I had learned the idea of absence, I was beginning to learn the idea

of 'trace.' There is always something left behind." "The Moment of the Discovery of America Continues," *The Lovely Treachery of Words*, p. 2.

10. *Ibid.*

11. *Ibid.*

12. "The Documentary Poem: A Canadian Genre," *Contexts of Canadian Criticism*, p. 267.

13. See Roland Barthes, *S/Z*, trans. Richard Miller (New York: Hill and Wang, 1974), pp. 4-6.

14. See *The Canadian West in Fiction* (1949), "The Prairie: a State of Mind" (1968), *Vertical Man/Horizontal World* (1973). The views of all three are included in *Essays in Saskatchewan Writing*, ed. Ed Dyck (Regina: Saskatchewan Writers' Guild, 1986), pp. 33-78.

15. "The Wreck of the Deutschland" (1875), *The Poems of Gerard Manly Hopkins*, ed. N.H. McKenzie (London: Oxford University Press, 1967), p. 54.

16. "What is in the Pot," *The Long Poem Anthology* (Toronto: Coach House Press, 1979), p. 11.

17. *Narrative Poems from the Swampy Cree Indians*, trans. H.D. Norman (Santa Barbara: Ross-Erikson Pub., 1982).

a/long prairie lines:

AN ANTHOLOGY OF LONG PRAIRIE POEMS

Homage, Henry Kelsey[1]

Jon Whyte

the river flows both ways

Henry Kelsey: His Poem[2]

Now Reader Read for I am well assur'd
Thou dost not know the hardships I endur'd
In this same desert where Ever y^t I have been
Nor wilt thou me believe without y^t thou had seen
The Emynent Dangers that did often me attend
But still I lived in hopes y^t once it would amend
And makes me free from Hunger & from Cold
Like wise many other things wch I cannot here unfold
For many times I have often been opprest
With fears & Cares y^t I could not take my rest
Because I was alone & no friend could find
And once y^t in my travels I was left behind
Which struck fear & terror into me
But still I was resolved this same Country for to see
Although through many dangers I did pass
Hoped still to undergo y^m at the Last
Now Considering y^t it was my dismal fate
for to repent I Thought it now to late
Trusting still unto my masters Consideration
Hoping they will Except of this my small Relation
Which here I have pend & still will Justifie
Concerning of those Indians & their Country
If this wont do farewell to all as I may say
And for my living i'll seek some other way

In sixteen hundred & ninety'th year
I set forth as plainly may appear
Through Gods assistance for to understand
The natives language & to see their land
And for my masters interest I did soon
Sett from y^e *house*[3] y^e *twealth of June*
Then up y^e *River I with heavy heart*
Did take my way & from all English part
To live amongst y^e *Natives of this place*
If god permits me for one two years space
The Inland Country of Good report hath been
By Indians but by English not yet seen
Therefore I on my Journey did not stay
But making all y^e *hast I could upon our way*
Gott on y^e *borders of* y^e *stone Indian Country*
I took possession on y^e *tenth Instant July*
And for my masters I speaking for y^m *all*
This neck of land I deerings point did call[4]
Distance from hence by Judgement at y^e *lest*
From y^e *house six hundred miles southwest*
Through Rivers w^{ch} *run strong with falls*
thirty three Carriages five lakes in all[5]
The ground begins for to be dry with wood
Poplo & birch with ash thats very good
For the Natives of that place w^{ch} *knows*
No use of Better than their wooden Bows
According to y^e *use & custom of this place*
In September I brought those Natives to a peace
But I had no sooner from those Natives turnd my back
Some of the home Indians came upon their track
And for old grudges & their minds to fill
Came up with them six tents of w^{ch} *they kill'd*
This ill news kept secrett was from me
Nor none of those home Indians did I see
Untill that they their murder all had done
And the Chief acter was he y^{ts} *call* y^e *Sun*[6]

So far I have spoken concerning of the spoil
And no will give acco.^{t} of that same Country soile
Which hither part is very thick of wood
Affords small nutts wth littele cherryes very good
Thus it continues till you leave ye woods behind
And then you have beast of severall kind
The one is a black a Buffillo great
Another is an ougrown Bear wch is good meat
His skin to gett I have used all ye ways I can
He is mans food & makes food of man
His hide they would not me it preserve
But said it was a god & they should Starve
This plain affords nothing but Beast & grass
And over it in three days time we past
getting unto ye woods on the other side
It being about forty sixe miles wide
This wood is poplo ridges with small ponds of water
there is beavour in abundance but no Otter
with plains & ridges in the Country throughout
Their Enemies many whom they cannot rout
But now of late they hunt their Enemies
And with our English guns do make y^{m} flie
At deerings point after the frost
I set up their Certain Cross
In token of my being there
Cut out on it ye date of year
And Likewise for to veryfie the same
added to it my master sir Edward deerings name[7]
So having no more to trouble you wth all I am
Sir your most obedient & faithfull Servt at Command

Henry Kelsey

Part ye First: List

The material relating to Henry Kelsey is so meagre that even the most commonplace fragments may be worthy of record.

Arthur G. Doughty and Chester Martin,
Introduction, *The Kelsey Papers*, xxiv

Ungava[8]
not the land Ungava
beyond horizon where man feels home
but
ungava
in the eye's lee
until a
moment grasps man   by his imagination
stretching in yearning   relaxing his thoughts

Ungava
is sallied forth from
England is an ungava

and in the reek of spring's melting
    in summer's florescence
    in patch-spotted swathing
    in maturing
here is not a land beyond the eye or memory
    in winter's dim and still
    beyond vision's rim
    but   here

I

am
Ungava
quickened by paddle's brush
gliding canoe
through silent lake and riverrush

If this wont do farewell to all as I may say
And for my living i' ll seek some other way

Speaking to himself, he speaks to us

In sixteen hundred & ninety'th year
I set forth as plainly may appear
through God's assistance for to understand
The natives language & to see their land
And for my masters interest I did soon
Sett from ye house ye twealth of June

out of isolation

Then up ye River I with heavy heart
Did take my way & from all English part
To live amongst ye Natives of this place
If god permits me for one two years space

Seekwan[9]
and the trumpeter swan returns
the long-beaked whimbrel[10] shores to summerhome
curlews whisper in the lengthening dusk and dawn of
spring
as seekwan is noise again
nostrils twitching odours from the snow's melt
the sun felt is seekwan
beneath the daily climbing sun
seek wandering
eyes rise
to the blunt horizon

it is
spring rivulets creeks flooding anew rivers flowing
forcing their ice to pack, crush, melt, overflow,
rumbling the heart stirring in the bosque[11] of
seek wondering

spring in the spring of birds and their song returning
buds, birds, cubs, calves, fawns and dawns warm
and incredible in the sparkle, ooze and hues of green,
seeping, washing waters and the rotting mosses' reek
seek wander
and be born again beyond
the sun setting lustwandering
no time for rest
stir, step, stride, walk, wander, follow, pursue,
sequent seekwan

Between the tangent drawn aslant the dream's nivation[12]
of sense: the ways things seem: locus of history about
a centre
a vision forming landscape
a manner of seeing
in the current of circumstance
by the south branch of the middle road

From ye house six hundred miles southwest
Through Rivers wch run strong with falls
thirty three Carriages five lakes in all

(by the Knee, Oxford, Walker, Cross, and Moose)[13]

to travel and to penetrate into the country
of the Assinae Poets,[14] with the Captain of that Nation
to call, encourage, and invite the remoter Indians
to a trade with us

the Echimamish[15]
flows both ways

West to the Nelson East to the Hayes

in time

dawnhunter in barrens
hunter of mastodon, mammoth
fear of the soft-stepping tiger
the giant bear lording his domain
at glaciers' toe

Upon
the debacle in spring
frazil[16] surfacing in autumn's decline
in the rivers' sinews beneath the sun-dogged sky

Kelsey stands

Hail Kelsey, come: the land is not barren,
land of little sticks, caribou lichen, musketers only;
come to the land: the land is not barren,
the land that is mused, is browsed, is fused
by mooseways over, among, between, and through
the muskrat-slickened banks of oozing mud,
its list aboil, aswarm with mosquitoes,
the must of melting and dispersing such a wonder
of flying, biting, cloud turmoiling things;
come to the land: the land is not barren;
the glaciers' scores on the rusty rock reveal
that life withdrew but has returned;
come, Kelsey, come to the land.

The Inland Country of Good report hath been
By Indians but by English yet not seen
Therefore I on my Journey did not stay
But making all ye hast I could upon our way
Gott on ye borders of ye stone Indian Country
I took possession on ye tenth Instant July
And for my masters I speaking for y^m all
This neck of land I deerings point did call

Name, namer, new master now
with fame ill-fit on Rupert's Land
trading across three centuries

> *for the use and benefitt of the Gov*^{r}
> *and Comp*^{y} *of adventurers of England*
> *trading into Hudsons Bay and their Successors*[17]

ourselves as well, who cannot be so easily assured,

> *Thou dost not know the hardships I endur'd*
> *In this same desert where Ever y*^{t} *I have been*

Just   In the web and texture of the land
is woven more than we can understand

> *Nor wilt thou me believe without y*^{t} *thou had seen*
> *The Emynent Dangers that did often me attend*

It does not begin nor end, hence we converse:
hunger, the stomach shrinking, the masked rocks of rapids,
the abuse of anger, the flare of feelings amid fear
and companions' enemies, canoes overturning, fire,
starvation peering through the lankness of the clouds,
fear of murder in the insolence of midnight,
being lost in uncharted woods in winter
where rivers fall away to darkness,
gestures of friendship taken as defiance,
unfamiliar beasts, unknown customs, the undiscovered hemlocks,
unease, disease, and always the threat
the land's maw will swallow a man
nor leave a trace of him on swamp or grassland,
in trees or in the woodland meadow,
deceiving man who thinks he knows himself

Language falls behind in the rivers' newness,
rumoured to run red as murderous blood in summer's flood,
of flesh-smooth land as soft as youth,
as old as archaic stone the glacier bared to sun.

But still I was resolved this same Country for to see
Although through many dangers I did pass
Hoped still to undergo y^{m} at the Last

It flows both ways

Calving glacial ice,
the blue-green dragon
meets in gravel
lichens breaking the greyness in golden rust,
and south, as the ice-chilled wind warmed,
came soft-spring-green grass
rooting in the till and rotting, forming soil
for hunter to walk upon softly, silently
as great cats walk.

The woods creep north to where they grow no higher
and who would live there hunts without hiding.

Rivers meander
grey in the misted morning: thick daybreak

Silence is born of the marriage of deep wonder and winter

Morning song of meadowlark
rejoicing from wild rice stalks

Sky blueness blunts the horizon

Stillness
the centre of wonder

Is
Ungava
obscured within the mind
beyond a loon-called loneliness?

The fog clings to the slow waters

It is time to shuck the hides, tighten muscles,
slide the canoes from the slick banks into the musty air,
glide on the ripples, seek the misted sun through oblique shadows

seek the river

in the muskrat country
between the tracks
upon a pan of snow

seek Miss-Top-Ashish
Little Giant
Henry Kelsey[18]

The land you saw we cannot begin to see
'til what you see reveals the world,
and we have just begun to be aware of an Ungava
about to brim up in our eyes and solitudes

in the wildlands and in your Ungava yet

we see you

now
standing in the
world alone
you made

Part ye Second: Etomami[19]

. . . he had been so near to ye sun at ye going down
y^{t} he could take hold of it when it Cut ye Horrizon

The Kelsey Papers, 23

Once we know where once he was,
we cannot tell when he was there;
whither once he went we know,
we cannot tell when he was thither.

Where
and when

Then
and there

at the mind's edge
at its edges
beyond me
is no substance
unstriking light
at the warmth's edge
where the
last shadow
standing
I fancy
I see movement
I hesitate
in the gloom

it is always dark
I squint
my shadow
dissipates
in darkness
I turn my back
trees glimmer
engulfed in shadow
peering into darkness
I see
I hope
my eyes darting
I thought it black

now it's night
darkness
more than mute
absorbent
adumbrated
directionless

bleak
mute
carbon silence
unrelinquishing
deep
bearingless

I could turn   back to blackness
gaze into the fire   my hands bask in
its pale phantoms   cold comfort
attract   in the chill
the edges   fade
the dark's ways   into luke-dim
unending   silence

But still I lived in hopes y^{t} once it would amend
And makes me free from Hunger & from Cold
Likewise many other things wch I cannot here unfold

knowing   which way they'd gone
I'd not be lost   in terror
not knowing   if their way is
doubting   alert to absence
in skepticism   to retrace steps
dusk falling   into night
night sounds   stars emerging
owls calling   rodent rustle
bittern booming   dark shape
not finding   turning back

Now Considering y^{t} it was my dismal fate
for to repent I Thought it now to late

In
a forest
of similarities
we find our path by slight distinctions
the aberrant, the taller tree
lush moonferns beside a spring
a slight displacement
a witch's broom[20]
a tree's growth slowed by fire scorch
a line of fire
a paler green in slightly younger spruce
except

when strangers are
in strange uncertainty,
dark forests' certain strangeness,

nothing is knowable

the echoes taunt
seem to "Holloa!" assuredly
in willows, cinquefoils, Labrador tea[21]
cougar, wolverine, or bear
or some unknown worse thing rustles:
I must be still:
friends'll shout:
I must shout

And once y^{t} *in my travels I was left behind*
Which struck fear & terror into me

Being lost
where you seem
ignorant
wandering
plunging on
dissembling
grievance, grief, gratitude
no longer figure

knowing
to be
where the others
ahead
think you ahead
laughing at fear
assume an attitude
in sullen valour

Because I was alone & no friend could find

alone
the lost
in circles
come upon their own fear
fatally

remembering
aimlessly
stumbling
snaring themselves
in a question

But still I was resolved this same Country for to see

Fixed, still waiting
quarry seeks you
as you seek it

For many times I have often been oppresst
With fears & Cares y^{t} I could not take my rest

lank after long walking the tendons chafe,
in the cold the rib cage caves,
in snow stumbling,
partaking in ritual and blaspheming,
belly weak after long hunger,
eating the dogs,
gluttony in the after-kill excess,
belly's sore swelling
heaving in sickness,
damp powder, wet moccasins,
feet blue cold beside the ashen embers,
blindness in the light after the storm,
an all-white vacancy
in whiteness lost
lost
in the wrong language speaking
knives flash

reverting to English,
ground blizzards,
the stench of the middens by noon thaw,
maggots crawling from the roasting meat,
bears devour carrion,
silence overwhelming
and at my side
her
the long night
lengthening nights and
always in strength and in warmth

Impossible, impassible winter walls us,
return to the fort now a failure
kindling their laughter

Soft bog sucks moccasins by the beaked sedge,
ducks through the pondweed emerge,
mudroots in their bills,
wind sways the long-stalked cattails drying,
the bright eyes of muskrats gleam at the water's edge.

Woods thin,
temper thins,
untempered muscles
twitch under skin

The women gather the last berries for pemmican:
autumn rots, decays.

The ground begins for to be dry with wood
Poplo & birch with ash thats very good
For the Natives of that place wch knows
No use of Better than their wooden Bows
According to ye use & custom of this place

A weapon of dexterity and grace,
supple from summers' faster growth and hard
and tight from winters'; by bole of branch unmarred;
in fall selected for the straightest bough,
shaped to a thumb's thickness where a left hand now
holds it erect, but narrowing to its ends
where harp-strung sinew tightens, bends
its flexing, tautens it to muscles' tension
against their own, as if their own intention
hewed their weapon from their thews; its swift
and pointed sapling arrow the bow can lift
a tree's height in arc and plummet from that height
into a moose's heart, darkening its flight;
sustains their enmity they will not cease.

In September I brought these Natives to a peace

no willows wail
nor night wind rises

But I had no sooner from those Natives turnd my back
Some of the home Indians came upon their track

moccasin silent
the blade silent

And for old grudges & their minds to fill
Came up with them Six tents of wch they kill'd

knife-slit throats
the warm blood flows
men's and women's

This ill news kept secrett was from me

their gore is the same

Nor none of those home Indians did I see

whispering in the reeds

Untill that they their murder all had done
And the Chief acter was he y^{ts} call ye Sun

It better were   he ran away
as history held   for centuries

Thus it continues till you leave ye woods behind
And then you have beast of severall kind
The one is a black a Buffillo great
whose size would call forth titan's tumult
summoning trumpeted speeches from dumb mouths

and in his majesty the thunderheads
roil in his cumulus hulking shoulders' mass
of curls that become the robe in winter will
sustain us in the sharp winds' blast;
his great horned head is higher than mine own
and bears his pride, even when lazily he grazes
the eared grass, champing delicately;
then when he rolls the dust he raises
darkens the sky; he snorts like bellows in a forge;
he drums in running like the sound of deep waves
pounding on the shores of this inland sea of grass;
in spring their bodies filled the rivers
and on the banks their bodies piled up
and ravens sat and ate their eyes and brains.

At the last of summer's false return the bison
clouded the plain turned sky unto horizon
and at their burrows' entrances the squirrels
awaited licks of wind, dustdevil whirls,
to sully the yellow, golden, pale blue flowers
of asters, ragweed, bergamot in hours
drying, reseeding this land "of good report,"
so pale, once bountiful, unlike the fort
I left in spring's onset to undertake
this inland journey for my masters' sake.

Trusting still unto my masters Consideration
Hoping they will Except of this my small Relation
Which here I have pend & still will Justifie
Concerning of those Indians & their Country

Rarely is it given to a man to find
a continent to which his homeland's blind,
and wander in it freely two swift years
of joy and awe and wonder, yet in fears
he'll not return; and carefree yet, unheeding
terror, disentangle what is needing:
commerce, comfort, shelter, peace in the land,
all of which the Indians little understand.

But still I was resolved this same Country for to see
Although through many dangers I did pass
Hoped still to undergo y^m *at the Last*

Mind is
wide and trackless
overwhelms
us
despairing
as
under
clouds
uncontained metaphor
prairie is
coursed
shaped
asundered
till what is left
is primacy

atoms of
irreducibility
in
plain
force
what he feels
prosaically

as later
he wrote

prairie
earth and air
inculcate
a calculus of
moving
homunculi
accumulate
the unanswerable
mind
doubt
by rivers
by glaciers
by wind
diminishes
and rebegins

thought
conjoins
concept
speech
utterance
must express itself
in poetry

secrets
in Indian tongue

they have but two or three Words in a song
& they observe to keep time along with him
y^t is ye leader of ye song
for Every man maketh his own songs
by vertue of w^t he dreams of

systole[22]

golden autumn
shrinks seed

diastole

rose hips wrinkle
leaf mulch

systole

burnt red
willow tips

diastole

cold clarity
in the stream

systole

aspen ignite
yellow, birch yellow

diastole

grassyellow, passing yellow
burnished willow

systole

pigeons shot
wood sounds dying

diastole

mourning, soughing
lowing, moaning

systole

crowd crows
raucous, murderous

diastole

eve of migration
owls' ululation

systole

piebald ermine
weasels vary
diastole

geese vee
hare vary
systole
hawks depart
bears den
diastole

quietus
silence
systole
distance
water
diastole

The tracing wavering of a skipping pen
on frail and fraying, ancient, greying paper—
a splotched gooseberry on snow

Distance from hence by Judgement at y^e *lest*
From y^e *house six hundred miles southwest*

Nothing is knowable except uncertainty

His direction known whence did he come

Place unknown when he was there

& at y^e *Conclusion of every song*
they give thanks all in general to him
y^t y^e *song belongs too*
So likewise if any one hath crost or vext them
y^t *they owe him any grudge*
they will pretend to set w^t *they dream of to work*
& it shall kill the offender at his pleasure

Trace
place of beginning
place of end
and
the one who returns
is not who went out

circuit incomplete

He disappears
gains momentum, escapes
vanishes
in the ways of likeness

is lost

Define thyself
consider thy autumns
keep silence

The muskrat inhale the bubbles, faces beneath the ice,
then back down into the black water vanish;
loon swimming in a shrinking circle of closing ice
bargain till the room for taking flight is gone;
a cacophony of scavengers—jays, ravens, coyotes, carcajous—[23]
argue over the scraps of the wolves' kill.

(Listen:)
the air is quiet
(Listen:)
the melody attenuates
largo notes fragmenting
drone dirge
concealing lethargy

life's almost silent
music's yet in silence
shapes silence
in which it is at rest
sweet

spontaneous

silence

Insurgent wave, ocean journey, the hyperboreal strait

lost in time   in wilderness unending
lost in world   in time expanding
lost   becoming

something other
forgotten and reclaimed

Etomami, its two ways clear
South to Assiniboine, north to Red Deer

The river flows both ways

where it reverses   unexplorably shifts

great eddies wheeling
capture flotsam
suspend it at the torrents' edges
an unstill point that stays
borne in current by the current
stilling time in motions' space
against the frisson of the flowing
while whirling
smaller eddies whirl around
and at their edges
still smaller
until still points of spinning
nothing
nothing turn and wheel away

Time vanishes   in the flow of metaphor

Tone slows   lean in richness

margin   zone of grey   disappearance   horizon   fade

simultaneity
similarity

plucked into present
from behind grey castle walls
bleak backdrop to Irish fields[24]
where cattle champ
a castle kept
secrets
and profits from the furs

synchronicity
spontaneity

systole

the bright secret

diastole

plangent in bushes
the dry leaves
crabbed letters in an old hand
two centuries
memory of Dobbs
not smashing the link
the lad, nineteen

accomplishing
coming back alive

cabinet or closet
paper rustlings
the writing decipherable
the suppression
willing to conceal but
that would reveal
difficult to remember
in the stature
just
not failing in commerce

Red blood the red water
flowing in the runnelled surface
ripples, swells
in standing waves and ice
coats the boulders

changing the shapeless torrent of life into a discrete quantity

language is a vehicle the universe decrees
for its description creating spaces
for another space to exist
silence between utterances in space
in which are acts acts begetting facts
in which words form totem, factotum
fact, act, fiction the thing made
in space a journey made
made journeyman's creation
time isolating
into Autumn the declining sun
narrows river day by day
before after
here and there
are abstracts
without meaning
there is a point at which
something is nothing
and nothing is something
clear water at sunset encased
silver ice sluggish beneath mica
stored willows wavering the current
wind wane leaf gold near stillness

black blossoms rose hips the flatness

ground mist glisten deer listen

berry-eating bear in the cool aspen

in the dark spruce forest

primeval mind until

one by one the stars appear

eldritch spruce silhouette fantasies

magnify the slipping sky

owl calling season eyes

in the darkness staring

query quarry keenly

qwho quiver

shivering taut

drum snare canopy

singing chant

beyond meaning

Part y[e] Third: Nivation

History begins in Novel and ends in Essay . . .

Macaulay, "History and Literature"[25]

Winter is wolf waiting for man to falter;
lowing wind, flowing moon, blowing snow;
o stray and wandering words, stay
    with me a while

O strange, bewildering thoughts
bred of the tempest, borne by the storm
born of winter

    The blue wolf howls

The savage faces of the land,
masks of fir, eyes of ice and mystery
salvage my spars

    The spruce tree cracks

Yet above me, over reader as over writer,
wheel the sustaining stars

    O God, be merciful

Sparks rise in the fire's night flare;
warmth and memory cling to the embers.

The wind is singing in a woman's voice,
dark and mysterious is the wind;
the land lies fertile yielding to me,
the sun is silver and the sky is bright,
and I am called by the wind to the land,
the wind which is singing in a woman's voice
and the land that lies like a woman lying
beneath the sun which burns in the air
bared to the warmth of the hovering sun
which clings like a burr in the sky,
and the wind is singing, soft as moaning—
"There is a meaning, meaning meaning"
soft in the hush of summer wind
soft as the sweetgrass flows like hair
in the wind that hesitates in its harmony
ever returning as a memory,
waving and washing the clouds and sky,
brushing the cottonwoods under the sun;
wishing wind will come as a woman,
soft as fair as sun of summer and brushing
as the wind is hushing a soft and summer day.

Summer and winter, river and wind:
I am adrift on smoke;
wind that between the nunatuks[26] blew
blows where the ice is gone.

Here Oomingmuk persists the pale red dawn,
raises the bearded one his hornwall head,
blue eyes searching through the arctic smoke,
for over the long night's gulf
he hears the rising howl of a wolf.

Time is rising on the fire
into the winter night;
summer and winter, fire and smoke,
my eyes discern no light.

The ice plate wanes
and the mammoths and mastodons, tapirs and mylodons,
tigers and horses fall on the bier of time;
and only the muskox lives on the arctic edge
where to the howl of the wolf and the wind
he raises his ancient head.
Fluid in summer with the grass he flows with,
in lichen patina on ancient rock;
in winter bull and herd are one.

June 25th 1689	*forc'd ashore by ye Ice* *now we Judged our selves to be about 20 Leagues* *from Churchill River*
y^{e} *29th* *Thursday*	*This days Journey most part ponds & hills . . .* *found an old Cannoe of those northern Indians* *abundance of Musketers*
y^{e} *30th* *friday*	*travelled all within Land it being all hills* *& more barren then before* *ye hills being all stones wth a coat of moss over y^{m}*
July y^{e} *2^{d}* *Sunday*	*it Raind hard* *having no shelter but ye heavens for a Cannope* *nor no wood to make a fire*

Bending north to summer's sill, winter's threshold
face to face

ye 9th *sunday*	*Setting forward good weather* *& going as it were on a Bowling green* *in ye Evening spyded Two Buffillo*[27] *left our things & pursued y^{m}* *we Kill'd one* *they are ill shapen beast* *their Body being bigger than an ox*

leg & foot like ye same
but not half so long a long neck & head a hog
their Horns not growing like other Beast
but Joyn together upon their forehead
& so come down ye side of their head & turn up
till ye tips be Even wth ye Buts
their Hair is near a foot long

On the wind the howl of the wolves,
their circle pack and the snow hard, crusted, and the wind:
always the wail on the wind.

Borne to the bearded ones, wail within wail,
is the mingled odour of fear and hunger,
and the herd of muskoxen, heads in the lee of the storm,
snow coning about the hollows of their bulk, wait,
hearing the keening, turn toward struggle in shadow.

The form of the enemy is memory,
recollection, not form,
forced into shape by instinct's code,
the old intrinsic coping within drama.

Round and insistent is the dream and the ring
of the herd and the pack and the rising wind;
the barrier of buttress behind which instinct dwells,
guard ring of bulls about cows and calves.

The tyranny of instinct fails.
Bulls, calves, cows, all fall

What wolves are these,
striking and biting from unseen hills?

Phalanx of instinct fails.

Smoke traces smoke;
seek smoke and find flare.

It had been undertaken to send *the boy Henry Kelsey*
to Churchill River with Thomas Savage because . . .
he is a very active Lad delighting much in Indians Company
being never better pleased than when
he is Travelling amongst them

Who recognized the stranger returned?

Kelsey *was not sensable of ye dangers.*
Those to whom he reported now were strangers.

Two summers since,
a winter in the fort between,
now wintering darkness.
Who could be aught except insensible?
Look back to the boyhood now you are beyond:
you discerned it, enriched it, lived it
when your beard was no darker than
the land of little sticks in sifting snow.

In 83 I went out in ye ship Lucy Jno outlaw command^{r}[28]
an ocean's breadth between your home and land
in 88 after 3 indians being employ'd for great rewards
to carry letters from hays river to new severn[29] *they return'd*
wthout performing ye business altho paid
then was I sent wth an indian boy
& in a month return'd wth answers

Memory surges as the water in the wake of the canoe,
veering scintillas away from the prow;
the darkness opens now:
In 89 Capt James young[30]
put me & ye same Indian boy ashore
to ye N^{o}ward of Churchill river
in order to bring to a commerce ye N^{o}thern indians
but we saw none altho we travell'd above 200 miles
in search of y^{m} : finding darkness in the summer

Perhaps it should stand: "I ran away."
It might as well have been.
Ran to the mystery the shore concealed,
ran to the forest darkness, or from Geyer[31] and his punishment,
as some would say, upon some *Boyish misbehaviour* chastised, I fled
and Geyer made *a Merit* of my *going up*
which Geyer undertook it was his own idea.

To him to whom the wind has sung orders mean little.
Honour I accorded his lord shagginess,
peering from beneath his hornbrow eminence,
serene in the loneliness of the unpeopled barren,
awe and respect as for no man.

Oomingmuk
bearded, sage, wise, and woeborn
wears the cloak of winter's hovering
waiting wolves
the forming of the ring
the closing of the ring
about the ring
Oomingmuk
bearded one
with the others
his head raises
into the wind whine
hearkens the tightening of
one of many circles

As rivers
etch patterns
time etched response in
Oomingmuk
obdurate, obstinate

and England
Kelsey, died
in you when you
beheld him
and you *kill'd one*

Oomingmuk lies
unmoving in a puddle of blood
oozing into tundra
redder than lichen
the lichens soaking
a precious wetness

Above the land always death hovers;
death and the barrens lie like lovers
intertwined, spent of their desire;
but the barrens knew not death as fire.

Time, depth, and distance fall away;
a cozened reader in a future age
will find a calmness in a rage
of rivers flouting time and space,
in meeting wildness face to face.

I stand in the haggard wind of winter,
turbulent air and colder times,
considering the depths of nights,
the distance travelled, the stars' cold light,
the muteness of my mouth where language fell away from me
until my silence forced me to reach
for any utterance, any speech
my chafed hand might render :
Now Reader Read for I am well assur'd
Winter has forted us, and us immur'd
Thou dost not know the hardships I endur'd

It is a beginning;
the wind is singing,
fire is dying:
the voice of the land is the wind,
the wind is the voice of the land, and

when you have heard the wind and its singing,
you shall have begun to understand.

Interlude: Dreambearer

In more than arctic darkness
no day begins as the long day begins

no music moves
where no thing moves
where nothing is
but the dream of the bear is dreamt

no word moves
as the great bear's mind forms in night
in cold beyond cold
the absolute
stillness
the world's long climb to daylight and delight
begins

form mind bear idea dream
breaking while a thought breaks
the word moves within the dark
the bear's form is borne in the great bear's mind

the void
begins to heave
weight and mass
slowly and critically
coalesce

form and idea
collide and collapse

the first trickling warmth

a word, a wind
breath, motion, swift light
hurled in a widening arc
thrusts through the dark
in the slow coition of universe
and the world's conception
in the wind behind the word
in an archaic dream

The sun is a fiction
under the rim of white light in indigo
the pale pink hope of warmth
spirit of rock
storms of creation
cloud chaos music words dreams
in white fragmenting light

beneath the stars
that one by one
form while the word is light and
move through mind to light and shape

out of the sleeping dreambearing night

Part ye Fourth: Flensing[32]

. . . one might almost say that metonomy corresponds to the order of events, metaphor to the order of structure.

Claude Lévi-Strauss, *Totemism*[33]

Sweat flecks the tawny hide, urging
the ecstasy the buck dies in, surging
ecstasy, crumbling on its legs splaying,
slaughter's dreary darkness replacing
the surgent rapture.

The larynx tightens; the word is drawn back;
before the utterance is thrown, the breath is drawn;
the heart's cords and the hand's tendons tighten;
song brims in the tension of silence.

Let my song fly; the arrow is true.

If at any time they are in want of victuals
they will fit a young man out wth *something of their own making*
as it may be half a dozen peruant[34] *stones*
w^{ch} *they have gott from y*^{e} *factory*
or Else a pipe steam
now these pruant stones they scrape smooth & burn spots,
or y^{e} *shape of any thing as their fancy leads y*^{m}
now if happens y^{t} *this young man w*^{ch} *is fitted out*
should kill a Beast y^{t} *day*
then they will impute it to y^{e} *things he carried about him*
& so it passes for a God Ever afterwards

The blade scores the soft belly flesh
and the guts of the buck spill out;
the knife flickers by the legs' tendons
revealing the pale yellow wax of fat.

After winter's hunger slaked by small birds only,
after the trials of hunting on spring's collapsing snow,
after the ribs of spring poking lankly,
summer seems good

Midsummer, sixteen hundred ninety one
ye floods past ye Snow eat by ye Sun
Near to Starvation obtaining from ye Govr
ye powder shott Tobacco for our Endeavour
wch items for all of which I asked
As necessary for my inland task
We sett out again seeking for to find
ye Stone Indians being ten days travell behind
at Deerings point and by cannoes we past
By creeks and brooks, ponds deepe in grass
wch like our English oats is ear'd
Leaving our cannoes Inland we veer'd
& made an hole as storehouse in ye Ground
wch when we pass hence next Spring will be found
A Bagg of Powder Tobacco & ye nettline
One tin show a hatchet & 2 skains of twine
In a rundlett[35] wch in ye Ground we placed
& abandonned in our Hunger & our Hast
For to journey further & to track ye Stones
Who by Evidence of ye scraps & Bones
Were 4 days only farr in front of us
& better victualled so catch up we must

In 9 days trek we came up with y^{m} at last
After heavy mossy going we had past
& they had kill'd both swans & muse
ye Chief gave me ye Gut he had cut loose

But now no Beast they kill
but some part or other is allotted for mans meat
wch ye women are not to tast of upon no acco^{t} . . .
by reason they think it will be a hindrance
to their Killing any more Beast
nay if a woman should eat any of this mans meat
wch is called in their language Cuttawatchetaugan
& fall sick in a year or 2 afterwards & dye
they will not stick to say it y^{t} kill'd her
for all it was so long ago she eat it

Now if they have a mind for to make a feast
they will pitch a tent on purpose
& after y^{t} ye tent is made & fixt
then no woman Kind y^{t} hath a husband
or is known to have been concern'd wth a man
must not come within the door of ye tent afore^{sd}

The gore warms stiff fingers,
palpable intestines fall in black heaps
on the crimsonned snow;
a foreleg jerks a last twitch.
The knife dances in glints
severing integuments and the hide's off-gloving
reveals a more naked, strangely dry and gangling body;
the blood deserting the fallen body
drips into baskets placed there as catchbasins
and frost invades the moments before warm tissue.

A word spumes on the baby's lips; the child does not cry;
words bubble on the rocks of rapids; incoherent murmuring;
words echo in the waking dream.
Drum tight tension: the forming words.

concerning their singing of their songs
& from whence they think they have y^{m}
those that they reckon Chiefly for gods
are Beast and fowl
But of all Beast ye Buffillo
& of all fowls ye voulter[36] *& ye Eagle*
wch they say they dream of in their sleep
& it relates to y^{m} w^{t} they shall say when they sing
& by y^{t} means whatsoever they ask or require
will be granted or given y^{m}
wch by often making use of it
sometimes happens to fall out Right as they say
& for y^{t} one time
it will pass for a truth y^{t} he hath a familiar
although he hath told never so many lies before

The drying bubbles blacken the snow;
the frame-stretched hide tautens;
the strands of tendon dry;
the spitted legs roast.

Our hungry bellyes were fill'd at great Feast
For now there was no want of fowl or Beast
Very glad were they y^{t} I had return'd
And by my promise else were it learn'd
I was dead the Nayhathaways w^{d} murder y^{m}
& Master of ye Feast I was for I had come[37]

then ye master of ye tent & one or two more
goeth in & Cutteth out a place for ye fire
about three foot square in ye middle of ye tent
& then ye fire being made they take a little sweet grass
& lay at every corner of ye said square
& then putting fire to it they perfume the tent so
Making a long speech wish all health & happiness
both to founders & confounders

One year's cycle spent;
dawn startled our onset
renewing us

Rested & wth pigeons & muse well fed
Proceeded we to y^{e} river y^{t} is Blood read
Where I should talk with y^{e} Naywatame
y^{t} had strong fear of harm in meeting me
For they 3 Nayhathaway women kill'd
A spring before and fear of revenge y^{m} fill'd

So far I have spoken concerning of the spoil
And now will give $acco^{t}$ *of that same Country soile*
Which hither part is very thick of wood
Affords small nutts w^{th} *little cherryes very good*
Through heathy barren land in fields we pitcht
y^{t} hath no fir but by fine groves of Poplo is enricht

The sun glimmers on the shores of that broad plain

One Indian lay adying and withall
A murmuring for warrs among y^{m} was ye call
In counsel said I to ye elder Dons[38]
Y^{t} was not ye way to use ye English guns

a smile radiates a face
brightening eyes' bleak hollows

& so by their singing
will pretend to know w^{t} y^{e} *firmament of heaven is made of*
nay some Indians w^{ch} *I have discoursed with*
has told me they have been there & seen it
so likewise another has told me
y^{t} *he had been so near to* y^{e} *sun at* y^{e} *going down*
y^{t} *he could take hold of it when it Cut* y^{e} *Horrizon*

Not knowing wch could Conquer Life or Death
Lay still and waited with held breath
Till y^{t} he died and then his body burn'd
& buried we made new camp and turn'd
They holding y^{t} it was not good to stay
Where y^{t} one died according to their way

Every man maketh his own songs by vertue of w^{t} he dreams of
as I have said before

And the dream of the bear is dreamt:[39]

Spirit
solitary
bearer of darkness
in man's sleep his grunting
his silver-dark pelt at the edges
melts
at the edge of sleep out of the darkness
robing him in thick-rilled silver
surmounting
the hump of his shoulders
down to the talons of his claws

Ride on the back of the great humped bear
to the stars in the night of the vast dark's sphere

Out of dream darkness and running
the bear pursuing the dreamer running
through silver-slipping birches waits
till the dreamer slipping falls

and in the eyes of the bear's great head
is reflected the diminishing realm he withdraws from,
driven back and retreating until

a high chill wind
on small willows
blows cloud wisps
the high silver clouds
and the rider
upon and within the
bear
sees
the world smaller

Bear, having borne him in his becoming the bear's eyes,
stands and surveys the sources of fear's pungence and terror.

Out of the heap of sleep
the breath of death bloody and bubbling
in the half-light of memory
the great bear strides across the sky.

The hills, the clouds, the poplar bluffs
he cannot reduce to parables of death
from the edge where he now sees
a bold simplicity where he finds himself standing

alone

Pitcht to ye outtermost Edge of ye woods
Where y^{t} ye silver haired Great Bear broods
His skin to gett I have used all ye ways I can
He is mans food & he makes food of man
His hide they would not me it preserve
But said it was a god & they should Starve
Neither white nor black like ye common Bear
But more like unto y^{t} our English Hare
Also Buffillo like the English ox their horns
Unlike those y^{t} to N^{o}tharward are born

We were in all now eighty tents
Together now on y^{t} our going hence
& full 200 of us proceeding at the least
To the woods y^{t} lyeth along West and East
Which at last we reached & there perforce
Y^{e} men requested y^{t} I let them to the warrs
W^{ch} I forbade the Govern^{r} would not it allow
But I y^{m} would reward should they seek now
Y^{e} Naywatame poets & if y^{t} they be found
Here where y^{t} ye Beavour do abound
September ye 1st their Enemies land we near'd
With 8 Indians who y^{m} greatly fear'd
& fill'd me with dread Anticipation
Of speaking with y^{m} and Interpretation
At morn & crying out just like the Crane
Young scouts arrived the Enemy they'd seen
& as if for Joy they had been stobb'd[40]
Y^{e} old men Served ye steam and sobb'd
While y^{t} ye young men sat without a sound
Showing y^{m} ye old Arrows they had found
Counselled I again they should not to ye wars
Y^{e} Comp^{y} preferring Peace to use of Force
But all my arguements little prevailed
For they believed the rout they sought availed

Four Strangers of the Naywatame poets
Came wch received kindly gave us notice
Of where their Capt was and so I went
To him and parleyed with him in his tent
& all ye Arguements then with him made
Concerning all ye Advantages of ye Trade
Saying he should forget his men were kill'd
Y^{t} were his Trade with us fulfill'd
We English should prevent it going further
& presented him with Gifts moreover
A coat & sash beads awls and whatnot

Tobacco & a gun wth Powder and some shot
Y^{t} pleased him well indeed & thus he said
My amends were enough for y^{m} his dead

In the heat haze
the sun rises
and the sun sets
streams gather
and flow to the sea

In the heat haze
mirage magnifies space
it is time to turn back now
beyond the bright flare of the day
to the foil of darkness

It is time to make the signs

The long swept grass gathered and dried; the sweet grass sustaining;
The long sweet grass burning sweetens the air with its smoke:
The pipe brims with the dried leaves of bearberry; seeds and sweet
herbs in a mound on a flat, scorched rock:
Coarse fingers bear coals from the fire, small coals igniting the leaves
grasses, seeds:
He calls through the haze of the tent: they enter and sit on a hide:
His fingers lift an ember which he places in the bowl of the pipe,
and the lit pipe he passes to the first of them who
turns its stem in his fingers; the bowl toward him, he turns the
stem to the northeast, the fort, where the old man has directed it:
Where the old man directs, he points the stem to the point of the
rising sun:
Where the old man directs, he turns it south to where the sun rises
highest:
Then to the sun's setting point, where the sun rests:
Tendrils of smoke cling in closedness as the old one another ember
places in the bowl:

The second who takes it repeats the points of the compass, pausing
and passing it:
Pausing and passing; taking and turning:
Sweet is the smoke, silent the ceremony till all have taken the pipe.

Sweet are the berries: we sing and rejoice in our singing.

I stand
in the middle
of the long grass
I turn
to the north and east
where the river flows
I turn
beneath the sun at noon
turn
to the ground
to the sky
draw
the sweet breath of the air
into my chest
and
like a giant heart ebb and flow with wind
and with seasons

It is time to turn back; time to turn from the mysteries; the hunt
is over.
At the sun's rising my shadow yearned itself into the tall grass:
At noon my shadow was short; I was unaware of my shadow:
Now in the dusk my shadow stretches and points toward home:
We will rise and walk early into the sun with the sun behind us
when day is done.
About the lone bear at the edge of the woods who nudged a stump
over to eat its grubs a noose of the sun tightens.

This plain affords nothing but Beast & grass
And over it in three days time we past
Getting into ye woods on the other side
It being about forty six miles wide
This wood is poplo ridges with small ponds of water
There is beavour in abundance but no Otter
With plains & ridges in the Country throughout
Their Enemies many whom they cannot rout
But now of late they hunt their Enemies
And with our English guns do make y^{m} flie

(I saw her with another woman;
like beaver kittens they were playing
beside the bank of the pond's still water,
splashing and raising a flight of ducklings,
then clambering up the slick grass and resting,
reclining and lying in the late summer warmth;
my heart was wandering with my mind.)

At deerings point after the frost
I set up their a Certain Cross
In token of my being there
Cut out on it ye date of year
And Likewise for to veryfie the same
Added to it my master sir Edward deerings name

Goldenrod, silverwood, water calla, dragonhead,
bunchberry, ragwort, paintbrush, and sedge,
Indian pipe, meadow rue, bur-reed, silverthread,
hornwort: growing at the water's edge.

Bog myrtle, sun dew, bracken and pincherries,
pitcher plants, touch-me-not, milfoil and brome,
twinflowers, bishop's cap, running pine, cloudberries:
garland the one who returns slowly home.

Frost fins the bog;
squirrels chatter noisomely;
And so another autumn, winter, long winter.

At Deerings point ye following spring
Y^{e} Naywatame chief having promised to bring
Down in aboundance ye Beavour pelts
For Trading gunns, powder and all else
All of wch y^{t} ye Captn & I did Agree
Eager our Endeavours fruit to see
At ye place of ye Resortance
Upon wch I had place a great Importance

But in ye Spring failed they to arrive
W^{ch} means our Goal we did not achieve
Y^{e} reason for ye failure being so
Y^{t} wch we hoped they would forego
After we had parted from ye Naywatame

An event I anticipated did dismay me
W^{ch} was y^{t} secretly ye Nayhathaway
Came up and two of y^{m} did slay
W^{ch} a new terror struck into y^{m}
Y^{t} they would not be let back again
If y^{t} they should leave to Deerings Point
All of my labours then was quite disjoint
Y^{e} Chief sent to me a pipe & steam
Of his own making wch I accepted y^{m}
& in return I sent him then a Piece
Of Tobacco from ye House with Pleas
He w^{d} come down ye following Year
Overcoming in desire for Trade his Fear

Having no more to trouble you wth all I am
Sir your most obedient & faithfull Servt at Command
Henry Kelsey

Part ye Fifth: Arbor

. . . because our languages have a future tense, which fact is of itself a radiant scandal, a subversion of mortality, the seer, the prophet, men in whom language is in a condition of extreme vitality, are able to look beyond, to make of the word a reaching out past death.

George Steiner, "Silence and the Poet"[41]

Given: plane surface
point moving locus

Point on the surface moving, tracing a line traces

Given: a tree
a mind concept

Mind on the tree is moving, locating a sign traces

On a pivot of consciousness balance: line and sign

From all points of the line regard the sign and

from the point of the sign regard the line and

marginal greyness
peripheral vision blurring

remove the plane, the point moving, the considering

the tree remains

take away the tree and what remains is poetry

If thou wouldst me define,
seek the blast that has thee bent,
seek the element in which thou grew,
seek the old supporting the new;
number the rings, tell the annuli of growth
in varying width: the cold, dry year's annular slenderness
between the two, wet, warm years of tenderness;
seek in the convoluted bark's drying like the skin
the lichen dryness where the rot set in
while fleshy soft and palpable the phloem
bears the sap, sweet liquid
that in capillaries welled from the green-black mosses and the rock;
look to the gnarls of the roots;
look to the shape of the insistent wind;
look with a persistent mind.

The bent tree
reveals
the force of land
wind
the climate's aridity
the snow's depth
the height of watertable
the lenten soil
roots scrabbling in the mossy
crack

Efflorescent the gathering prism,
the iris dilating
stares into the crescent tree:

vascular
rooted
branched
skeletal
leaflorn
hydrotropic, heliotropic
fixed, firm
still

Xylem, phloem, cambium,[42] bark,
branches, twigs, needles, sap,
scabs of scars, cicatrices on the blazemark,
chickadees upon the twigs,
ravens' vantage places on its plumes of branches,
a lynx peering from beneath its snow-heavy boughs,
the shadow of its height on a plane drawing the circle of a day,
drawing from the ground its water,
drawing from the air its sustenance,
flayed by snow in sharp crystals at the snowline,
its chlorophyll sapped away in autumn, its needles blacken,
its squirrel-shredded cones creating a midden of bracts,
its green spears of new growth in candelabra in the spring,
shining, silver ghostly tree in hoarfrost in the fog,
or glistening in apparitional dew at dawn;
sentinel, guideway, haven,
home to the squirrel, eyrie[43] for raven, harvest for woodpecker,
nest for flicker, outpost of owl, walkway for nuthatch;
bed by bed of boughs sundered from its trunk

stem
flowering
resinous
sweetly
scented
tree

Of this tree: take all away yielding poetry

Compass, mirror, kin
of persistent
roots
squeeze out from the moss
its rootlets
jamming growth

observer participant
growth
in rock
the germinated seed
seeking water
in durable stone

drawing substance
from sun, air, light
sustenance from
transparencies
shaped by them

a carven krummholz[44]

huddled in branches
it shows the wind
the winter wind
wind which flays
with sharp snow

in the lee, luke sun
weather-worn one
always the wind
its needles
finer needles

epitomizing place
as myth makes history meaningful
while making of it something else

Given: a sphere
point moving locus

Wherever the point is on the sphere, it is the centre of the circle

at the centre of many circles

Given: a sphere
point still locus

The radius of the circle equals a radius of the sphere

Sphere: a way of thinking
Sphere: a manner of perception location

Circle: a plane of intersection of two spheres
a way of thinking, a mode of perception
Circle: the intersection of a sphere and plane
the volumetric intersection of a pair of spheres: a lens

Sphere of the eye Sphere of the world
together a lens each focussing
the other

On the oblate disc
formed of two spherical sections
ringed by the circle's perfection
(recall, now, the ringed muskoxen)
aware of the dish-disc apposite
which forms the boundary
thinking and perception
the spheres' equivalences
and the spheres equivalent
(else the smaller would be consumed by
the larger)
at their identity
the universe is free
limited but unbound
horizoned but infinite

Substitute in the above any of the following:

your sphere, my sphere;
your sphere, Kelsey's sphere;
my sphere, Kelsey's sphere:

in articulate suspension

The spheres near each other
a pair of convex surfaces
diminishing the virtual we see
a point of contact

•

the gap breached
the void crossed
zeroed in upon
and
that which was made small's enlarged
the eye of the beholder fills the lens
and
that which is beheld is held to be fulfilled

the lens that magnifies and concentrates
expanding sun
distilling it
to a bright white spot that lights
upon dried grass
blackens it
before the curling smoke
ascends

The gesture of the journey, the long line,
the dust of the continuum,
the particular the point points
binding but infinite
unbound yet finite
as he ceases to be
the luminous eye
brightens
the simulacrous self burns
until he vanishes in its combusting
the fire the earth
the air
uniting
in spirit, the unspoken, the lens

all that remains is flame, the speaking flame and passion,
corolla of gold, crown of crimson enveloped in evanescence,
flames that out of nothing rise nothing to become beyond,
but while they flicker they embrighten our swift passage.

Landscape delitescent
diminishing he becomes a giant
disappearing he dissolves in us
diverging from horizon

Eighteen when he was sent on his first journey
into the barrens with Thomas Savage, Indian,
their long days in anxiety as they scanned
the shore for the ship that would take them home;
the travels fruitless, the "stars for cannope,"
came back alive, accomplishment sufficient
to send him out again; and so "the twealth of June"
in '89, he left the fort, canoed six hundred miles
upstream to encourage the inland Indians
to bring their furs to trade downstream;
and nineteen then, his company's age,
from one of two forts on the Bay's bare shore
into the unknown land, himself unknown,
for two years' wandering, eloigned[45] of language
except for Indians' words he had picked up
in his four year apprenticeship;
forayed with them, ate from their baskets,
took one of their women to bed and wive,
made ceremony with them, hunted with them,
undertook to bring them peace, and failed;
came back alive . . .

silence

needle crunch punctuates
a beaver slaps its tail[46]
the doves murmur
then the murmuring subsides

into river

loon laugh

the parenthetical

silence

. . . the silence growing until

it is shapeless, undefined light only

suffusing mind, land
winding river
within the brightness of the blanked out

caesurae of the crescent cusp of moon
the land seen in the smallness of the eye
the circular
shape of things
imputed by the shaping of the mind
that in great wheels thinks it finds itself

until upon the river in descending he meets himself ascending
failing to recognize even in himself the stranger
who in boyish manner set out with heavy heart
in his escape from time, came back younger than the one who left
and older than the stranger

beyond
the full, dull November twice
February's seering brilliance twice
beyond the muck of trickling spring
twice
beyond

until in the specula,
in the discovery of the aspiring breath,
vaporous, spirant breath,
the soft wind singing the primitive,
the archaic words seething on the brim
of the old leather pot in which the hot stones are dropped

words pulse like birds pulse in the pulse arrow
singing pulse like the heart pulse in the body pulse
the rhythm pulse the wind pulse
till in the heat of your transformation pulse

all and all else
escapes inertia

little matters

will

Epilogue: Scab

Scar in space scabbed by time

The book ever open will close, fold in upon itself,
the deck be cut, shuffled, reshuffled,
footsteps soft in the forest fall,
leaves lost in the fall of time;
lacunae in which beaver build fill in; foxing will occlude;
water will stain; torn from the past the present.

Hailed in health upon the river,
the river runs in sundered splendour
between the caving banks of memory,
between the rough edge of the trees,
between low hills of lowlands;
beyond the clouds, beyond the day
the slow stars wheel, wheel bear beyond:
he slips, streams, dreams, deems, deeps, deposits,
    posits, pairs, peers, glistens,
    listens beneath the flood
    he cannot plumb.

Raw land rumour etches:
    the synapse[47] opens, wan memory;
    bleaches the image of the golden plain
    to the paper on which he writes
as brightness blanches shadows on the snow.

So after it's all over he becomes another line,
a line on a map that shows a loop that may approximate
his path and passage or may err a thousand miles or so,
                    and what's the difference?

A bearing become   baring a nerve
                    bearing
without   knowing
                    history
becoming first his verse   indelibly scored
                    scorched by time
shored himself   in poetry
                    became his life
his line   remembering
                    the embering beneath
                    his kindling
became   beyond
                    us, an ungava

The story continues, the story is ended.

The story continues, "The story is ended . . ."

The story continues

---

1. Reprinted from *Homage, Henry Kelsey* (Winnipeg: Turnstone Press, 1981). This book contained nine striking ink drawings by Dennis Burton, one of which appears on the front cover of this anthology. They were done in Chin-Chin and Pelikan India Ink and in Dr. P.H. Martin's concentrated transparent water colour (inks), on cartridge paper, 18" x 24", and photographed by Edward Cavell. Two Notes were also included. The first, a letter of appreciation from Burton to Whyte and Kelsey, is omitted. Part of the second note, written by Whyte, follows:

> In the autumn of 1967, I started a poem about muskoxen. . . . In 1968's autumn, home in Banff, I took up the notes for the poem, and read some more, finding that Henry Kelsey had been the first to describe the pleistocene relic. Even more interesting, he had been the first English poet of the Canadian prairies, an ancestral voice. "Poet?" I liked him, thought his poetry doggerel. . . . But, as I reread him, I kept hearing in his poem the genuine. He took over the poem about the muskox. The poem began to shape itself into epic. My academic work on the medieval poem *Pearl* [late fourteenth century] started to inform what I was doing: I would, like the jeweller of that poem, put his poem into a new setting. Hence "homage."
>
> Kelsey in 1690 took his journey to the plains and wrote his couplets about that trip upstream. The rest of his journal consists of brief notes. In finishing my poem I took his notes and finished for him his journey in poetry in my part IV, "Flensing." The reader of *Homage, Henry Kelsey* may distinguish his text from mine, for his is in italics throughout. His text is taken from *The Kelsey Papers*, edited by Arthur G. Doughty and Chester Martin [Ottawa: The Public Archives of Canada and the Public Record Office of Northern Ireland, 1929].

Jon Whyte was born in 1941 in Banff where he now lives and where his grandparents were pioneers. He has published some fifteen books of poetry, biography and non-fiction. He is curator of the Heritage Collection of the Museum of the Canadian Rockies.

2. In the Turnstone edition Kelsey's own poem appeared as a postscript. Historians disagree a great deal about the geography of Kelsey's travels and somewhat about dates. According to Gerald Friesen in *The Canadian Prairies* (1984), "he accompanied an Indian back from the Bay to the region of . . . The Pas . . . in 1690 and

. . . in 1691, toward the vast plains that probably had never been visited by Europeans." In 1689, however, accompanied by a young Native boy, Thomas Savage, he had already made another journey inland 20 leagues beyond what he calls "Churchill River" (probably Fort Churchill at the mouth of the River on Hudson Bay).

3. This is York Fort or York Factory, located near the mouth of the Hayes River in northern Manitoba on Hudson Bay.

4. A point of some contention, Deerings Point may have been at the site of the present-day The Pas or at Cedar Lake, just north of Lake Winnipegosis. From either place Kelsey could have proceeded up the Saskatchewan River and then inland.

5. Carriage is Kelsey's word for portage, the carrying of boats or goods over land between two navigable waters.

6. Sun is the Indian's name here.

7. The Honourable Sir Edward Dering was Deputy Governor of the Hudson's Bay Company from 1685 to 1691.

8. Ungava is used for its Inuit adverbial meaning of "beyond," not as the place name.

9. Seekwan is Cree for the season of spring.

10. Whimbrel is a term applied to various small species of curlew.

11. "Bosque" is probably a variant of the archaic "bosk," which is a bush or small wood, according to the *O.E.D.* (1989).

12. According to the *Random House Dictionary of the English Language* (1987), "nivation" is a geological term describing erosion which results from the action of frost beneath a snowbank. Nivation can also mean resting or sleeping or growing under snow, the winter (Canadian) equivalent to aestivation.

13. These lakes are situated north of Lakes Winnipeg and Winnipegosis.

14. The spelling of Assinae Poets is from *The Kelsey Papers* where Kelsey transliterates his Cree guides' name for the Plains Nakodah or Dakota (the two forms are cognate), the people we know as the Assiniboines (cognate with Assinae Poets) in Saskatchewan and Manitoba, the Stoneys in Alberta. The name is the typically pejorative type of name an enemy tribe uses: Assinae means "stone," Assinae Poets, the "stone-cooking people." Whyte's use of "poets" in a poem about mental space and myth-making is not inappropriate.

15. The Echimamish is a Manitoba river which connects the courses of the Nelson and Hayes Rivers. The Cree name encompasses its characteristic of reversing its direction of flow depending on which source course is higher. Whyte says he and Margaret Laurence (*The Diviners* [1974]) happened upon the trope of a river flowing two ways coincidentally, that the figure of enantiodromia concerns both her and himself although the two of them use it in different ways, and that his source was *Fur Trade Routes of Canada* (1984) by Eric Morse.

16. Frazil is defined by *The Random House Dictionary of the English Language* as ice crystals formed in turbulent water.

17. On May 2, 1670 the Royal Charter of the Hudson's Bay Company was issued to "The Governor and Company of Adventurers of England Trading into Hudson Bay."

18. Joseph Robson, a contemporary of Kelsey, passes on the information that "Miss-Top-Ashish" (little-giant) was a Native name Kelsey earned by killing two grizzly bears when they attacked him.

19. The Etomami is another reversing river, one located in eastern Saskatchewan, again named for the Cree "river which flows both ways" in a different transliteration. Jack Herbert, a Saskatchewan history buff, now dead, told Whyte that in his opinion Kelsey more likely reached the Etomami than the Echimamish.

20. Witches' broom is *Arceuthobium americanum,* mistletoe.

21. Labrador tea is *Ledum groenlandicum,* a shrub with leathery leaves which can be used for a bitter tea.

22. Systole and diastole are terms applied to the contraction and relaxation of organs, especially the heart and arteries.

23. According to the *O.E.D.*, the word carcajous, apparently of Native origin, is accurately applied to the wolverine and erroneously applied to the badger and the Canada lynx.

24. In 1926 *The Kelsey Papers* were given to the Public Record Office of Northern Ireland by Major A.F. Dobbs of Castle Dobbs, Carrickfergus. His ancestor, Arthur Dobbs, had been an administrator and traveller in North America. Doughty and Martin point out that he was also frequently a critic of The Hudson's Bay Company.

25. This comment can be found in an essay entitled "History," *Essays, Critical and Miscellaneous* by T. Babington Macaulay (New York: D. Appleton and Co., 1864), p. 51. It originally appeared in the *Edinburgh Review* in 1828.

26. Nunatuks is an Inuit term. Scarps of rock surrounded by ice, the tips of otherwise glacier-buried mountains, are called nunataks in the western Arctic.

27. These are the muskoxen Kelsey saw on the journey of 1689. He appears to have been the first white man to see or hunt them.

28. According to Doughty and Martin, Kelsey arrived in 1684 in a ship called *The Lucy,* the captain of which was John Outlaw. Kelsey had been apprenticed to the company on April 14, 1684. He was 14 years old.

29. New Severn is probably Severn House, located at the mouth of the Severn River which is east of York Factory.

30. James Young was captain of a sloop called the *Hopewell* in which Kelsey travelled to the Churchill River.

31. George Geyer was the governor of York Factory during Kelsey's stay.

32. To flense means to flay or strip off a skin.

33. Trans. Rodney Needham (Boston: Beacon Press, 1963), p. 27.

34. Peruant, and pruant which follows, may be cognates of either pruinose (in the *O.E.D.*, covered with hoar-frost), or the obsolete pruant (shaped like a plum).

35. Rundlett is probably roundlet—in the *O.E.D.*, a small circle.

36. Voulter is probably the turkey vulture which is still common in Manitoba.

37. The sense is this: "The Nayhathaways were gladdened by my returning as I had promised. For if I had died and they had learned it they would murder those who had been accompanying me (the Naywatame). Because I had returned I became Master of the Feast."

38. Whyte uses the word "dons" both as a rhyme for guns and as what he describes as "a kind of joke about writing doggerel: rhyme leading sense more frequently than sense leading rhyme."

39. To many people of the North-West the bear was a creature possessed of especially potent spiritual motive power. In Rudy Wiebe's *The Temptations of Big Bear* (1973), Big Bear is guided by the bear spirit of whom he dreams, "the most powerful spirit known to the Cree." See also *The Sacred Paw* (1985) by Paul Shepard and Barry Sanders.

40. Stobbed is Kelsey's original word—possibly stabbed, possibly sobbed.

41. *Language and Silence* (New York: Atheneum, 1967), p. 38.

42. These are all terms with botanical ramifications. Hydrotropic and heliotropic refer to plants which respond sensitively to water and to light respectively. Xylem is the woody tissue of the plant. Phloem is the softer portion of the fibral vascular tissue. Cambium is the cellular viscid substance beneath the bark of some woody plants.

43. Eyrie seems to be a version of aerie, or nest.

44. Krummholz is German for "crooked tree" but used by botanists as a term for the bent, twisted trees which grow at tree limit, both at the edge of the alpine and the northern tree line.

45. The past participle, *eloigné*, of the French verb from which this word is derived means "far away." The sense here, then, seems to be "alienated from language."

46. The slap of a beaver tail is a warning of the presence of danger.

47. A synapse is the junction of two nerve cells.

The First Woman[1]

Lorna Crozier

✿

The first white woman in the West
Marie Anne Lagimodière[2]
born 1782
she did exist
her reality stops me

who am I to tell
her story?
what is it
I want to know?

I am not the first
white woman in the West
I am not Catholic
I am not French
but in this wilderness
I cross
I am the first
woman   these words
            my signs
for those
who went before

✿

He was a voyageur come back
to Trois-Rivières
every night he told stories
all of us come to listen
and who cares
            it was not the truth
but exciting

his voice rose
and fell with the fire
shadows in the room
were Indians
            or wild animals
that tore us apart
if we leaned too far back
in our chairs

when he proposed
I never thought
            of asking
if he would stay
in the village
nor did my father
everyone so sure
he wasn't thinking
of wandering again
all those stories
death and the long wind
that had no trees
to stop it

but a month after the wedding
he was pulled by spring
onto the rivers
                    and me
what was I to do?
not young   twenty-five
become a housekeeper
for Father Vinet
or go with him?

✿

The first man to cross this river
to climb this hill   to write
his name in stone
the first man to be held
in the eyes of a doe
that did not know
to run

did these stories
draw you to him?
or while others listened
did you feel desire?
watch the gestures
of his hands, his face
his lean body moving
through your eyes
through the village
that was the world

✿

After the water
I didn't mind the trip
so much
but the canoes
they were dangerous

on Lake Superior   no need
for tales of monsters
wind and wave rose
from the cold
with foaming mouths
we rowed from bay to bay
praying in between

the canoe just ahead
flipped over   men thrashed
grasping the air
for the hand of God
                    grown men
crying for *Mary*   for their mothers

sucked down
          into the black
cold belly of the lake

I bruised my palm
clutching the beads
so tight

✿

These things protect you
: the holy beads
: God
: a fire
: the single-shot
rifle
: your husband

but he keeps changing
shape
he is a wolf
a lynx a muskrat
a weasel a cougar
a silver fox
filling your doorway
after the long season

✿

Sitting around the fire
Bouvier on the other side
screams *Mon Dieu*
Mon Dieu this is just
across the fire we think
it can't be animals
the fire makes us safe
my husband grabs his rifle
we see a bear sow
drag Bouvier into the bush
Shoot shoot
Don't let me be eaten alive

she batters his head
my husband clubs her
with his rifle   fires
she drops her prey
rears at him
he runs for his other gun
the bullet strikes
she does not rise again

no screams   no words
just gargling sounds
from Bouvier
                    the bear has torn off
his face as if it were a mask
nose eyes mouth all gone

✿

What remains when the fire
no longer holds back the fear
when the gun will not go off
when the healing herbs are poison
what remains?

beads to bruise the palm
the words of the priest from the lost village
the man who sleeps with you
under the skins of what he has killed
the living cooking washing mending
saying your prayers
praying

            little enough
but enough to keep you going

when Indians try to buy your child
and your husband moves
from trap to trap
                                        across the snow

It was the custom
you know
but he never told me
he took a squaw
the four years he stayed
at Pembina

and this woman was kind
she visits me every day
shows me herbs for healing
tells me with her hands
she'll make a drink
to take away the weakness
I've carried
since the first baby

she helps me
with the hides
shows me how
to scrape away the flesh
how to rub the liver
brains and fat into the skin
for a jacket
that will please him

her knife goes *snik snik*
across the surface
I am clumsy
leave spots of blood
like cricket tracks
across wet clay

she gestures
                soon she'll have this drink
for me

I speak only French
she Blackfoot
hands shape our thoughts in the air
hers are dusty swallows
she wants to tell me
    my husband will like
    this skin we work on

when she forms the word
for *husband*
                I know
she has known him
as only a wife can

and I do not take the drink

While an Indian wife waited at Pembina[3]
softening his skins with her spittle
he returned to the village he left behind
married a woman of his kind

did he desire
                    your piety?
your very name *Marie* his mother's
his sister's   memories one needs
to press into the heart
when the canoe tips over
the gun jams   a bear grows out of fire

did he want you
                    to stay in the village
until he returned old and tired
his children strangers   his wife
a grey woman to pray away his sins?

but you demanded
to go with him
                    the first white woman
the Indians had seen
worth many horses hides and guns

you waited
at the end of the trapline
hands that worried beads
touching the images you shaped of him
in the dark unholy hours

✿

Never in one place long
by spring he wants to go
this time
          to Fort of the Prairies[4]

from an Indian trader
he buys me a horse
a good one   gentle
but strong for a long journey

by twilight we crest a hill
a herd of buffalo
grazes in the valley
my horse stiffens
too late I know
he's a buffalo runner
throws himself
                    down the hill
splits the herd
buffalo explode around us
my horse running
                    running

later on the saddle blanket
that stinks of dust and sweat
the new baby tears from me
                    rips me in two
flies settle on his head
                    I name him
Laprairie

Twelve years
of following your husband
from place to place

until the priests arrive
at Red River
they build a church
your husband builds
a house from wood

    bells divide time
    into hours and years

at the bedside
he asks you to keep
his gun
his leather jacket
hangs on a nail
beside the door
until your son
packs it away

you blow sparks
in the black stove
stack pieces of wood
around a weak flame

Would I have lived otherwise?
what a question
                    of course
I would have had a priest
to baptize the children
a mother near
a father   uncles   cousins
sisters   a village and trees
old as the land

people who shared
                    my tongue
fires built only for warmth
and the closeness of stories
a husband
who did not think
he was a river
who didn't think
he had to fill the sky
or stretch his shadow
                                        so far
across the snow

but then
I could have married a village boy
covered with dirt from the fields
ah   who knows
                              who knows
would I have lived otherwise?

I lived   I had children
I am old

Sharing this place
you call *desert*
outside of the country
you came from
country old enough
to have a name
                         Canada

sharing this body
this human fear
                                        of being
alone
            of living
in another's house

this made you
leave the known behind
                                                    I leave
what I know
like strips of red cotton
tied to branches

if you listen   first woman
you will hear the steps
of one who follows
far in the back of your mind
moving out towards your eyes

---

1. Reprinted from *The Weather* (Moose Jaw: Coteau Books, 1983). The poem was inspired by Lise Perrault's book, *The First White Woman in the West* (Saskatoon: Western Producer, 1980), translated from a book written in French by George Dugas in 1883.

Lorna Crozier was born in 1948 in Swift Current, Saskatchewan. For several years she wrote under her married name, Uher. With *The Weather*, she reclaimed her lost Crozier. She is currently Writer-in-Residence at the University of Toronto, but her permanent home is in Saskatoon.

2. According to the *Dictionary of Canadian Biography,* Louis Riel's mother Julie Lagimodière was the daughter of Jean-Baptiste Lagimonière [sic] and Marie-Anne Gaboury. Marie Anne Lagimodière, then, was the grandmother of Louis Riel. It seems appropriate to include Riel in this book as both a future possibility and part of the historical past. In his book on *Gabriel Dumont* (1975), George Woodcock speaks of Riel as a mythic figure who, more than any other in the Canadian past, manifests the Canadian psyche. In an interview (*Journal of Canadian Fiction* I, No. 3 [Summer 1972], 49), Robert Kroetsch has compared Riel to other similarly apocalyptic prairie politicians:

Douglas, Aberhart and Diefenbaker. It also seems appropriate to allow Riel to speak implicitly, since his oracular voice is so much a part of the scar tissue in the prairie identity.

3. Pembina was probably located close to the site of present-day Pembina, which is on the American side of the North Dakota-Manitoba frontier.

4. Historians seem uncertain about the location of this fort. Many speak about it; no one locates it. It may have been in northern Saskatchewan.

Wild Man's Butte[1]

A Stereophonic Poem

Anne Szumigalski & Terrence Heath

Voices: NARRATOR
HENRI BEAUBIER—junior surveyor
TOM GREENAWAY—senior surveyor
AYEE—young Indian woman
MAN—mythic man
WOMAN—mythic woman

A summer electrical storm approaches. Peals of thunder echo down the valley, but there is no wind or rain.

NARRATOR: At the beginning of time before time
There was the earth, and there was the sky.
The sky cracked in a chaos of thunder,
Lightning ringed the valleys,
Crashing on the circling hills,
Splitting open the white sky like rocks.
Out of this light came man, the warrior,
Looking far to the North and South, to the West
And East for game; measuring the distance
Of his stride on the hilltops. The cleavages of
Boulders were his only house. His shoulders
His only strength.

Out of the earth,
Out of the treed coulees cut in the prairie floor
Came woman, the preparer,
Seeking and finding a use for fire, and making

Ready herbs and berries, roots, seeds
And bark, the salt of lake beds,
The minerals of rocks, the lichen and even soil
For the time when they might be needed.
She pressed her spittle into animal hides
And tanned soft garments in the fire's smoke.
The man called down to her, huddled on the edge
Of a lake, rocking herself in the acrid smell:

MAN: Woooooomaaaaaaaaannnnnnnn! Come,
Bring me up a sinew for my bow.

NARRATOR: The woman turned her head away, and whispered:

WOMAN: Man, you come down here. And bring me the sky.

NARRATOR: She took the longest and toughest thong she had
And, holding tight to one end, threw it skyward.
He grasped it, but she did not let go.
She pulled with all the strength prepared in her
And toppled the mighty warrior from the butte.
Man fell from the sky like a star
And lay screaming at her feet.

MAN: You she-devil.
You source of deceit.

WOMAN: But, Lord, do you not see that my sinew is strong and good?

The storm rumbles away and there is silence. Then, the wind rises.

NARRATOR: At the beginning of time, about 1910,
When the surveyors came and pricked
The dried scabs of prairie with their rods,
At that time, the butte had no name;
It was a jut of rubble and pointing shale.
In the cracks of rocks grew brown Coreopsis,[2]

Blazing Star and False Mallow.[3]
With hard small centres like stones,
Their dusty heads dragged against the scarce dirt;
Their roots twisted among the pebbles of the butte—
A mat of clinging fingers; their stalks, red
And wiry, recoiled from the rising winds.
For the surveyors, it was a topographical elevation,
Separating the three bitter lakes
From the weed-green mud of sweet water
In the fourth lake. It was a
Feature of Townships 1 and 2, Range 19,
West of the 2nd Meridian, an outcropping
To defy their gridded mapping. It had no name,
Indian or white. From the height of the cliffs,
Southwards, the wide land rolls greyly
Into the distance, strewn with heavy boulders,
Smudged with salt flats and stale
With the smoking lakes and the heavy
Stink of rotting sulphur. There is no green
Southwards. But northwards it is a hill
To catch first sight of the watering hole,
A peak of jubilation. No buffalo run,
No practical use, no mystery or magic,
A rise for prowling coyotes, nameless.

Wind fades.

BEAUBIER: Dear Sir:

I have the honour to acknowledge the receipt of your letter dated August 23rd. I am being so bold as to answer this letter in the stead of Mr. Thomas Greenaway, Dominion Land Surveyor, since he has been missing from our party some ten days now and has not been seen. He left the main camp to search out fresh water on the last day of August as our supplies had become low, due to breakage of three of the four barrels.

A search party has been sent out—several labourers, chainers, and the reckoning boy, who is very much attached to the person of Mr. Greenaway. The cook refused to go. We have been taken to a spring by passing Indians.

I am proceeding with the surveying as per original instructions, but you will appreciate, I am sure, the tardiness in our progress due to the absence of Mr. Greenaway.

I have the honour to be, Sir,
your obedient servant,
Henri Beaubier,
Evening, September 10, 1910

POST SCRIPTUM: This land is desert, not fit for farming.

The aspen grove rustles. Birds sing. Twigs crack. Somewhere an Indian woman sings a lullaby.

NARRATOR: The coulees here are fissures in the ground;
Edges slant down into the long, uncommon grass,
Brush of red roseflesh and honeysuckle, and at the bottom,
Wet, with trees and lush, soft grasses.
The deer come to shed their spikes in the
Shadowed bottoms of the coulees. Weathered deer-scat[4]
By the bushes. The earth is soft,
Spongy, everything here leaves tracks.
Nothing passes unnoticed. Below the level of the prairie
But high in the sky of the short coulee days,
The dead are buried in the treetops.
Night is close and eternal.
The mummied dead in the maples, the mummied dead

In the aspens and birch, soughed in the air drafts,
Like cocoons, the bark ties frayed, disentangling.
The dead will settle into the lush grass.
Children are laid on the low shrubbery
Like small, wrapped mists of the dank coulee
    morning,
And the trees are alive with the songs of birds.
Here, the prairie nomads camp;
The men, weary from the hunt,
Their women, bringing hot fires to the coulee
Bottom. When they come, the deer trembles
In the thicket and stands motionless
Over her fawns, while the moaning women
Bundle up their failed births for burial
And bundle their live ones for sleep.
In the encampment one woman's heart
Beats with the heartbeat of the deer;
Sightless, she listens to the thud of her own heart.
She is among the women but the closeness
Of the doe tears her away from the women's talk,
And she trembles.

AYEE: He calls me Ayee,
But my name is "the deer".
I have hidden afraid
In the coulee trees,
I have trembled.

Lullaby louder.

NARRATOR: In the sweet air of a summer morning
The deer anxiously struggle up the slopes,
Through the brush of the coulee sides.
Rusty thorns catch in their hide.

AYEE: I am torn
By a tangle of roses.

NARRATOR: They graze on the young spring grass,
Lying on the prairie among the crocuses
With their backs to the wind, chewing
The new cud of succulent growth.
The winter scent of their faded grey coats
Rises on the soft winds.

Prairie wind.

AYEE: There, on the prairie,
He found me,
The man who marks out
The starpoints of the earth,
Who measures the land
With the long eye
Of his instrument.

The wind rises and drowns out the quiet morning sounds.

He came at the sound of morning
When the deer struggle
Up from the coulee.
And I went with him.
It is a year
I last heard birds
Quarrelling in the trees.
A year since I found
In my breast
The deer's heart
And bounded away
From my people.
All winter I whispered
In his ear like a spring breeze,
And his heart bent.
First, he said,
I must chain the prairie,
Then, I will run with you,

My Ayee.
Now he is gone;
He left behind
The glass that sees
Everything near.
He is lost in the distance.

Around the marsh can be heard the raucous call of gulls.

NARRATOR: Willets walk, one or two together,
Along the salt-crusted stones of the water lines,
Pecking disdainfully at the stinking
Lakes, where only small brine shrimp breed.
Amongst the gravel grow bright Samphire
And Glasswort,[5] the colour of water,
Their small flowers embedded
In bitter, juicy stems, their roots
Weakly holding them to the brackish wetlands.
The bowl of sky clamped tight to the bowl
Of earth. Rocks heave out of the ground.
Single clouds scrape close to the horizon.
Everything is sucked to the brackish centre
Of the world and the walking willets,
Not a feather out of place.

TOM: Salt again!
Three lakes of stinking, putrid water
Foul as a witch's arse.
The fresh must be further south.
That ignorant, old bastard didn't know how to make a map.
Look, he shows the sweet water two miles east
Of here, in the middle of that desert
I walked across this afternoon. Christ,
My bladder shrivelled in that terrible sun
And he found water? I can still feel
The burn of that cracked, grey earth
Through the soles of my boots.

Well, Tom, maybe he saw the same
Lake and trees you did, floating
Two feet above the ground.
Mirages!
Wish young Beaubier'd been with me—
I'd sent him off after it with a pail.
I should have brought more water.
Canteen's half empty already *(Pause)*
And me with a thirst that'd drink buffalo stale.
Tom, it's a stupid, bullheaded pride
You've got. Goin' off lookin' for water
At 56 years of age, when you could
Have sent that greenhorn Frenchie out.
He'd've carried along a bottle of his fancy brandy.
Don't begrudge him it, Tom,
He needs it to keep him warm at night.
I should have brought Ayee with me—
A woman keeps a man warm.
He wouldn't've even known how to make a fire
Out on the bald prairie. So what do you get, Tom,
For all your knowledge? A night in a blanket
On ground already frozen hard,
Ground that pukes up the dead. No wonder
The Indians hang them up in the trees close to the sun.

That great butte there's not even on this map.
What use is a map like this? I'll use it
To light a fire to-night and might it
Add a little warmth to his old surveyor's soul
That's surely burning in hell. Ayee
Always says, This land don't want to be charted.
Well, Tom, nothing to do but head for that butte
And have us a look-see. Christ and Tarnation,
There's no rest for the wicked.

NARRATOR: On the abrupt sand face of the crag
Bank swallows have punched
Nesting holes in the crumbling wall.
They shoot out of the sheer facet
Of sand, flashing white breasts
As small as heartbeats, strike
Upward, turn in long parabolas of
Soundlessness: hundreds of them,
Knifing the blue.

AYEE: Why did the skyman
Go by himself?
I felt his retreating footsteps
Across the prairie,
Heard him shout out
Something not for me.
They said to get water.
We do not need water.
In two days it will rain.
The air is troubled
Tonight.
The air pulls at my feet
Like the wind
Of winter, scraping
The ground.
The callings of owls and coyotes
Resound like shadows over the stars.
I hear the movements
Of sleepless deer.
Even now my head is hot
From the fanged sun.
Oh, the man was a running stream
That could not be dammed.
I feel troubled tonight.

The night releases its sounds.

TOM: Getting dark. Maybe I can see something
From the top. Better be careful.
This time of year probably rattler young 'uns around.

NARRATOR: The prairie rattlesnake is a timid reptile,
Light sandy, greenish or greyish brown,
With dark brown patches on the back
And small patches along the sides; it
Passes unnoticed. But if aroused
Or surprised, it rears and
Its fangs flick out of hiding
Places along the roof of the mouth
And, guided by heat-sensitive pits
Between the nostril and eye on either side,
It spears its warm-blooded enemy with unfailing
Accuracy, even in total darkness.
If you are careful where you walk
And wear high boots, it is unlikely
You will run afoul of the coiled buzz.
But "there is no more foolish act
When climbing in the badlands
Than placing one's hands on ledges
Without being first able to see
If they are inhabited. These are
Favourite rattlesnake resting places."[6]

AYEE: I hear him call;
I must go to him,
Leave silently, not wake
The camp curs.
I will follow
The track of his voice
On the night wind.

TOM: Men have survived snakebite. On the neck?
If I lie still, rest, let the warm venom
Work itself out of my system.
Shite, Tom, you've got yourself
In a fine mess. Go sticking your head
In a snake's nest. You could have
Tried the butte in the morning. In
The morning, when you could have seen better.
Snakes, I hear them moving over the hot stones
In the dark. Their tongues flicking, flicking.
Those old rattlers get a mite cranky, Tom,
When you rub eyeballs with them.

AYEE: He's come this way.
What does he seek
Of these lakes?
These running sores?

TOM: I have water for another day—maybe.
My throat! Getting hard to swallow.
Oldtimers say no one ever need die of snakebite.

AYEE: Dryland, why
Do you lure him
To the poisoned waters
Seeping from your core?

NARRATOR: Venoms are proteins related to the albumin
In the white of an egg. They contain both toxic
And anti-toxic substances. Among the toxic,
A coagulin, a haemolysin, a haemorrhagin and
A neurotoxin have been isolated.

TOM: All you have to do is kill the snake,
Cut out its liver and eat it.
That'll cure any bite.

NARRATOR: The coagulin
Is a diastase, which comes from the white
Blood corpuscles, and acts within the blood vessels
Inducing clots which may lead to death through
Embolism. Its action is transient since it is
Offset by that of the haemolysin, which breaks
down
The red corpuscles. Haemorrhagin acts on the walls
Of the capillaries, allowing blood to pass into
The tissues: especially of the skin, lungs,
Intestines and bladder.

TOM: He stabbed me before I even seen him.

NARRATOR: Neurotoxin has a
Selective action on the nervous system. It acts
On the brain, bringing about stupor and
A dazed condition. By attacking the spinal cord,
It causes first, paralysis, and, after reaching the
medulla,
Nausea, sickness and profuse sweating.

BEAUBIER: Dear Sir:

I have the honour to acknowledge the receipt of your letter dated September 19th. In the matter of Mr. Thomas Greenaway, I am grieved to advise you that I must file a report of his demise.

TOM: If I just lie here quiet, breathing slow.
There's your lake, Tom, to the north,
Two, three miles. And southwards, the salt lakes,
Steaming, smell the stink from here.
Water, have to drink. Have to drink. Just a little.
There! Still lots if I save it.
Ah, Ayee, bring me water in your brown hands;
Cup me in your cool hands like dew.

BEAUBIER: Tuesday last we captured an Indian who had in his possession Mr. Greenaway's compass which said Indian carried in an ornate shoulderbag, which men in my company assure me is a medicine bag. It is therefore to be assumed that the prisoner attached some sort of superstitious value to the object in question. Subsequent to our discovery, we elicited a more complete account of his gaining possession of the compass.

He told an improbable tale of having seen several weeks ago at sunrise, a man dancing and writhing on top of a high butte north of three salt lakes. He took this dance to be one to placate the angry sky god. For at that time, an electrical storm encircled the hills of the valley and seemed to turn on the centre of the butte's height. He remarked on the unusual time, early morning, of this phenomenon. And it is true that such violent storms usually come in the evening, as an aftermath of the building up of heat in the valley during the day.

TOM: Ducks fly over without stopping.
Nothing, nothing finds me here. Tom,
What's the matter with you? They know
Where you've gone. Tomorrow night
They'll organize a search party.
Wind here on the butte strong, no cover.
Tomorrow, sun. If I could sleep!
My tongue swells to choke me, choke off
Sleep. Nothing sleeps here, everything is still,
Nothing sleeps.

AYEE: It is a year
He has stridden before me.
He bound the wild land
With his steel thongs.

Now, I feel a weariness
In his steps.
The earth is slowing
Him, his feet drag
In the heat of the land.
He kicks the dirt
And grey dust rises
To choke him. He tramples
The rocks, they turn
And strike him
With their teeth of stone.
Why did he follow
The stink of the bitter lakes?
Why did he not go north
To the watering hole?
The earth pulls him down
To her sour caves.
There are freshwater lakes,
Treed coulees, where he
Could find water,
But the earth hides them from him.
I feel him move;
He turns in his sleep
But cannot sleep.

BEAUBIER: Subsequent to obtaining this information, I organized yet another search party of six men including myself, the Indian and the boy, who was so close to Mr. Greenaway and who would not be left behind. On arriving at the butte, the savage pointed to a cairn of rocks at the top, but refused to make the ascent with us. The boy, two others and myself climbed to the peak. The rocks were piled pyramidically with some care at the highest point of the butte, from which place we gained a panoramic view of the entire countryside.

NARRATOR: The symptoms of rattlesnake poisoning
Are as follows: the painful wound
Is speedily discoloured and swollen.
As a rule, constitutional symptoms appear
In less than fifteen minutes.
Prostration, staggering, cold sweats, vomiting,
Feeble and quick pulse, dilation of the pupil,
And slight mental disturbance. In this state
The patient may die in about twelve hours.

BEAUBIER: Against the cairn, we found Mr. Greenaway's canteen, binoculars and rifle. At the bottom, and about six inches from the ground, was a flat, projecting rock. On this ledge, we discovered Mr. Greenaway's sidereal watch. I am bound to report that the watch was still running. I am at a loss to explain how this could be since it has been now over a month since Mr. Greenaway left camp — excepting that someone has regularly wound it.

TOM: All night I hear the movement
Of animals; they come close, they wait,
They breathe the frosted air,
They creep out from the shadow of boulders,
Along the ridges of the peeled earth's surface,
Shifting their weight in the spiked grass,
Watching me from black eyes, stopping
Me from sleep. Watching . . .

AYEE: His body is blinded:
The sickness of my eyes.

BEAUBIER: This I believe to be the case. I decided that it was inadvisable at this late date to disturb the remains, and so I returned to camp.

I am packing and shipping to the Department the effects of Mr. Greenaway, excluding the following items, which I am retaining to complete the survey:

one sidereal watch
one transit theodolite (Keuffel and Enser)
one aneroid barometer
one clinometer
one 100 foot steel band chain

If it is agreeable to the Department, I shall proceed with Contract #23 of Mr. Greenaway and expect to complete the work by the end of October.

I have the honour to be, Sir,
your obedient servant,
Henri Beaubier
October 2, 1910

Dear Sir:

Pursuant of my letter of October 2nd, I beg to report that further questioning of the savage by the Mounted Police revealed that Mr. Greenaway's death was occasioned by a self-inflicted and mortal wound.

TOM: (*Groaning*) my head aches with dark lucifers night
beasts prowling crawling breathing on me
ECHOES Echoes echoes light dims the stars my
hands swollen black dirt on the rim of the valley
hands thick as necks fingers strangle the sun with
black ropes brass sun suns suns a circle of
cold suns god have mercy on me the wind blows me
my feet far away down on the earth far below me
my feet move far above me my voice cries out I
call to you. sun, hear me sun's in my head Ayee
your smoky eyes your slow grey tears

BEAUBIER: It is claimed by the prisoner that he and several other savages saw Mr. Greenaway, astride the butte, place the rifle to his head and pull the trigger.

TOM: get away from
me they're crawling over my body where's my rifle
up up christ I can feel them on my legs around my
chest can't breathe stand up my rifle up there
go away get off they're tightening can't breathe
off off they're trying to kill me I can feel them
inside my gut in my gut the sun is spilling snakes into
the sky over top of me my shells where's my
shells one-two-three uh, four five that'll do
it Tom I'll shoot them off the sun BAM BAM BAM
too many of them BAM I can't get them all they're
inside me in my head coiling in my skull
Aaaaarghh tightening they're swallowing my
eyes BAM

The long, echoing shot fades away like distant thunder. The wind whines quietly; horned larks call.

NARRATOR: Against the dawn, at the rounded
Edges of the sand cliffs, snakes
Slide out and over, down
The face, flicking their tongues, scenting
The warm staleness of mothered nests,

BEAUBIER: This story seems to me a shameless prevarication, designed, in all likelihood, to conceal some crime that might be attributed to the prisoner if the body were exhumed. Mr. Greenaway's character was not such that he would have chosen this ignominious end. Nor do I know of any cause in his life immediately before the unfortunate events which would have led him to choose such an unnatural demise.

NARRATOR: The brown-spotted eggs of the swallow left
By terrified birds, that screech
In the wind, swooping at the stretched,
Sucking lengths of reptile. The snakes
Swallow the eggs whole and withdraw.

BEAUBIER: Also I should like to report in strictest confidence, to shield the sensibilities of Mr. Greenaway's immediate family, that while in the field, and during the past winter, when he did not return East as was his wont, he had taken to himself a young squaw.

An Indian woman begins her lonely song of mourning, first quietly, then, rising in pitch and intensity.

I am sure that she meant very little to him, the needs of the flesh sometimes outweighing the more civilized principles of social behaviour. But she did leave camp two days after Mr. Greenaway set out, which I thought strange at the time, seeing that he was due back in camp that evening. I do not wish to suggest that she was in any way implicated, but the coincidence of her departure, just before the presumed time of his death makes it incumbent upon me to report this information for your consideration. Mr. Greenaway did not mention her name or treaty number to me, nor can I find them amongst his papers. I am, therefore, at a loss to know how she might be traced, if the Department desires to do so. I might add that the young squaw was blind, although not totally so.

I have the honour to be, Sir,
your obedient servant,
Henri Beaubier
October 3, 1910

POST SCRIPTUM: The savage claims that the body was a black colour when they reached it.

TOM: Crusts of blood, dark streams . . .
A deer comes to me in the waves of heat,
Hooves moving over the salt-matted sand.

I wipe her away from my eyes but always
There, the same, floating over the flatland
To this butte. Am I dreaming
A last time? Shite, Tom,
You could have blasted away the half
Your head that didn't do the dreaming.
The deer comes, her pelt is tanned
And beaded like the garments of my Ayee.
Poor, blind doe,
Picking her way up this cliff,
Searching between darkness and light,
Staring through the grey milk of her eyes,
She comes so slowly, drops
Of her blood smear on the rocks.
Ayee? Is it you?
Have they hurt you
In the monthly cycle of the hunted?
Your sewn pelt is dry and grey, turning
To dust. By the time you reach
Me, you'll have powdered
And blown across the spikards of grass.
But your blood is still bright and red,
Like water.

Mourning song fades. The sound of thunder brings with it the rain of autumn.

AYEE: My hunter, warrior,
Star man.

I was coming.
I heard the thunder
Of your weapon from the hill.
From across the valley
I heard you fall
Like a wounded beast.

You have brought the sky
Down with you.
The sun trembles
In the black clouds;
The earth rumbles.
It is the beginning
Of the day.

Who has killed this?

I touch your head,
Blood, dust,
A stillbirth
Wrenched from my womb.

Who has killed this one?

Sun? Morning wind? Earth?
Earth.

BEAUBIER: Dear Sir:

I have the honour to acknowledge the receipt of your letter dated October 20th. This is to inform you of our discontinuance of the surveying of Range 20 for this season. The unusually early cold and snow have prevented us from completing the contract, and I send herewith the last Progress Report for Subdivision Survey made under Contract #23 of 1910.

I took the occasion of our returning in the vicinity to visit the cairn and last resting place of Dominion Land Surveyor, Thomas Greenaway. The peak of the butte was bitterly cold and I only stayed a few moments. I regret it was not possible to have his earthly remains shipped East where he might have had a decent burial by those who loved him. Upon my return, I shall most certainly carry

my condolences to his wife and children.
The deer are surprisingly plentiful this
autumn and we have enjoyed a good supply of meat
from this source for the past two months.

I continue to be, Sir,
your obedient servant,
Henri Beaubier
Late Afternoon, November 2nd, 1910

NARRATOR: September is rutting time.
The drylands are cooled by the rains of autumn.
Now, under the trees of the coulee, the bucks stamp
Out their territories and fight for chosen places,
Antler against antler, they bellow into the cooling air.
Under the yellowing leaves, they bellow
In the evening, stamping the ground.
The doe comes from the dew of the morning,
Lifting her feet, sniffs at the stamped
And straggled grass blades, feeling
The heat in her white haunches,
Answers the buck with a gentle bleat.
There, on the stamped field, she lies down
And waits. Together they will find a place
Near water.

AYEE: He called me Ayee;
My name is "the deer".

NARRATOR: In the dark of the coulee,
The days are short.
Curled in the grass, the doe
Is content to be with her mate
At this end of the year.

AYEE: The rains of autumn
Are cold.

NARRATOR: Long ago, the people of the coulee moved
To another valley. A place marked out for them.
They left their dead in the trees.

The rain pours down.

AYEE: Between two thin poplars,
In a swaddle of soft skins,
In a sling of bark,
I have hung him
Close to the stars
With his face uncovered.
He looks straight at the sky,
Scans it with his eyes,
With his salt water eyes.

I guard him all day
From crows; all night,
From the whirr of owls.
He looks forever
Into the heavens,
Forever he watches the sky.

Silence.

NARRATOR: And, another time, the woman said
To the man:

WOMAN: My fire has gone out.
You are a son of the sky. Go up there
And bring me a star.

NARRATOR: But man sat, bent, huddled
To the earth, clutching his cloak of warm skins
Close to him.

MAN: Woman

NARRATOR: He said.

MAN: I have grown old and blind,
I cannot see the sky.

---

1. Reprinted from *Wild Man's Butte* (Moose Jaw: Coteau Books, 1979). The poem was originally written for radio where it was produced by Irene Prothroe for CBC's "Anthology" in January 1977. The cast included John Neville as Narrator, V. Poland as Ayee, Robert Koons as Tom and David Sherman as Beaubier.

According to the authors' introduction to the Coteau book,

> *Wild Man's Butte* is set in the southern Saskatchewan badlands, "The Big Muddy" country, shortly after the beginning of this century. The "natural" story came from Harley Rakestraw, who was a cowboy on the Big Muddy in the 1930s. He had heard it from ranchers, for whom he worked. The story went that a surveyor was cut off from his party, lost his way and went mad from thirst and heat. Some said he shot himself; others, that Indians had murdered him. In any case, a cairn of stones marks the supposed place where this "wild man" danced and was later buried. Ironically, the butte, on top of which this cairn is built, lies within view of a body of fresh water.
>
> We have woven into this story the story of his love for a blind Indian woman and his "discovery" of the rattlesnake nest.
>
> The mythic plot, which acts as a frame for the story of the surveyor, is based on an Assiniboian creation myth, adapted for the purposes of this piece.
>
> Although the surveyor letters and other material and references are fictional, we have used materials from the Saskatchewan Archives and the Public Archives of Canada in preparing sections of the poem which relate to the activities of the surveyors.

Anne Szumigalski was born in 1922 in London, England. In 1951 she transplanted herself to Saskatchewan where she has flourished as a poet. Terrence Heath was born in 1936 in Regina. He is a writer and curator in visual arts and has been Executive Director of the Saskatchewan Western Development Museums and Director of the Winnipeg Art Gallery. At present he lives in Toronto and Niagara-on-the-Lake.

2. *Coreopsis tinctoria*, the common tick seed, is a small weed.

3. *Liatris punctata* and *Malvastrum coccineum* are both small plants native to the prairie provinces.

4. Scat or scats is a wilderness name for animal droppings.

5. Samphire is probably red samphire (*Salicornia rubra*), a prairie plant with small leaves often found near sloughs. Glasswort (*Salsola kali*) is often called Russian thistle.

6. This quotation comes from *Resource Reader* (Saskatchewan Department of Natural Resources), #411.

The Wind Our Enemy[1]

Anne Marriott

I

Wind
flattening its gaunt furious self against
the naked siding, knifing in the wounds
of time, pausing to tear aside the last
old scab of paint.

Wind
surging down the cocoa-coloured seams
of summer-fallow, darting in about
white hoofs and brown, snatching the sweaty cap
shielding red eyes.

Wind
filling the dry mouth with bitter dust
whipping the shoulders worry-bowed too soon,
soiling the water pail, and in grim prophecy
greying the hair.

II

The wheat in spring was like a giant's bolt of silk
Unrolled over the earth.
When the wind sprang
It rippled as if a great broad snake
Moved under the green sheet
Seeking its outward way to light.
In autumn it was an ocean of flecked gold
Sweet as a biscuit, breaking in crisp waves
That never shattered, never blurred in foam.
That was the last good year . . .

III

The wheat was embroidering
All the spring morning
Frail threads needled by sunshine like thin gold
A man's heart could love his land
Smoothly self-yielding,
Its broad spread promising all his granaries might hold.
A woman's eyes could kiss the soil
From her kitchen window,
Turning its black depths to unchipped cups—a silk crepe dress—
(Two-ninety-eight, Sale Catalogue)
Pray sun's touch be gentleness,
Not a hot hand scorching flesh it would caress.
But sky like a new tin pan
Hot from the oven
Seemed soldered to the earth by horizons of glare . . .

The third day he left the fields . . .

Heavy scraping footsteps
Spoke before his words, 'Crops dried out—everywhere—'

IV

They said, 'Sure, it'll rain next year!'
When that was dry, 'Well, next year anyway.'
Then, 'Next—'
But still the metal hardness of the sky
Softened only in mockery.
When lightning slashed and twanged
And thunder made the hot head surge with pain
Never a drop fell;
Always hard yellow sun conquered the storm.
So the soon sickly-familiar saying grew,
(Watching the futile clouds sneak down the north)
'Just empties goin' back!'
(Cold laughter bending parched lips in a smile
Bleak eyes denied.)

V

Horses were strong so strong men might love them,
Sides groomed to copper burning the sun,
Wind tangling wild manes, dust circling wild hoofs,
Turn the colts loose! Watch the two-year-olds run!
Then heart thrilled fast and the veins filled with glory
The feel of hard leather a fortune more sweet
Than a girl's silky lips. He was one with the thunder,
The flying, the rhythm, of untamed, unshod feet!

But now—
It makes a man white-sick to see them now,
Dull—heads sagging—crowding to the trough—
No more spirit than a barren cow.
The well's pumped dry to wash poor fodder down,
Straw and salt—and endless salt and straw
(Thank God the winter's mild so far)
Dry Russian thistle crackling in the jaw—
The old mare found the thistle pile, ate till she bulged,
Then, crazily, she wandered in the yard,
Saw a water-drum, and staggering to its rim
Plodded around it—on and on in hard
Madly relentless circle. Weaker—stumbling—
She fell quite suddenly, heaved once and lay.
(Nellie the kid's pet's gone, boys.
Hitch up the strongest team. Haul her away.
Maybe we should have mortgaged all we had
Though it wasn't much, even in good years, and draw
Ploughs with a jolting tractor.
Still—you can't make gas of thistles or oat straw.)

VI

Relief.
'God, we tried so hard to stand alone!'

Relief.
'Well, we can't let the kids go cold.'
They trudge away to school swinging half-empty lard-pails
to shiver in the schoolhouse (unpainted seven years),
learning from a blue-lipped girl
almost as starved as they.

Relief cars.
'Apples, they say, and clothes!'
The folks in town get their pick first,
Then their friends—
'Eight miles for us to go so likely we
won't get much—'
'Maybe we'll get the batteries charged up and have
the radio to kind of brighten things—'

Insurgents march in Spain

Japs bomb Chinese

Airliner lost

'Maybe we're not as badly off as some—'
'Maybe there'll be a war and we'll get paid to fight—'
'Maybe—'
'See if Eddie Cantor's on to-night!'[2]

VII

People grew bored
Well-fed in the east and west
By stale, drought-area tales,
Bored by relief whinings,
Preferred their own troubles.
So those who still had stayed
On the scorched prairie
Found even sympathy
Seeming to fail them
Like their own rainfall.

'Well—let's forget politics,
Forget the wind, our enemy!
Let's forget farming, boys,
Let's put on a dance to-night!
Mrs. Smith'll bring a cake,
Mrs. Olsen's coffee's swell!'

The small uneven schoolhouse floor
Scraped under big work-boots
Cleaned for the evening's fun,
Gasoline lamps whistled.
One Hungarian boy
Snapped at a shrill guitar,
A Swede from out north of town
Squeezed an accordion dry,
And a Scotchwoman from Ontario
Made the piano dance
In time to 'The Mocking Bird'
And 'When I Grow too Old to Dream',
Only taking time off
To swing in a square-dance,
Between ten and half-past three.

Yet in the morning
Air peppered thick with dust,
All the night's happiness
Seemed far away, unreal
Like a lying mirage,
Or the icy-white glare
Of the alkali slough.

VIII

Presently the dark dust seemed to build a wall
That cut them off from east and west and north,
Kindness and honesty, things they used to know,
Seemed blown away and lost
In frantic soil.
At last they thought
Even God and Christ were hidden
By the false clouds
—Dust-blinded to the staring parable,
Each wind-splintered timber like a pain-bent Cross.
Calloused, groping fingers, trembling
With overwork and fear,
Ceased trying to clutch at some faith in the dark,
Thin, sick courage fainted, lacking hope.
But tightened, tangled nerves scream to the brain
If there is no hope, give them forgetfulness!
The cheap light of the beer-parlour grins out,
Promising shoddy security for an hour.
The Finn who makes bad liquor in his barn
Grows fat on groaning emptiness of souls.

IX

The sun goes down. Earth like a thick black coin
Leans its round rim against the yellowed sky.
The air cools. Kerosene lamps are filled and lit
In dusty windows. Tired bodies crave to lie
In bed forever. Chores are done at last.

A thin horse neighs drearily. The chickens drowse,
Replete with grasshoppers that have gnawed and scraped
Shrivelled garden leaves. No sound from the gaunt cows.
Poverty, hand in hand with fear, two great
Shrill-jointed skeletons stride loudly out
Across the pitiful fields, none to oppose.
Courage is roped with hunger, chained with doubt.
Only against the yellow sky, a part
Of the jetty silhouette of barn and house
Two figures stand, heads close, arms locked,
And suddenly some spirit seems to rouse
And gleam, like a thin sword, tarnished, bent,
But still shining in the spared beauty of moon,
As his strained voice says to her, 'We're not licked yet!
It must rain again—it *will*! Maybe—soon—'

X

Wind
in a lonely laughterless shrill game
with broken wash-boiler, bucket without
a handle, Russian thistle, throwing up
sections of soil.

God, will it never rain again? What about
those clouds out west? No, that's just dust, as thick
and stifling now as winter underwear.
No rain, no crop, no feed, no faith, only
wind.

---

1. Reprinted from the Ryerson Poetry Chapbook Series (Toronto: Ryerson, 1939). Probably more than any other Canadian poem, "The Wind Our Enemy" is identified with the harshness of the Canadian prairie experience during ten years of drought and depression, 1929-1939. Even non-literary people not only know it, but also consider it a classic in the Canadian cultural tradition.

Anne Marriott was born in 1913 in Victoria. She wrote "The Wind Our Enemy" after spending the summer of 1937 with relatives near Forgan, Saskatchewan.

2. Eddie Cantor was a popular American singer and comedian on the radio.

Seed Catalogue[1]

Robert Kroetsch

1.

No. 176—**Copenhagen Market Cabbage:** "This **new introduction, strictly speaking,** is in every respect a **thoroughbred,** a **cabbage** of **highest pedigree,** and is **creating considerable flurry** among **professional gardeners** all **over the world.**"

We took the storm windows/off
the south side of the house
and put them on the hotbed.
Then it was spring. Or, no:
then winter was ending.

"I wish to say we had lovely success
this summer with the seed purchased
of you. We had the finest Sweet
Corn in the country, and Cabbage
were dandy."
—W.W. Lyon, South Junction, Man.

My mother[2] said:
Did you wash your ears?
You could grow cabbages
in those ears.

Winter was ending.
This is what happened:
we were harrowing the garden.
You've got to understand this:
I was sitting on the horse.
The horse was standing still.
I fell off.

The hired man laughed: how
in hell did you manage to
fall off a horse that was
standing still?

Bring me the radish seeds,
my mother whispered.

Into the dark of January
the seed catalogue bloomed

a winter proposition, if
spring should come, then,

with illustrations:

No. 25—**McKenzie's Improved Golden Wax Bean:** "THE MOST PRIZED OF ALL BEANS. **Virtue** is its **own reward.** We have had **many expressions** from **keen discriminating gardeners extolling our seed** and **this variety.**"

Beans, beans,
the musical fruit;
the more you eat,
the more you virtue.[3]

My mother was marking the first row
with a piece of binder twine, stretched
between two pegs.

The hired man laughed: just
about planted the little bugger.
Cover him up and see what grows.

My father didn't laugh. He was puzzled
by any garden that was smaller than a
¼-section of wheat and summerfallow.

the home place: N.E. 17-42-16-W4th Meridian.

the home place: 1½ miles west of Heisler, Alberta,
on the correction line road
and 3 miles south.

No trees
around the house.
Only the wind.
Only the January snow.
Only the summer sun.
The home place:
a terrible symmetry.[4]

How do you grow a gardener?

Telephone Peas
Garden Gem Carrots
Early Snowcap Cauliflower
Perfection Globe Onions
Hubbard Squash
Early Ohio Potatoes

This is what happened—at my mother's wake. This
is a fact—the World Series was in progress. The
Cincinnati Reds were playing the Detroit Tigers.[5]
It was raining. The road to the graveyard was barely
passable. The horse was standing still. Bring me
the radish seeds, my mother whispered.

2.

My father was mad at the badger: the badger was digging holes in the potato patch, threatening man and beast with broken limbs (I quote). My father took the double-barrelled shotgun out into the potato patch and waited.

Every time the badger stood up, it looked like a little man, come out of the ground. Why, my father asked himself—Why would so fine a fellow live under the ground? Just for the cool of roots? The solace of dark tunnels? The blood of gophers?

My father couldn't shoot the badger. He uncocked the shotgun, came back to the house in time for breakfast. The badger dug another hole. My father got mad again. They carried on like that all summer.

Love is an amplification
by doing/ over and over.

Love is a standing up
to the loaded gun.[6]

Love is a burrowing.

One morning my father actually shot at the badger. He killed a magpie that was pecking away at a horse turd about fifty feet beyond and to the right of the spot where the badger had been standing.

A week later my father told the story again. In that version he intended to hit the magpie. Magpies, he explained, are a nuisance. They eat robins' eggs. They're harder to kill than snakes, jumping around the way they do, nothing but feathers.

Just call me sure-shot,
my father added.

3.

No. 1248—**Hubbard Squash:** "As **mankind** seems to have a **particular fondness** for squash, **Nature** appears to have **especially** provided this **matchless** variety of **superlative flavor.**"

Love is a leaping up
and down.

Love
is a beak in the warm flesh.

"As a cooker, it heads the list for warted squash. The
vines are of strong running growth; the fruits are large,
olive shaped, of a deep rich green color, the rind is
smooth . . ."

But how do you grow a lover?

This is the God's own truth:
playing dirty is a mortal sin
the priest told us, you'll go to hell
and burn forever (with illustrations)—

it was our second day of catechism[7]
—Germaine and I went home that
afternoon   if it's that bad, we
said to each other   we realized
we better quit   we realized

let's do it just one last time
and quit.

This is the God's own truth:
catechism, they called it,
the boys had to sit in the pews
on the right, the girls on the left.
Souls were like underwear that you
wore inside. If boys and girls sat
together—

Adam and Eve got caught
playing dirty.

This is the truth.
We climbed up into a granary
full of wheat   to the gunny sacks
the binder twine was shipped in—

we spread the paper from the sacks
smooth sheets   on the soft wheat
Germaine and I   we were like/one

we had discovered, don't ask me
how, where—but when the priest said
playing dirty we knew—well—

he had named it   he had named
our world   out of existence
(the horse   was standing still)

— This is my first confession. Bless me father I played
dirty so long, just the other day, up in the granary
there by the car shed—up there on the Brantford Binder
Twine[8] gunny sacks and the sheets of paper—Germaine
with her dress up and her bloomers down—

— Son. For penance, keep your peter[9] in your pants
for the next thirteen years.

But how—

Adam and Eve and Pinch-Me
went down to the river to swim—
Adam and Eve got drownded.

But how do you grow a lover?

We decided we could do it
just one last time.

4.

It arrived in winter, the seed catalogue, on a January
day. It came into town on the afternoon train.

Mary Hauck,[10] when she came west from Bruce County, Ontario,
arrived in town on a January day. She brought along
her hope chest.

She was cooking in the Heisler Hotel. The Heisler Hotel
burned down on the night of June 21, 1919. Everything
in between: lost. Everything: an absence

of satin sheets
of embroidered pillow cases
of tea towels and English china
of silver serving spoons.

How do you grow a prairie town?

The gopher was the model.
Stand up straight:
telephone poles
grain elevators
church steeples.
Vanish, suddenly: the
gopher was the model.

How do you grow a past/
to live in

the absence of silkworms
the absence of clay and wattles[11] (whatever the hell
they are)
the absence of Lord Nelson[12]
the absence of kings and queens
the absence of a bottle opener, and me with a vicious
attack of the 26-ounce flu
the absence of both Sartre and Heidegger[13]
the absence of pyramids
the absence of lions
the absence of lutes, violas and xylophones
the absence of a condom dispenser in the Lethbridge Hotel, and me
about to screw an old Blood[14] whore. I was in love.
the absence of the Parthenon, not to mention the Cathédrale de
Chartres[15]
the absence of psychiatrists
the absence of sailing ships
the absence of books, journals, daily newspapers and everything else
but the *Free Press Prairie Farmer* and *The Western
Producer*[16]
the absence of gallows (with apologies to Louis Riel)[17]
the absence of goldsmiths
the absence of the girl who said that if the Edmonton Eskimos won the
Grey Cup[18] she'd let me kiss her nipples in the foyer of
the Palliser Hotel. I don't know where she got to.
the absence of Heraclitus[19]
the absence of the Seine, the Rhine, the Danube, the Tiber and the
Thames.[20] Shit, the Battle River ran dry one fall. The
Strauss boy could piss across it. He could piss higher
on a barn wall than any of us. He could piss right clean
over the principal's new car.
the absence of ballet and opera
the absence of Aeneas[21]

How do you grow a prairie town?

Rebuild the hotel when it burns down. Bigger. Fill it
full of a lot of A-1 Hard Northern bullshitters.[22]

— You ever hear the one about the woman who buried
her husband with his ass sticking out of the ground
so that every time she happened to walk by she could
give it a swift kick?

— Yeh, I heard it.

5.

I planted some melons, just to see what would
happen. Gophers ate everything.

I applied to the Government.
I wanted to become a postman,
to deliver real words
to real people.

There was no one to receive
my application.

I don't give a damn if I do die do die do die do die do die
do die do die do die do die do die do die do die do die do
die do die do die do die do die do die do die do die do die
do[23]

6.

No. 339—**McKenzie's Pedigreed Early Snowcap Cauliflower:** "Of the many **varieties** of **vegetables** in **existence, Cauliflower** is **unquestionably** one of the **greatest inheritances** of the **present generation, particularly Western Canadians.** There is **no place** in the **world** where **better cauliflowers** can be **grown** than right here in the **West.** The **finest specimens** we have **ever seen,** larger and of **better quality,** are **annually grown** here on our **prairies.** Being **particularly** a **high altitude plant** it **thrives** to a **point** of **perfection** here, **seldom seen** in **warmer climes.**"

But how do you grow a poet?

Start: with an invocation[24]
invoke—

His muse is
his muse/if
memory is

and you have
no memory then
no meditation
no song (shit
we're up against it)

how about that girl
you felt up in the
school barn or that
girl you necked with
out by Hastings' slough
and ran out of gas with
and nearly froze to
death with/ or that
girl in the skating
rink shack who had on
so much underwear you
didn't have enough
prick to get past her/
CCM skates

Once upon a time in the village of Heisler—

— Hey, wait a minute.
That's a story.

How do you grow a poet?

For appetite: cod-liver
oil.
For bronchitis: mustard
plasters.
For pallor and failure to fill
the woodbox: sulphur
& molasses.
For self-abuse:[25] ten Our
Fathers & ten Hail Marys.
For regular bowels: Sunny Boy
Cereal.[26]

How do you grow a poet?

"It's a pleasure to advise that I
won the First Prize at the Calgary
Horticultural Show . . . This is my
first attempt. I used your seeds."

Son, this is a crowbar.
This is a willow fencepost.
This is a sledge.
This is a roll of barbed wire.
This is a bag of staples.
This is a claw hammer.

We give form to this land by running
a series of posts and three strands
of barbed wire around a ¼-section.

First off I want you to take that
crowbar and drive 1,156 holes
in that gumbo.[27]
And the next time you want to
write a poem
we'll start the haying.

How do you grow a poet?

This is a prairie road.
This road is the shortest distance
between nowhere and nowhere.
This road is a poem.

Just two miles up the road
you'll find a porcupine
dead in the ditch. It was
trying to cross the road.

As for the poet himself
we can find no record
of his having traversed
the land/in either direction

no trace of his coming
or going/only a scarred
page, a spoor of wording
a reduction to mere black

and white/a pile of rabbit
turds that tells us
all spring long
where the track was

poet . . . say uncle.

How?

Rudy Wiebe: "You must lay great black steel lines of fiction, break up that space with huge design and, like the fiction of the Russian steppes, build a giant artifact. No song can do that . . ."[28]

February 14, 1976. Rudy, you
took us there: to the Oldman River[29]
Lorna & Byrna, Ralph & Steve[30] and me
you showed us where
the Bloods surprised the Crees
in the next coulee/ surprised
them to death.[31] And after
you showed us Rilke's word
Lebensgliedes.[32]

Rudy: Nature thou art.

7.

Brome Grass (Bromus Inermis): "No amount of cold will kill it. It **withstands** the summer suns. Water may stand on it for several weeks without apparent injury. The roots push through the soil, throwing up new plants continually. It **starts quicker** than other grasses in the spring. **Remains green** longer in the fall. **Flourishes under absolute neglect.**

The end of winter:
seeding/time.

How do you grow
a poet?

(a)

I was drinking with Al Purdy. We went round and round
in the restaurant on top of the Chateau Lacombe. We
were the turning center in the still world, the winter
of Edmonton was hardly enough to cool our out-sights.

The waitress asked us to leave. She was rather insistent;
we were bad for business, shouting poems at the paying
customers. Twice, Purdy galloped a Cariboo horse[33]
right straight through the dining area.

Now that's what I call
a piss-up.

"No song can do that."

(b)

No. 2362—**Imperialis Morning Glory:** "This is the wonderful **Japanese Morning Glory,** celebrated the world over for its **wondrous beauty** of both flowers and foliage."

Sunday, January 12, 1975. This evening after rereading *The Double Hook*:[34] looking at Japanese prints. Not at actors. Not at courtesans. Rather: Hiroshige's[35] series, *Fifty-Three Stations on the Tokaido*.

From the *Tokaido* series: "Shono-Haku-u." The bare-assed travellers, caught in a sudden shower. Men and trees, bending. How it is in a rain shower/ that you didn't see coming. And couldn't have avoided/ even if you had.

The double hook:
the home place.

The stations of the way:
the other garden

Flourishes.
Under absolute neglect.

(c)

Jim Bacque said (I was waiting for a plane,
after a reading; Terminal 2, Toronto)—he said,
You've got to deliver the pain to some woman,
don't you?[36]

— Hey, Lady.
You at the end of the bar.
I wanna tell you something.

— Yuh?

— Pete Knight—of Crossfield,
Alberta. Bronc-Busting Champion
of the World. You ever hear of
Pete Knight, the King of All
Cowboys, Bronc-Busting Champion
of the World?[37]

— Huh-uh.

— You know what I mean? King
of *All* Cowboys . . . Got
killed—by a horse.
He fell off.

— You some kind of a nut
or something?

8.

We silence words
by writing them down.

THIS IS THE LAST WILL AND TESTAMENT
OF ME, HENRY L. KROETSCH:

(a) [yes, his first bequest]

To my son Frederick my carpenter tools.

It was his first bequest. First,
a man must build.

Those horse-barns around Heisler—
those perfectly designed barns
with the rounded roofs—only Freddie
knew how to build them. He mapped
the parklands with perfect horse-barns.

I remember my Uncle Freddie.
(The farmers no longer
use horses.)

Back in the 30s, I remember
he didn't have enough money
to buy a pound of coffee.

Every morning at breakfast
he drank a cup of hot water
with cream and sugar in it.

Why, I asked him one morning—
I wasn't all that old—why
do you do that? I asked him.

Jesus Christ, he said. He was
a gentle man, really. Don't you
understand *anything*?

9.

The danger of merely living.

a shell/exploding
in the black sky: a
strange planting

a bomb/exploding
in the earth: a
strange

man/falling
on the city.
Killed him dead.

It was a strange
planting.

the absence of my cousin who was shot down while bombing
the city that was his maternal great-grandmother's
birthplace. He was the navigator. He guided himself
to that fatal occasion:

— a city he had
forgotten
— a woman he had
forgotten

He intended merely to release a cargo of bombs on a
target and depart. The exploding shell was:

a) an intrusion on a design that was not his, or

b) an occurrence which he had in fact, unintentionally,
himself designed, or

c) it is essential that we understand this matter
because:

He was the first descendant of that family to return
to the Old Country. He took with him: a cargo of bombs.

Anna Weller: *Geboren* Cologne, 1849.
Kenneth MacDonald: Died Cologne, 1943.

A terrible symmetry.

A strange muse: forgetfulness. Feeding her far children
to ancestral guns, blasting them out of the sky, smack/
into the earth. Oh, she was the mothering sort. Blood/
on her green thumb.

10.

After the bomb/blossoms
After the city/falls
After the rider/falls
(the horse
standing still)

Poet, teach us
to love our dying.

West is a winter place.
The palimpsest of prairie

under the quick erasure
of snow, invites a flight.[38]

How/do you grow a garden?

(a)

No. 3060—**Spencer Sweet Pea:**
Pkt. 10¢; oz. 25¢;
¼ lb. 75¢; ½ lb. $1.25.

Your sweet peas
climbing the staked
chicken wire,
climbing the stretched
binder twine by
the front porch

taught me the smell
of morning, the grace
of your tired
hands, the strength
of a noon sun, the
color of prairie grass

taught me the smell
of my sweating armpits.

(b)

How do you a garden grow?[39]
How do you grow a garden?

"Dear Sir,

The longest brome grass I remember seeing was one night in Brooks.[40] We were on our way up to the Calgary Stampede, and reached Brooks about 11 pm, perhaps earlier because there was still a movie on the drive-in screen. We unloaded Cindy, and I remember tying her up to the truck box and the brome grass was up to her hips. We laid down in the back of the truck—on some grass I pulled by hand—and slept for about three hours, then drove into Calgary.

Amie"

(c)

No trees
around the house,
only the wind.
Only the January snow.
Only the summer sun.

Adam and Eve got drownded—
Who was left?[41]

---

1. "Seed Catalogue" was originally published in 1977 in *Seed Catalogue* (Winnipeg: Turnstone Press). The poem was printed over the vague background of the 26th Annual Seed Catalogue of the McKenzie Seed Co. It is, after all, a garden poem operating in loose association with a tradition of garden poems extending back to at least Andrew Marvel and John Milton. "Seed Catalogue" is now part of *Field Notes, The Collected Poetry of Robert Kroetsch* (Toronto: General Publishing Co., 1981).

The impact of this poem on the development of an indigenous prairie voice has been enormous. Several of the authors in this book consider their work to be the result of the enKroetschment of "Seed Catalogue." In fact, it was dedicated to two of them: David Arnason and Dennis Cooley.

Robert Kroetsch was born in 1927 in Heisler, Alberta. He now lives in Winnipeg where he is Professor of Canadian Literature at the University of Manitoba.

2. Kroetsch speaks about his mother in *Labyrinths of Voice*, ed. S. Neumann and R. Wilson (Edmonton: NeWest Press, 1982), p. 22.

3. Kroetsch has changed the last line of this verse. "The more you toot" is the "correct" final line.

4. These words recall the oxymorons in both William Blake's "The Tyger" where the tiger has a "fearful symmetry" and W.B. Yeats's "Easter 1916" where the executed leaders of the Easter Week Rebellion possess "a terrible beauty."

5. In 1940 the Reds beat the Tigers in seven games.

6. This appears to be an echo of Emily Dickinson's "My Life had stood—a Loaded Gun."

7. Kroetsch was raised in a Catholic family and received normal Catholic religious instruction.

8. Brantford Binder Twine was used to tie cut wheat into bundles. Farmers put the sacks that the twine came in to many uses.

9. "Peter" is an informal word for the male sexual organ.

10. The Hauck family also appears in *The Ledger* (1975). Hauck is the "maiden" name of Kroetsch's paternal grandmother.

11. This is an allusion to the second line of W.B. Yeats's poem "The Lake Isle of Innisfree" where, living amid the concrete of London, Yeats longs for the simplicity and the spiritual motive power of the Irish countryside, and resolves to build on an island in Loch Gill a cabin "of clay and wattles made." Wattles are stakes intertwined with small branches.

12. Lord Horatio Nelson (1758-1805) is probably the greatest Naval hero in British history. The Battle of Trafalgar, where he defeated the combined Spanish and French fleets, was his greatest victory, although he died in it. He was also a rather famous adulterer. James Joyce calls him the "one-armed adulterer" in *Ulysses* (1922).

13. Jean-Paul Sartre (1905-1980) and Martin Heidegger (1889-1976) were

twentieth-century Existentialist philosophers associated with the political left and the political right, respectively.

14. The Bloods are an Alberta Indian tribe.

15. These are two well-known symbols of the European tradition of high culture. The Parthenon, a temple to the Greek goddess Athena, is considered by many to be the supreme achievement of ancient Greek architecture. Chartres Cathedral is similarly considered to be among the most sublime artistic expressions of the Middle Ages.

16. *The Western Producer* calls itself Canada's largest weekly farm newspaper since 1923. *The Free Press Prairie Farmer* started in 1883 as the *Manitoba Free Press* and underwent various name changes. In *The Diviners* (1974), as a girl Morag Gunn dreams about publishing her story "Wild Roses" in *The Free Press Prairie Farmer.*

17. According to George Woodcock in his book *Gabriel Dumont* (1975), the martyr Riel, more than any other historical figure, manifests the qualities that fascinate Canadians. Although he was an American citizen at the time, Riel was executed in 1885 for having betrayed his "allegiance, fidelity and obedience" to the queen.

18. The Edmonton Eskimos football team won the Grey Cup, emblematic of the CFL championship, in 1954, '55, '56, '75, '78, '79, '80, '81, '82, '87, and they threaten to win every year. Kroetsch's female friend dare not reveal herself.

19. Heraclitus (c. 535-475 B.C.) was a famous Greek philosopher who believed that reality was composed of ceaseless change and binary oppositions, and that no one possessed an individual soul.

20. These are all much-romanticized European rivers. Until now the Battle River has not had the same international resonance, although it is often a point of reference in formal Canadian history and the Native oral tradition. The powerful Chief of the Plains Cree, Poundmaker, lived on a reserve on the Battle River. Fort Battle, threatened by the Cree during the Riel Rebellion of 1885, was located there. Battleford, where the Battle River joins the North Saskatchewan, became the capital of the North-West in 1877. Wetaskiwin, the town which appears so often in Kroetsch's novels, is located on the Battle River in Alberta.

21. Aeneas was a legendary Trojan who survived the fall of Troy, became the lover of Dido, Queen of Carthage, and through his descendants founded Rome. His exploits are the focus of Virgil's epic *The Aeneid.*

22. In the 1940s and '50s A-1 Hard Northern was the top grade of prairie wheat. "No. 1 Northern" is also the name of a piece of sculpture by John Nugent done in 1977 and placed in front of the Canadian Grain Commission Building in Winnipeg, but now situated on Stapon Road and Lagimodiere Blvd. near the Revenue Canada Taxation Data Centre, a perhaps appropriate location when one considers the noun that ends Kroetsch's line here. Equally apt is the fact that *No. 1 Northern* (1977) is the title of an anthology of Saskatchewan poetry edited by Robert Currie et al. Kroetsch is quick to admit poets to the realm of "bullshitters."

23. This is a line from a Country and Western song often sung by Johnny Cash. It is sometimes associated with masturbation.

24. In *Paradise Lost* Milton invokes the Holy Spirit to help him write his epic poem and "justify the ways of God to men." Kroetsch is, of course, operating against the grain of the European epic tradition in producing his own indigenous prairie epic. Here he invokes the local listener, "you," involved in stories about vaguely sinful activity. Extended linear narrative and formal language are not provided with their Miltonic priority.

25. Self-abuse is a euphemism for masturbation.

26. Sunny Boy cereal, a variety of grains, is still used by many farm families as fortification against the ills of the prairie winter. "It'll keep you going in the winter."

27. Gumbo is a prairie word for the particularly malicious muck encountered in many prairie regions.

28. See Wiebe's essay "Where is the Voice Coming From?" in *The Narrative Voice*, ed. John Metcalf (Toronto: McGraw-Hill Ryerson, 1972), p. 259.

29. The Oldman River is the last free-flowing river in southern Alberta. Kroetsch has written a series of poems called "Old Man Stories" which appear in *The Stone Hammer Poems* (1975).

30. Lorna Uher (Crozier now), Byrna Barclay, Ralph Ring and Stephen Scriver are part of the Moose Jaw Movement of Writers that also included E.F. Dyck, Robert Currie and Gary Hyland.

31. See Wiebe's story "Along the Red Deer and South Saskatchewan" in *Wild Rose Country* (1977), ed. David Carpenter.

32. R.M. Rilke only used this word once in his work: "Auf einmal faβt die Rosenpflückerin / die volle Knospe seines Lebensgliedes, / und an dem Schreck des Unterschiedes / schwinden die [linden] Gärten in ihr hin." See *Sämtliche Werke*, ed. E. Zinn et al (Wiesbaden: Insel-Verlag, 1966), Vol. 2, p. 435. A translation of the passage, by Claus Lappe, follows:

> And suddenly the girl picking roses
> Grabs hold of the full bud of his life-member
> And with the fright of the difference
> The gentle gardens in her fade.

33. The Canadian poet Al Purdy (b. 1918) has written a poem called "The Cariboo Horses."

34. *The Double Hook* (1959) by Sheila Watson is a novel that intrigues Kroetsch. Watson, like Kroetsch, is interested in daring and unusual forms. Binary oppositions run throughout the work of both writers. *The Double Hook* is a kind of Western (set in the Cariboo country) and is interested in notions of home.

35. Hiroshige (1797-1858), also known as Utagama and Ichiyusai, was a Japanese artist. *Fifty three Stages on the Tokaido* is a series of paintings done between 1833 and 1834 of the fifty-three stations on the Tokaido, the eastern sea road by which

travellers went between Tokyo and Kyoto. Hiroshige saw himself as an interpreter of man's role within the landscape. *Shono-Haku-u, Thundershowers at Shono* is number forty-six in the series.

36. Jim Bacque (b. 1929) is an Ontario novelist whose work often deals with social upheaval. Kroetsch has commented that Bacque provided a great deal of encouragement when he first started to write.

37. Pete Knight was born in Philadelphia in 1904, but came to Alberta when he was eight. He was World Champion in 1926, 1935 and 1936. He was one of the few to ride the almost unrideable Midnight, but he died in 1937 shortly after being bucked off an ordinary horse called Slowdown. "There never was a horse who couldn't be rode / There never was a cowboy who couldn't be throwed."

38. A palimpsest is a surface carrying traces of previously erased texts. Here the word recalls Jacques Derrida's use of Freud's essay "Note on the Mystic Writing Pad" where the French critic points out that experience leaves traces in the language which inevitably influence immediate verbal apprehension and expression. The use of the word "erasure" in this context carries traces of Derrida's notion of putting verbal signs *sous rasure* in *De la grammatologie* (1967) in order to demonstrate that concepts no longer valid nevertheless continue to function as part of the cultural climate.

39. Is there an echo here of "Mary, Mary, quite contrary, how does your garden grow?"

40. Brooks, Alberta is located on the Trans-Canada Highway about half-way between Medicine Hat and Calgary.

41. The answer is, of course, "Pinch me" . . . WATCH OUT!!!

Homestead, 1914
(SEC. 32, TP4, RGE2, W3RD, SASK.)[1]

Andrew Suknaski

i returning

for the third spring in a row now
i return to visit father in his yorkton shack
the first time i returned to see him
he was a bit spooked
seeing me after eleven years—
a bindertwine held up his pants then
that year he was still a fairly tough little beggar
and we shouted to the storm fighting
to see who would carry my flightbag across the cn tracks
me crying: *for chrissake father*
lemme carry the damn thing the
train's already too close!

now in his 83rd year father fails
is merely 110 pounds now and cries while
telling me of a growing pain after the fall
from a cn freightcar
in the yard where he works unofficially as a cleanup man
tells of how the boss that day
slipped a crisp 20 into his pocket and said:
you vill be okay meester shoonatzki
dont tell anyvon about dis
commeh bek in coopleh veek time. . . .
father says his left testicle has shriveled
to the size of a shelled walnut
says there's simply no fucking way
he'll see another doctor—says:

the last one tried to shine a penlight up my ass
now son
no one's ever looked up my asshole
and never will
never

while we walk through the spring blizzard to the depot
i note how he is bent even more now
and i think: *they will have to break his back*
to lay him flat when he dies

in the depot
father guards my bag while i buy two white owl cigars
and return to give him one
we then embrace saying goodbye
and i watch him walk away from me
finally disappearing in the snowflake eddy near a pine
on the street corner
and then remember how he stood beneath a single lightbulb
hanging from a frayed cord in his shack
remember how he said
my life now moves to an end with the speed of
electricity

ii mother

her ship sails for the new land
and she on it
the fare paid by her brother in limerick saskatchewan

dancing in the arms of some young farmer
she remembers her polish village
the day her mother is fatally struck
by a car—
she remembers being 14
when world war one begins
remembers how she and another girl walk 12 miles

to work every three days
shovelling coal onto flatcars for sixteen hours
before returning home
along the boundaries of wolves (their eyes glowing
like stars on the edge
of the dark forest)
she remembers the currency changing as the war ends
her money and several years' work
suddenly worthless one spring day

all these things drift away from the ship carrying
her to the unknown
new land

iii father

arrives in moose jaw fall of 1914
to find the landtitles office
is given the co-ordinates for the homestead east
of wood mountain village—
and he buys packsack and provisions for the long walk south
sleeps in haystacks for the first few nights
(finally arriving in limerick
buys homesteader's essentials: axe saw hammer
lumber nails shovel gun bullets food
and other miscellaneous items)
he hires someone with a wagon and horses
to drive him to the homestead
builds a floor and raises one wall that day
and feeling the late autumn cold
nails together a narrow box in which to sleep
the first night

the following morning
he rises through two feet of snow to find
all his tools stolen (except for the gun bullets
and knife he slept with)
he searches for a spot on the hillside
to carve out with a blunted knife
a cellar
in which to endure the first few years—
he nails together a roof with a stone

philip well is his closest neighbour
and they hunt together
and through long evenings
play cards by light of the coaloil lamp
spin tales of old country wanderings
to survive 40 below winters till pre-emption time
is up
when the landtitle is secured
and a more suitable shack is built—
father walks six times between moose jaw and
the homestead
till haggling civil bastards give him the title
each time
he carries a $10. bill sewn inside his pocket across
the heart

iv parting

the day i walked fearless between horses' trembling feet
my father watching with hands frozen
to a pitchfork
is clearer in my memory
than the day he and mother parted
—she leading the children through the fall
stubble to wood mountain

in the following years
all i knew of father was the lonely spooked man
whom i met each autumn
in the back alley behind koester's store
while winter descended from the mountains—
it seems he always came during the first storm
and tied his team to the telephone pole
(their manes and nostrils frosted)
he always pulled a side of pork from the hay
in the wagon
and placed it on my sleigh

parting
we never found the words
simply glanced at one another's eyes and turned
something corroding the love in my heart
until i left wood mountain one sunday afternoon—
running away to the mountains
for what i thought would be forever
until another spring
i returned to see father
eleven years later

v the funeral

sofie in winnipeg
sends each member of the family a telegram announcing
the death of sister eve

mother who is 66 at the time
rides a greyhound bus from moose jaw to brandon
all night
father and brother louis drive from yorkton
arrive in brandon the night before the funeral
and get a hotel room—
louis goes out and buys father a pair of pants
and a shirt

returns wondering: *how the hell will i get*
father out of that sweater he's sewn himself into?
back in the room
he goes to the bathroom and turns on the water
and returns to subtly introduce the idea to father
who will have no part of it
louis loses his temper and pulls out a pair of scissors
from a shaving kit
and wrestles father to the floor (cuts him out of
the old sweater
while father cries:
okay okay — i'll take a bath)

the following day
the family is all on edge
everyone wonders how mother and father will respond
to one another
after 18 years of silence—
louis drives father to the funeral chapel
where mother is already viewing their daughter
they park outside
and father nervously climbs out as the chapel door opens
(he freezes
while mother emerges and also suddenly freezes
both stand motionless for 30 seconds and then
begin to run toward each other
they embrace
and she lifts him off the ground
he is 79 at the time)

vi birth certificate

carrying it in my pocket now as father carried
the worn $10. bill across his heart for the landtitle
i have crossed bridges of cities
hoping to find salvation
have gazed into the dark rivers of
spring where others found love
hoping to glimpse the face of some god—
and stopped by grey-eyed policemen
produced identification and tolerated their jokes:
what do these letters and numbers mean kid?
where is this place?
is this all you have?

vii epilogue

my father once said:
i might have murdered you all and gone
straight to heaven

and having arrived at all these things now
what is to be done with you and love
father?
what is to be done now with that other man who
is also you?
that other man so long ago on a hot summer day
far too hot for man or beast
the day mother at the well with the rope
frozen in her hands watches louis
who has ceased haggling with you
sadly carrying a bucket of staples to the barn—
you father something frightening
slowly sweating and walking after him
you slowly raising a fence post above your thoughts
swimming in familiar rage
over that day's fence posts' improper spacing—

louis stopping suddenly for some reason
not looking back
but merely gazing across to tall wheat growing
beyond the coulee's black shadow
(you suddenly stopping too and seeming afraid
and then lowering the fence post
as you turn around and return to the picket pile
to continue sharpening poplar pickets
with your newly sharpened axe)
that other man beating mother with a rolling pin
by the cream separator one morning
she pregnant and later sleeping in the late afternoon
to waken from a dream while the axe rises
above her grey head
her opening eyes staring into the eye of death
you father slowly turning away once again frightened
and ashamed

you once warning us of that other man within you:
when these things happen to me
do all you can and help one another save yourselves
from me

that other man once sharpening mower blades
when brother mike plays and suddenly tips
a bucket of water used to soak blades—
that other man suddenly drowning in black rage
grabbing a long scarf from a coat hook in the porch
then seizing mike to knot the scarf around his neck
and around the end of the grindstone's pulley
bolted high in the porch corner
the trembling right hand slowly labouring to turn
the crude sandstone
(mother and sister sofie fortunately arriving just in time
to fight you and free your son)

father
i must accept you and that other dark man within you
must accept you along with your sad admission
that you never loved anyone in your life
(you must be loved
father
loved the way a broken mother loves her son
though he must hang in the morning
for murder)

viii suicide note

silence
and a prayer to you shugmanitou[2]
for something
to believe in

---

1. Reprinted from *Wood Mountain Poems* (Toronto: Macmillan, 1976).

Andrew Suknaski was born of a Polish mother and Ukrainian father in 1942 near Wood Mountain, Saskatchewan, where he still lives.

2. Shugmanitou means "coyote" in the Dakota Indian language.

The Shunning[1]

Patrick Friesen

some praise God
some cry uncle

I.
his shunning

And they shall drive thee from men, and thy dwelling shall be with the beasts of the field. . . .

(Daniel IV: 32)

August 12

A hundred and one things to do, but anyways Tina is getting a little better. Her fever is almost gone and she can swallow already.

Started canning today. Finished 12 quarts of yellow beans. The two oldest girls picked a lot of raspberries for preserves and jam. Maybe I can do all the beans tomorrow.

Old Mrs. Friesen, my aunt Katie, died yesterday. The Lord giveth and the Lord taketh away.

August 13

Abe Neufeld came with his buggy in the night. The boy was born around 6 in the morning. Their first boy. It was a very easy birth. The boy was skinny, though, and will be sickly. He has a big nose like his father. So far this year I have brought 5 children into this world. All were healthy.

I did the last of the beans today. Altogether there were 20 quarts. I finished the raspberry preserves too. There weren't many this year.

Tina eating again today.

he had disobeyed. had waded barefoot in the creek before the weather was warm enough. you could easy have got a cold she said. she brought out a spool of #10 thread and tied his ankle to a tree with a 5 foot length.

break that and you get strapping.

mother hoeing

her red arms
her eight-month belly
her hair tied into a knot

then the bright hoe raised high
slashing down like a sun
again   again
and mother stoops to pick up the mangled snake
slings it over the fence   a yellow rope

she wipes her hands on her apron
nostrils wrinkling she turns to me   smell this
I inhale the musk and grease of her hands

his mother thought it was the second coming[2]   one taken   one left. her eye has wandered for a moment. when she turned back she alone stood in mid-garden   hoe in hand.

for that instant she stood bewildered. christ had returned and left her behind. that was not her horror   the taken son was. to lose her only child   the flesh she loved more than herself   the flesh that would be made word.

her eyes looked for directions in the garden in the sky. there were no flames or winds. everything was still as before yet all lost in a moment.

then she saw corn stalks wave at garden's end. she ran to hug the boy with corn silk for his beard. a prodigal son[3] a kind of ghost baffled by her love.

I asked father why the garden needed ploughing
and without thinking or raising his eyes
he said that for anything to grow the earth must be turned

somehow the unruly garden was always smooth and hard-packed
by mid-summer
and somehow the carrots and potatoes always grew in rows

and sometimes I stopped playing
to watch father on his knees among the gladioli
only his hands moving as if they were leaves the air breathed upon

long as I remember
someone listening at the door or
crossing the yard beneath my window

mother peering between crib slats for my next breath
holding her breath for me as I dreamed

long as I remember these people
open fields and the sun shaping a shadow of me
these people staring
and merciless light

longing as I remember
for night to blacken the sky

we climbed the hayloft
swallows skimmed out the door
we sat   feet hanging outside

father seeding a quarter-mile away

our creek shining in the sun
Peter said it was a silver S
a brand placed on earth by God

a hawk hanging high and black

swallows fluttered beneath eaves
their nests like pouches
Peter said they were purses holding gold coins
to pay the hawk as rent

red-winged blackbirds wagging on cattails
Peter said they were his favourite bird
they bleed but never die he said

and mother calling   as usual
to make sure we were all right

black horses
muzzles glittering with frost
chains like frozen chimes

black horses
dragging logs into the firelight
their shadows rear across trees

and I'm wide-eyed all night

voices shouting commands
echoing from farther forests
and no one in sight

and this is how I dream of emptiness

I latch the barn door
bend to pick up a pail of milk
then wobble through snowdrifts

a steel guitar cries from our house
I pause   the night below zero
and listen to Peter's nasal song

He lifted me up to a heavenly place[4]

I look up   there
icy sheets of northern lights
planets reeling above the barn

only words sung   the guitar
encounter this star-marred night
and utter folly

Uncle Peter had the farm beside ours. I remember him as a quiet, serious man. He seemed never to be happy. I know I always admired Aunt Helen for being so patient with him, for taking him through the bad times. I was young then and I remember him from the time when he was having trouble with the church. So I guess there was a good reason for him being unhappy. That was a bad time. For us too. Mother and father were not supposed to visit Peter. I remember some men from church talking to father once for a long time.

People said Uncle Peter had too much pride. That's all I ever heard, and father wouldn't talk about it. Peter sure was his own man. That I know. You should have seen him walking behind his horses. Just the way he walked, ploughing or seeding, was kind of proud. You never saw him stooped, even when he carried heavy feed bags.

And you know, he was not a big man, quite thin even. He had kind of a hooked nose, I would say, and blue eyes, like the sky in summer, or sometimes greyish, also like the sky. Father, I remember, sometimes called him *der blaue Engel*.[5] I always thought it was because of those eyes. It seemed a funny thing to call a man.

I remember now too that Uncle Peter had asthma. Especially in the winter, or on cold evenings in the fall, his breathing would get heavy and his voice scratchy. After an attack once he told me I didn't know how lucky I was to be able to breathe easily. Then, after he got his breath back, he sort of laughed and asked what I thought would happen to a fish that couldn't live in water.

Uncle Peter left people alone and he wanted to be left alone. He would go into the bush when he felt too strong about one thing or another. Like when he was angry. And you never saw a temper like his. I know about his temper because I sometimes sneaked up on him near Buffalo Field. You know when you're young with nothing to do and you roam around, finding out things? Well, I did that too, and I found the spot where Uncle Peter would walk back and forth when he was upset. Right on the edge of Buffalo Field.

Anyways, usually he was quiet. One time, though, he was swearing and punching a poplar tree with his fist. When I went to look at the tree after he had gone, there was blood smeared on the bark. I wouldn't have wanted to see his knuckles.

I guess mainly he just wanted grownups to leave him alone because he would let me help with his work. He would teach me to do things right. He did his work just right always and so quickly.

sometimes the sun glowers
burns me black into soil
so that I am Adam again   before sin
before creation's frenzy

Lord Jesus Christ breathe into me
make me man   make me flesh again
as God the Father did in the beginning
and take away all sin and shame

a cry

of some animal caught

no (my son stung
I spit on my fingers
salve the reddening bump
and he asking will I die?

I'm thinking we all die

but he runs before I answer
no he will not die yet
he is not a stranger to this earth)

woman what does she want?
she knows the work I do long hours
look at these hands
and the lines the sun has made at the corners of my eyes

what does she think the horses would do
if I didn't prop up the fence where it sags?
and the chickens can they live on stones?
when do I find time for the garden?
as if I don't see enough of the sun
and when do I have a minute for my sweat to dry?

one day I'll give her an earful straighten things out
what does she think a man can do in one day?
how many hours are there? am I not to sleep?

even these poplars know it's not easy
before she knows it I'll be bones too like Queenie here
I may as well lie down right now
she can visit lay flowers on me
let's see where the farm goes without me

at night she says she wants me for herself
one of these days she'll see how much of me is left

rivers

a woman sags in ropes
her hair seaweed

where horses ford
bridle and sword glinting

the river grandfather swims
naked in his slim strength

where mosquitoes cloud a paddlewheeler

these rivers flowing me back
and   as in a dream   I cross and cross

I kiss His hands His feet
and though my lips redden
I cannot taste His blood

to find love

to find love
I sit on the stone between tomb
and Christ risen   pale with hunger

to find Jesus   alone   in the garden
before the serpent crawls through the fence

child

his fine legs   bent at the knee
squeeze the horse
he hardly occupies the saddle
grasping pommel and mane
his hair like honey in the sun
brown eyes take everything in

the horse a white sculpture

father his eyes slit by light
stands beside horse and child
one hand clutches a lead rope
the other circles the neck
as if ready to wrestle the horse down

I lean in the doorway. Loewen with Penner and Funk behind and below him stands on the top step of the porch. His clean white shirt is buttoned to the throat but one shoelace is undone dangles off the step.

Loewen holds a black Bible before him and though he knows the verse by memory he reads with his finger.

> *And I will give unto thee the keys of the kingdom of heaven: and whatsoever thou shalt bind on earth shall be bound in heaven: and whatsoever thou shalt loose on earth shall be loosed in heaven.*[6]

I step out and close the door so mosquitoes won't get in. There is very little room so Loewen backs down right on Funk's foot moves up again until both Funk and Penner are on the bottom step. When he is settled on the second step he wets a finger and pages further into his Bible.

> *Know ye not that a little leaven leaveneth the whole lump? Purge out therefore the old leaven, that ye may be a new lump, as ye are unleavened.*[7]

Penner slaps the back of one hand with the other. A tiny scarlet splash there and a wreckage of black legs and wings. Funk waves his hat back and forth in front of his face. There are mosquitoes on Loewen's hands one on his cheek but he pages on and reads.

> *It is a fearful thing to fall into the hands of the living God.*[8]

Bible closes. They bow their heads and Loewen prays for my salvation and that they will do the right thing. I move toward Loewen as he prays. He backs down. Funk and Penner stumble off the porch. Loewen shuffles aside as I go down and walk to the barn.

it was july   and the sun
there was a *tsocka boum*[9] and a rope swing
Peter sat upright   motionless
all afternoon he gazed unseeing across his land
everyone else was inside   Helena   the children

only

two horses   muzzle to muzzle
stand against the fence   tails flicking flies

Brummer   hot on the trail   yelping in the trees

and Peter on the swing

that sunday was the first day of his shunning

It was never easy to know Peter. I never had cause to doubt his love for me, but I didn't understand some of his ideas. He said more than once that there couldn't be such a place as hell, not with a loving God. That's what started all the trouble with the church. Peter must have mentioned this to someone and the pastor got to hear about it I guess.

The first time Reverend Loewen came over alone to talk with Peter. They didn't want me to listen, but I knew my Peter. He didn't change his mind, and I think that's where the talk of pride started. Things just got worse and worse. The more Loewen talked to Peter, the more stubborn he got.

He was banned.[10] It was July. A very hot July and lots of mosquitoes. Loewen and two deacons talked to Peter at the front door. I remember Peter would not invite them in. He stood in the open door, letting in mosquitoes like crazy. Then Peter must have gone to the barn, and the three men asked if they could come in and talk to me.

I must not share our bed with Peter, they said. I would surely be damned if I did. Such matters were, of course, right only between husband and wife and only if they shared the true faith and were submissive to the church. Christ's bride.

This was very hard for me, to stay away from Peter. I loved him. I remembered our wedding, how I had vowed to submit myself to him. But he never pushed for it. He must have known what they told me, and he was so proud. He never asked to enter my bed.

We talked it over, and I was scared by what he had to say about the church. I told him that if he wasn't right with them something must be wrong. I said we should try it the way they said. For a while. And maybe he would find his way to a firm faith again. Maybe it would help him settle his doubts. Peter said nothing.

Of course he got worse when people stopped coming to get eggs. The eggs we couldn't use Peter threw on a pile beside the hen house. One morning he slaughtered all the hens. I don't want to say how he did it. I never knew people could do things like that. He hardly ever spoke to me anymore. We got farther apart. I wanted him, but I thought he was wrong. I thought he was wrong. And I did not want to lose my faith. My Christ.

the boys beg to help father pitch hay
peter hands them a hayfork
and stands aside   leaning on the fence
a bridle   a garter snake slung over the top rail

he pulls a red handkerchief from his back pocket
wipes his brow   blows his nose
boys   he laughs   that way it'll be christmas before you finish
all in one motion   using legs as well as arms
see   and he skims a forkful of hay from wagon to hayrick
not bending his back but turning at hip's fulcrum

helen calls her men for supper
peter unties a boot and shakes out chaff
he points at the darkening horizon
boys   see that   tomorrow it gives rain

Of course, father and Uncle Peter didn't once mention the shunning. How people no longer came to buy eggs or chickens. How, when Peter went to town to buy goods, the only people who would talk to him were Frenchmen he knew from La Broquerie.[11] How even grandmother and grandfather had almost nothing to do with Peter. And how Helen was getting thinner and crowsfeet grew around her eyes. Instead they talked about last year's yield, this year's weather.

Even though they were pretty sure no one would be dropping in, I was told to watch at the front window.

Uncle Peter sort of half-lay in an overstuffed chair with one leg draped over the arm. This was not like Peter. But it was good to see him like that. Sitting there in one corner, not saying that much, but his eyes smiling. He looked the way I thought everyone should look on the day of rest.

Mother and Aunt Helen were in the kitchen making *vaspa*.[12] Father talked and talked like he had saved up words for weeks. He talked about the stoneboat he had built, about the nuisance swallows were around the barn, about how he found the Heinrich Wiens boy killing crows with a slingshot then cutting off their legs for bounty.

I went for the kitchen, I remember. Heard mother saying that a woman owed her husband at least a little love even if she didn't feel like it. And Aunt Helen, nearly crying, saying it was not what she wanted but what they wanted. When the two heard me, Helen wiped her eyes with her apron, and mother said I should tell the men that the food was ready. At least if their hands were clean, it was.

her mouth's hungering held back
as she kisses my cheek at the doorway
then she is gone

I kneel to ease my belly's pain
strike my head on the floor
remembering her bare arms around me
how I went lost there
helpless as a baby
and I woke   a man again

forever   her flesh
and now winter

and memories can kill

where she is now   the church
hitching post
worn steps
the hard benches
and Helen
her black kerchief   her white face

sits apart   on fire

the snare tightens with struggle

I lie in bed
swaddled in moonlight
and someplace out there
a rabbit scrambles
shrilling   almost human in the snow
in raw december   in this lost year of our Lord 1914

if I could live
find something from my people
something to hold

the days that have fallen
that were months and years
when men broke the land
when women gave earth their children
when there was childhood
before the stoneboat before the calloused hand

something to hold
from all those days going back

if I could find a love
that grabs Loewen by his collar and shakes him
awake look again look
with eyes open see me hands touch at least
at last a love that sloughs the flesh
and we are reborn in Christ loving man

if I could know each day of our 400 years
take them in hand and say this is what it is

simply something
to hold to live for
to bring the kingdom here

and we not forsaken

rooster crows the sun
and I know what must be done
before it crows again

I dress quickly
walk out boots in hand

running for the henhouse
I smell the heap of smashed eggs
grab the startled rooster and twist his neck
throw him on the stinking eggs

hens flutter as I flounder   reaching
tearing with my hands   my teeth
spitting blood and feathers
fat headless hens dancing on broken shells
the room all dust and feathers
and my voice shaking rafters
my words sailing through walls
no   I bellow   no   no

and then it is still   so still

sun slants in at the windows
on the spattered floor   on my untied boots

from Johann's farm a cock crows
the sun will not be denied

this man   less than a man
stands these days in doorways
this man   my man   I
flinch at this distance I have run

where fields grow bones
and nothing breathes
a graveyard I have circled before
now stumble   stand in the middle
turning   squint at the apparent edge   the trees

this distance will not be forgiven

I must come back
sit on benches
if I am to be loved again

but how do I come back?

reverend loewen said his mouth was open. peter's mouth hung open and he stared toward the trees. he didn't seem to hear loewen's words. then loewen remembered peter said that he was cold.

all this light he said
all this cold cold light

You know I didn't let go of Peter through all the trouble. Not even when he went wild that time. I finally let go when he was standing in the backyard, facing Reverend Loewen telling Peter how he could make things right again, how he could return to the church, how he could be with me again. Peter said nothing. I was washing the supper dishes and Peter in the backyard saying nothing. Just looking over Loewen's head toward the bush. When he finally said something, I saw his lips move, but all I heard was something about light. All the light, too much light, or something like that. Then Peter turned slowly to the kitchen window. I don't think he could see me. I was too far back from the screen. And he went to the barn. I let go.

forgive them he whispers
limp hair and sweating
forgive them he says
then his eyes open ask why

of the world
mother weeps for him

his brother shivers at noon

a choir of soldiers sings shoulder to shoulder

he smells rope at his wrists
the approaching rain

raises his head in the dark
forgive he says
at last
me

I didn't see Peter leave the barn, but that wasn't unusual. Whenever he wanted to be alone, when he didn't want to be seen, Peter would go in the barn at the front and out through a back door. Then it was only a few steps into scrub bush. That barn was almost like a tunnel from the yard into bush.

What he did in the scrub I'm not sure. I saw him there only once. I was walking back from visiting my sister-in-law, Carolina. When I got to the clearing, we called it Buffalo Field because there were a lot of skulls and bones there, I saw Peter walking back and forth on the other side. He walked along the edge of the field, sometimes out of sight in the trees, then walking in sun. He didn't see me. I watched for maybe twenty minutes, and Peter just went in and out of the trees, the sun.

I was pretty sure Peter was in the scrub. This time I was worried because I had felt myself let go of him. Without deciding to do it I had let go. As if I had said "okay, you often go your own way. Now you can go forever because that's what you want even though you keep saying you love me."

When dishes were finished, I sat on the top step. Our boys, Henry and Leonard, were playing with Brummer, Johann's dog. They were throwing a stick, and he was fetching. It was still warm though it had rained in the day. The clouds were already going, and the sky over the trees grew red. The boys were singing "red sky at night, sailor's delight." I laughed and said "you mean farmer's delight," but they said no. It was "sailor's delight." I thought that here we are in the middle of scrub and, except for the Atlantic when our fathers came over, we haven't seen the ocean for four hundred years. Yet the boys are singing about "sailor's delight."

Then I remembered that father had once said that some of our people had been whalers back in the Lowlands.[13] I couldn't believe it. These people crushing grain between thumb and forefinger for ripeness, pulling at a cow's teats, or picking chokecherries from stepladders, who could imagine them bending as the ship bucked, harpoon in hand, and Leviathan ahead spewing and snorting through wind and waves. Oh how I wished then for a sailor to come calling, to taste the salt on his lips. How I wanted to sail away with my sailor to warm lands. I was pretty silly then. I must have been about ten.

Now I was over thirty, and the red sky became night. I called the boys and put them to bed. I wondered where Peter was. I fell asleep on the couch waiting for him. I remember that I dreamed of sailing in an old ship. Someplace where gulls floated, rising and falling with the waves. When they tried to fly, they couldn't. The water held them. I felt so tired, trying to fly with them. I woke.

Peter was still not in the house so I lit a lantern and walked to the barn. No one there. I went to the henhouse. Empty. Just dark splotches, and feathers stuck to the floor.

Then I hurried back to the barn and went straight to the nails where Peter's .22 hung. But it wasn't there. I was not surprised. It was dark, and I knew I wouldn't find him. I went inside and sat up the rest of the night, my mind empty of anything.

I heard the rooster first. Then I heard Henry talking in his sleep. I woke him and asked if he was dreaming. I sent him for Johann.

I told Johann about Loewen being there last night and Peter not coming in for night. I said "find him, the rifle is gone, and he had nowhere to go."

a silver fall water
fall arcing aching
cock crow

singing the hollow

hallow
the hollow singing

still
in that cold face
singing yes yes yes
singing still
at cock crow
at caught cock crow
in the face of

no god
know

black wings flapping

in one appalling twitch
here beside this creek

blood spilling worthless
blood seeping in earth and heaven this night

where tomorrow

red sky

at morning
sailor's warning

the crouped child choking
and mother holding him over a steaming kettle

the child sprawled on gravel   licking his blood

the child   rolling his pantlegs to the knees
wading down twin creek   cattails bowing
this boy   his feet and calves mud-smeared
is man here   the caught corpse

one hand in water
one boot off   the other untied
his white foot nudging the rifle stock

his temple   a blue hole the bullet made

June 28

Blue jays woke me. A beautiful blue sky this morning.

While I was talking to Mrs. Dyck about her gall stones, my wife came in and whispered that someone had been shot. I rode out with Johann Neufeld. It was his brother who was dead. I asked how it had happened, and he said quietly that his brother shot himself.

He was lying in the bedroom. The cause of death was a gunshot wound to the right side of his head. We placed the body in the back of a wagon. The man's wife and young sons stood watching us. Neufeld brought the body into town. I filled out the papers in my office.

I'm puzzled by this suicide. I imagine it had something to do with his trouble with the church. Though what that trouble was I don't rightly understand. Strange people.

This evening I trimmed the lilac shrubs. Then I found this year's first ripe strawberries. Very tasty too. I had to go in because of the mosquitoes. They are awful this year.

Rereading Mill's *On Liberty*.[14] Must reading for anyone claiming to be educated I would think.

living in another world
where mother lies stone cold
and father embraces us

living where the ghost is free

we were two boys
swaying in a *tsocka boum*

we chewed leaves and told the world's story
about the smell of rain   about blackbird's flying

two young men   courting women
you looking for someone to lose yourself in
I hunting for one that could make me shiver
and scent the rest of the world

but I almost forget   forgetting
that you were God's own
the kind of child that dies before he's grown

always out of breath

and I almost forget
you aiming a rifle at the sun
thinking you could bring night

we were two boys
like almost any others

Before Peter's death, in the months I slept alone, I was held in esteem. The leaders, like Loewen, praised me for my faith. In church I had the sympathy and respect of my brothers and sisters. I was being true to Christ. Some marvelled at my courage in living with a sinful man who had placed himself outside the church. They thought I feared and even despised Peter, but that I stayed in his house to give him a reason to come back to the Lord. I never feared him, though sometimes I feared for him. I loved him. They were right in thinking I was hoping to bring him back. But from where?

When he died something changed. They tried to comfort me by saying I had done what was best, that I had done the best I could for him. But very quickly they avoided me. Fewer and fewer women talked to me or, if they did, only in passing and about other things. They still said I had done God's will, but now I think they feared me. I felt sometimes like a witch.

And I lived in shame for many years. Maybe still. A shame that I had not behaved in a truly Christian way, in a human way, and that Peter had known and despaired for me. Johann called Peter *der blaue Engel.* Maybe we were two angels. I often thought Peter was not meant for this world. It could be that neither of us was. Though I am still here.

now his narrow home
a mound a stone

wild rose bushes
barbed wire
and headstones on the other side

Franz Reimer
Katharina Plett
Bernhard Dyck

until the trumpet
until morning cracks open his grave
he lies apart
his face to the sun going down red

a part of them Peter
who wanted so much what wasn't

if love could clothe his bones in flesh

II.
time happens

For thou shalt be in league with the stones of the field: and the beasts of the field shall be at peace with thee.

(Job V: 23)

Today. Everything just looks itself. No tricks. And the sounds   as if I tilted my head   banged it a few times with one hand   hopped on one leg and emptied my ear of water. I can hear again.

The horseshit   still steaming   even the horseshit smells sweet.

And those plums bending the branch   sweating juice where they split open. Their insides just busting to get out.

I tell you it's amazing. On these church steps   service over and sun bringing the afternoon. Hilderbrandt and Klassen comparing crops   their wives deciding whose turn it is to visit. And Barkman over there   sitting on the rail   not talking at all. I think   if I know him at all   that he's remembering an afternoon like this   thirty years ago   when he could have tumbled a brown-eyed beauty   grey and lumpy now   five children   her husband's hands black from machines. Maybe he did. I've heard things.

But tell me something that tastes better than a strawberry. Something that makes your eyes squint and puckers your mouth. In July   when you're herding the cows home across Swallow Bridge and they turn off the dirt track to dip their muzzles in the creek   or like Peter used to say   when sun aims his bullets at us   is there anything you could want more than a handful of fat red strawberries?

Or this.

a woman walking home from church
her shawl loosens and slips to her shoulders
she pauses removes combs and pins
lifts her face to the sky and shakes out her fiery hair

behind her the sun and golden withers
of a horse reaching for grass
beneath the bottom strand of barbed wire

a horse the sun
and almost everyone shielding their eyes

on a sunday

thursday afternoon thunder
I come in from seeding
hoping to work other fields

and my Carolina's willing

I scrub at the basin
comb back my wet hair

cool air rustles at the window
we undress and stand
shivering staring at flesh

the deep rift of her spine curving to buttocks
her fingers like feathers raising hairs on my arms
my flat stomach her soft-bellied urge

Carolina takes my hand
and draws me beneath the quilt

I smell rain at the window

How she bunches freshly-cut gladioli in one quick hand and thrusts them into a pitcher. Her familiar fingers spreading the long stalks fluffing petals open.

How she walks   straight as a hollyhock   a milk-pail in each hand.

How she curves her head forward and to one side to watch the young one suck.

How like a girl she looks even though she is young.

rib-bones curving above grass
sun-painted skulls   like white wood
grained by wind and rain

these were cows and horses
carted here by Queenie or Bucky

chains around their hind legs
bloated bodies dragged into the weather

father's favourite   his first Prince
is bones here   his black hide his intestines
vanished like leaves   his stench lost in grass

my tongue tells names
and these bones speak their epitaph

a gopher rises
front legs at his chest
Brummer darts from my side
and suddenly nothing is there

November 21

The war is over in Europe but not here. Five of the patients I saw today have the flu. People are stunned by the ferocity of this epidemic. It is the invisible enemy.

It's been a long, wet fall. Today is cold, though, and an inch or more of snow has fallen.

November 22

Below zero today. The horses don't like this any better than I. They haven't grown a winter coat yet.

Since Mrs. Elizabeth Friesen and young Cornelius Siemens passed away on the 20th, there have been no new deaths. Henry Doerksen is over the worst. John Neufeld and his wife, however, are both seriously ill. Their daughter, Anna, and an aunt from Blumenort[15] are taking care of the young children.

Tonight I read Carlyle. *Sartor Resartus. Doubt of any sort cannot be removed except by Action.*[16]

November 23

The weather is clear and cold. I spread crumbs on the feeding stand for the sparrows. If I could be as hardy as they are.

November 24

Mrs. Neufeld passed away in the early morning. She was a young woman, only thirty-two, and left five young children. She had been asking for her children during the night. Apparently the youngest was at her breast and she stroking its hair. Her husband is unconscious. With their mother dead, the children need him now more than ever.

I read more Carlyle tonight.

Also repaired the door-jamb. Snow was drifting in.

My horses are worn out. J. Hiebert, my neighbour, offered the use of his team. I may have to take him up on that tomorrow.

to wake   finding november at the window
my wrist shrunk to bone
but to wake   again

earth   still fat with october
shivers beneath white wind

here   on this farm
between la broquerie and steinbach
now   in this hardening month   1918[17]
they say she has gone
and though I hear myself say it isn't true
I know it is because the house is cold

I dream a blizzard

Barney and Prince flounder
snow whirling from treetops
spinning where wind twists one way then another
snow drifting to their chests
melting on muscle   forelegs driving
and wallow   and Barney strikes the rise where snow is thin
leans against a poplar   deadstill

I turn my eyes back to the hollow
snow rising like pillars as wind swoops
but there is no Prince
and when I look to the trees there is no Barney

snow fluttering against glass
and I'm wondering how hard the earth
shovels flashing at noon   iron strike iron
how they lowered her then
snow and dead leaves wheeling across her casket

I lie facedown on her side of the bed
the warmth   the musk of her
this I cannot bear

a mirror face a stone behind glass
hanging there almost silver almost splintered
like a thin moon you can see through into dreams

eyes see themselves
everywhere they look

her hands grasp beneath armpits wrinkling baby's skin
as she lifts the dripping child (I remember

the towel sea blue) threads dangling
where it was torn from the larger cloth

she wipes her fingers on the apron

there is no getting away from the eyes
flat and cold
and the thin man they show me
his mouth slack with staring
in his eyes are dreams to stun me

her legs open to land him
he flops at her breast gaping
(I remember my dream of her
limbs flung caught beneath a white sheet
I crawled in beside her the fever of her flesh
vanished only her cold skin against my lips

I remember our daughter crying in another room)

she straddles him on knees and palms
then lowers proudly to her elbows
he sucks at hungry nipples (I remember
the child woke I remember light from the other room
seeping in through a crack all around the door)

she stands sideways before the mirror
combing her hair with long fingers
half-sings *mirror mirror on the wall*[18]
then turns away laughing

at 2 a.m.
our daughter   suddenly awake
sways at the end of her bed
eyelids drooping   her eyes prowl the room
peering for the comfort of her mother's breast

her mouth remembers
and she listens for footsteps

I want to tell her about absence
how the mouth learns to crimp
I want to say that her mouth will know the world
and that sometimes she will hear silence

father will hold you   I say
and walk her past tears to sleep

Today one of the boys came running in calling "Mutti Mutti." He saw me at the stove   stared for a moment. Sitting down he just looked at me   a blue scarf around his forehead   crossing his mouth and nose   and wet where he breathed. Then he said "Papa   come and see my snowman   behind the house. It's finished." I put on my parka and went out to see. There it was   three balls of snow   one on top of the other   branches for arms   the eyes were coals. I said what a fine snowman but what are you going to call him? He thought   then said "his name will be Johann   yes   if you give me one of your hats to put on his head he will be Johann."

When I was a young boy I once froze my feet. Father filled a tub with snow   brought it in and began rubbing my feet with it. I remember how I cried. I said the snow hurt. Father said the snow made it hurt less. Nothing could take the pain away completely unless I wanted my feet to stay frozen. Then   he said   when the feet turned black they would have to be cut off with a crosscut saw.

january 21

neustadtgasse[19]
narrow deserted
six men four in pairs two alone
sad men determined
too proud to crouch yet
walking cautiously in the shadows of houses
each man careful to walk in the tracks of the one who went before
and the tracks getting bigger their shapes vague

moonlight

(but I don't know this a dream
of facts or maybe a memory
I saw in my double tracks today
as I walked back from barn to house

remember?

yes the snow that's what
and the sound boots make in fresh snow)

snow squeaking
clouds of breath
a door opening light and the door closed
that's all

inside I don't remember a table? a candle?
or words muffled near the window?

it's dark
snow falls moonlight
filling my tracks between house and barn
this house alone
and me looking out

Loewen that same Loewen who spoke to Peter who spoke for the church with all the weight of the brotherhood behind him a brotherhood of brothers who would never condemn a man on their own who could almost all wash their hands and mourn Peter erring and falling Loewen died today beneath a load of logs. The logs were not yet properly fastened when the horses shied and broke the load. Maybe a bird near their feet they said or just something spooky in the air. And Loewen in red snow breathing his last a log across his chest. The men rolled one log off his legs but couldn't move the other before he sputtered blood and frozen air and died.

to have you to stem time
not when the camera blinked
and you bled in through its eye
but a moment before you
standing among wild rose bushes
when you snatched a horsefly from the air
released it and turned into the photograph
squinting

curling at its edges
like paper the yellowing moon
breaks when I touch it

like my red heart
like a leaf like dreams
the morning interrupts

I dream what was apparently
a woman almost thirty hoeing weeds
a jar of water on a fencepost
her throat as she drinks a glass vase

and walking in a dream at noon across the bridge
the white stroke of her arm
drops of water colliding silver with air
her hair dark and sleek like an otter

eyes remember what was flesh
a dress brushing against russian thistles
shoes scuffing stones
a white finger bleeding from roses

I reach for the moon
to plant it like a seed
beside the porch   in the night
plant it and grow a sun
maybe   in the morning
a woman waking beside me

my wife lies quietly
so   just like we always did sleeping
yes   so beautiful   her shawl
roses on her black shawl
still   and still her violet eyes
and those worn hands   you wouldn't believe
how soft   soft   on my mouth
my eager mouth kissing   those fingers
those slender arms   those breasts

she moved with me   her hands on my hips
she twisted   we were so young   so
she twisted   spun on top of me   calling
Johann   Johann   she called me   she found me
yes   called in the night   through the whole world

we lay awake together
as winter tried to get in beneath the door
and that was long ago
we were young   even though
we were so young
things weren't always like that

black branches scrawled on air
a mumbling underfoot
and sun ringing in my ears

snow looks for a hole to crawl into
stalks bleed bark swells and bursts
blasting winter to kingdom come

a time for thawing that's for sure
a time to seed

easter's thorns
daffodils
hollyhocks leaning away from the house

I clear my throat
and begin to sing
softly *amazing grace . . .*

how sweet the sound . . . brightshining
as the sun[20]

I wasn't thinking of the child
swimming in the stone shell of her belly

I remembered cattle
how they lowed uneasily in labour
how scrawny legs stuck out like branches
how father tugged
as if he might tear the calf apart
how things were born no matter what

no ceremony

only the animal butting into sight

I remembered smells
camphor or the slough
where the new one splashed   bawling like a calf

I remember the infant   her lank prince
animal or fish
wriggled at her breast
waiting pale-eyed for the waking kiss

I had been thinking of calling the child Franz. Carolina said why not call him Peter. But that's too much of a burden   to grow up with that name   to live with that story. At least that's what I said. I was thinking too that the name was unfinished   that somehow the name should be taken by someone and lived through until it was done. That name still had life in it.

It didn't seem fair though to ask this of a child. I kept my thoughts to myself. Carolina said that it would be an honour for the child   after all Peter had been a good man who hadn't lived a false life   only his own life. That made me think it over. Carolina was right   Peter had lived his own life and maybe it was complete. Things couldn't have gone any differently. How could I say he was brave or not?

Well all the thinking and talking came to nothing. The child was a girl   our Elizabeth. The full moon tonight makes me remember. I went outside after her birth. What seemed funny to me was that there were sundogs[21] around the sun and Brummer was barking like crazy someplace in the fields.

Brummer howls me out of my dream. There is a sound like rain on the roof but light flickers at the window. Night begins to glow.

The boys are still asleep in the next room. I shake them awake and lower them from the window. Anna is already outside with the little one. Everyone is quiet. There is only the fire's crackle and Brummer howling.

Flames have hold of the summer kitchen and the porch where Brummer always sleeps. The boys are still half-asleep and try to crawl back through the window. I drop the pail I have just hauled from the well and run to pull them back. Anna stumbles across the ploughed field going for the neighbours.

Near the creek I cover the boys with horse blankets and tell them to sleep. And Brummer is quiet. I turn to the flames roaring like a wind fire stars floating on the night. Dog is dead I think I smell its burning flesh and my eyes all flames sparks shooting through my brain and Carolina dead just six months and shadows leaping against the barn. Voices somewhere. I break the kitchen window reaching in at the phone sill on fire the house buckling and me reaching to save the telephone. Flames at my arms my hair on fire I wrench the cord then I'm tumbling like a planet through heaven.

Father was rushing about. Getting the boys out of the way. He threw a few pails of water from the well onto the fire. He dragged the boys to the creek. He was shouting for Brummer to shut up. He was shouting "the dog can't get out, Brummer burns." I ran across the field with the youngest, my sister Elizabeth. I looked back over my shoulder and could see father's shadow running back and forth, and the flames rising higher, and the sky full of sparks. I left Elizabeth with Mrs. Plett and hurried back with Plett and two of his sons. Every part of the house was on fire now. At first I couldn't see father. Then I saw him standing at the edge of the fire, reaching through the kitchen window, and then falling in a fit. I got to him first, grabbed his ankles and pulled him to the middle of the yard. He was staring, his lips drawn back like a dog, and his legs trembling. In one hand that crazy man held our new telephone. We never figured out why he did that, and he never said.

After the fire? There's not much to say. When I fell it seemed that I fell through air. I never felt the ground.

I don't remember night after that. Only the morning ashes and beams leaning against each other. Anna sat beside me. The boys poked at the ruins with sticks and called Brummer. Maybe he's still alive they said.

I had no eyelashes. On my arms and head hair was melted into knots. Some hairs broke when I touched them. Anna said there had been fire on my head that she put out with her nightdress.

I felt there was something to say like after a dream and there's a story in your head you can't quite remember it but I hadn't dreamed and there was nothing to say.

Anna helped me to the creek. I knelt to wash my face stood up dripping brushed off ashes then saw for the first time I was naked. I laughed how I laughed. What a sight to have seen a wild man running around without clothes on fighting fire with a pail of water from the well.

Peter once told me that the stars were on fire. He knew a lot about stars about what shapes you could find at night. I don't know about stars burning they're still up there but that house is gone and the dog long buried.

the creek still flows every spring
though cattails have spread
and now as summer settles like dust
the water stands green and thick
slumbers through a memory of war

days flow too
and I wade downstream
ten years to the day
when I kneeled   here
praying rushes to hold Peter
rock him tender until the sky opens

when I raised him   pale as angels
and carried him home

here the spirit left flesh behind and ascended

here there is no forgetting
before he became broken man
the boy with yellow hair   clothed in seasons

and here the blackbird
rising from a cattail
still bleeds

each spring I seed
and each summer the farm grows stones

if it doesn't make you cry   it makes you laugh

a cairn for each acre
or   from a distance   tombstones
nothing alive here but the horses
and me sweating for dirt   talking to myself

unload the stoneboat
make a living with what you have

One of my boys in the poplar tree at the end of the section. He thinks I can't see him. He's been there for an hour at least. I'll have to think of something for him to do. No   just pretend I don't see him. Next load   when I pass the tree   take out the axe like I'm going to chop the tree down. Let's see how long he keeps quiet that little snake in the grass.

hangs there like a cross   stiff-winged
between earth and sun
I bend to the stoneboat and forget
until his sudden shadow slides across the horses

I look up
he slants   braking descent with hard wings
his talons reaching   the animal twisting
and wings fanning dust
then he rises with the kill dangling broken-backed
an arch in the sky

Yellow storm all day   straw billowing like clouds. You had to stop sometimes and blow the dust from your nose. Wheels spinning   the belt turning round and round   shining black at midday. Your ears roaring   you could still hear it at night though the tractor was shut down   and I was feeding the machine   stooping and rising between the bandcutters' knives and the hungry machine.

And Ruth calling us to dinner. Ruth   an old maid with working hands. Ruth   who I'd known for years   who never married   and now Ruth standing at the pump asking if I would like to duck my head into the spouting water. I thought then she would be my wife   would share my life. Us growing old together.

Later she said to me that where I was   where my home was   her home would be.

So we married. And she was a good wife. We worked hard. She was a blessing to the children still at home. They had a mother. In the evenings we sat together. She would always be doing something with her hands   knitting maybe or mending. I guess I was remembering. And then   when I was remembering less   she gave me her gift. She gave me back feelings I thought I had buried. And she gave me a daughter. From our bed a daughter. It was a little while yet before we grew old together.

mother washing dishes
her head turned slightly
so she can hear what we're saying in the living room

father's birthday
and he's sitting in his proud chair
holding forth

and you know what that means

he and Henry Penner   stark naked
hanging onto their horses
swimming some russian river

that story

or Henry untying the neighbour's team
the neighbour being in the store
and father throwing stones
until the horses bolt
potatoes flying from the wagon   scattering along the street

that story too

and the one about the Jew who borrowed a raincoat

but I know stories as well
though I don't have 75 years to remember from

The Jewish pedlar Feldman making his regular trip to New Bothwell carrying everything from thread to oilcloth and even tobacco for the Frenchmen. The sun is setting and Feldman begins packing up. Jake L. Barkman's boy Nick not even 20 years old sidles up to the Jew and says he has a confession to make.

Feldman looks up then goes back to packing. Maybe you want the priest from St. Pierre he says I don't take confessions though I can give you a good price on broadcloth for a suit. This flusters Barkman's boy and he says it isn't a joking matter. Feldman figures it must be something pretty serious then because most things you can laugh about.

Two years ago the boy says I stole a can of chewing tobacco from you. I have since made things right with the Lord. I am a different man now and want to ask your forgiveness. Who am I to forgive you asks Feldman you've made things right with God you say? Yah but I need your forgiveness as well. You're forgiven says the Jew. But that's not enough for Barkman's boy. He wants to pay for what he stole. How much do I owe he asks. Well sighs Feldman if you want to pay me a can of Red Man is worth 10¢ to me. 10¢? says the boy. How about a nickel?

the house floating across fields
rain in sheets clattering on windows
then shifting abruptly with the wind and the house still
black clouds roil twist like fish
the bulk of whales sounding rising
water sprays through the screen

I close the inside door turn
to Ruth reaching a hand for me
smiling she loosens a plait of hair with her free hand
I undo buttons slowly
her plump breasts her breathing beneath the cloth

the dress falls to her waist
we nuzzle
my fingers trace her fleshy hips

we crawl under the old blanket

her toes wiggle   tickling my feet
our legs entwined like vines
her hair smelling of cloves

what else can one do but make warmth

rocking easily in the verandah
my eyes closed

the sun   flies buzzing
and the chair squeaking each time it rocks back

of a sudden my mouth wrinkles   my tongue squirms
as I bite and juice trickles

I open my eyes   light
and Ruth   her apron full of raspberries

old woman

I have known you always
even when you were someone else

the swirl of your dress
as you turn angrily from me
your eyes growing big and soft
when you make ready to cry

your body that seems too thick sometimes
and the hair too grey
so that I wonder how you looked when you were young

but youth lies in the grave

and I know though you never say
that you don't like the stubble on my chin
I don't have all my teeth
my cheeks are hollow and not all my hairs have stayed with me

yes old woman there is not much to choose between us
there are no others for you or me

I know

your calloused hands on the hoe
your arms around me

the grass grows too long around the house let it
and if there is no time to paint the barn
well that's one job less

When Aaron and I got married, there was a supper at my in-laws, the Reimers. Both our families were there.

My father-in-law, Klaas, now there was a rare man. He didn't know his real father, that I know. Much else, even his children didn't know. He would talk of his mother, her hard life, her family, but never of his father. You know, as well as I do, there are different kinds of fathers.

I heard awful stories, that when Klaas was a baby, just months old, his father held a shotgun to him. I guess he got talked out of it, or something. He ran away after that, the father did, and was never heard of again.

Klaas's mother, though, woke up one morning when she was in her fifties, and said that now her husband was dead. She had dreamed, saw her husband lying in a ditch beside a railroad track.

From such a start Klaas didn't grow the same as other boys. I've heard that most of the children could not play with him because he had no father. I guess, too, because his mother didn't seem too sorry. So are the sins of the fathers visited upon their sons.

Klaas was a dreamer, cut towns and animals out of paper. He didn't even play the usual games. Klaas told me of his only try at baseball. Someone gave him a mitt and stood him in the field among the gopher holes and cowpies. When the ball was hit his way, he said, all he could see was the sun. And that sun came down faster and faster, and Klaas forgot to lift his mitt. The ball struck him on the forehead. He said he dropped that mitt and walked home.[22]

Anyways, I could keep telling stories. Klaas was a wise man, a quiet, dignified kind of man with white hair. Yet he liked to laugh and tell stories. I heard him tell my first boy about an Indian ghost that flew backwards. Don't ask me where he got such an idea or what it meant.

He was short, and I think that's why he tilted his head back a little, so he could look people in the eye. I remember, too, that he liked to come over on Monday mornings to eat chocolate cake left over from Sunday.

What I wanted to say was something else. Let's see. It was about our wedding supper. Oh yes. Klaas. How I always wanted to make a good impression on him. He had shelves full of books in both German and English, although lots of those were cowboy stories. But he spoke very clearly, very exactly. I was always careful in talking with him, to say things right. Although he only had grade eight, or something like that, he seemed quite educated.

My father, though, didn't care what impression he gave, as usual. I expected him to be himself. Laughing at the wrong times, and such a cackle like you can't imagine. Eating with his fingers because food tastes better with a little salt, or so he said. But what I didn't expect was for him to make a crude joke in front of everyone while we were eating.

Klaas was talking about the CNR and wondering why it didn't stop near father's farm. After all, he said, there was a sawmill in the area and a pretty big dairy farm. Father said that the train didn't stop exactly because of the dairy farm. He said there's too much cowshit, that's what he said, too much cowshit on the tracks and, when the train tries to stop, it just slides right by and doesn't stop till it gets to Giroux.[23]

It was the most embarrassed I had ever been, and I quickly told father he shouldn't talk like that. Like what he asked. My face was beet-red. I looked at Klaas and saw that he really enjoyed what was going on. Not just the joke, but my embarrassment. Those two men got along just fine.

What do you want to know about Mennonites? What don't you know? Do you want to know about good people or not such good ones? Do you want to know about those that went to Africa or Asia to save the souls of heathens? Or do you want to hear about the quiet ones who live their faith so you never really notice until they're dead?

I can tell you about my daughter who was a nurse until she got married. She always lived for others. Even when she was a little girl she saved every cent she got her hands on. Not to buy something nice for herself but to send to missionaries. Always doing what she thought was best for others.

I can tell you also about the son that never learned anything from me especially about farming. Yet he has some kind of farm. His sons and his wife break their backs to keep the farm going. He drives to town every day for coffee. Sitting around with his cronies telling stories and jokes. I don't know what's in his head.

You know about some of our businessmen. The sharp ones who pay their workers dirt. Who live in their big houses and say God has blessed them. I always thought we were to share give our only coat to the man without one. We were to build a heavenly mansion[24] not an earthly one. Yet I have heard one of these sharpies boast about how he gives work to the poor. That's sharing for him I guess. I sometimes wonder if these sharpies know where they would be without workers. You see how I don't understand things anymore.

ukraine
poland
netherlands
belgium
switzerland

from the shed blood of
Manz
Eberle
from Blaurock   his blue coat flapping at the knees
from lonely Denck   who believed that love would never hurt
from Pastor Philips[25]
from Simons   running   hiding behind his priestly collar
from Grebel   on neustadtgasse

and we've come from rivers
rat
red[26]
molotszhna   where father used to swim
rhine
limat[27]   that swallowed a few of us

You can read about those things in books. I've read some   but mostly what I know has been told to me   or I have heard in sermons. Lots of countries and names. Sea of Galilee   Palestine   Beersheba   Babylon   Dead Sea   Absalom   Elijah   Job. And don't forget it all comes down to Jesus. Not just for us. For the Frenchman too   and the Englishman. For the Jew, God's chosen.

And do you understand we've come from memories?

simlins[28] cowshit fires
horses wandering home through blizzards
Toews or Reimer frozen in the sleigh
grasshoppers in plagues
those born on oceans those buried there
steppes that father often talked of
with their yellow waves of wheat
the swamps of danzig[29] where no armies could come
whaling ships yes whaling ships
and some of our people sailors
horse and foot blade flame and iron
those driven from home
and there being bears in the mountains
and soldiers in the countryside

do you understand?

those are my memories father's
his mother's maybe her mother father
their friends their neighbours

here in the brush by this creek where the limat flows
an overgrown orchard near poltava[30]
or a wharf smelling of fish

do you understand this? where we came from?
it all adds up
figure it out for yourself

You say you've read about Simons. Now what do you know about him? Do you remember J.J. Fast? No of course not. You were only a boy when he died. But if you had known him you would know something about Simons. Fast was a blacksmith one of the last but he was just like Simons. That kind of man. Always serious. Even the few jokes he cracked weighed a ton. What mattered most to him more than his family I think was that the church should always be right that no one put himself above the church. And you never saw someone who could hide better. Behind the preacher. Behind the Bible. Behind God. Yes if you knew that man you knew something about Mennonites. Not everything mind you.

We had the telephone father saved when the house burned. But father would not get a car. Well, actually, he bought a Model A, but after trying it once, running through a flower garden, and finally stopping in the pig pen, boards all over and pigs squealing like crazy, he parked it and it didn't move again until years later when someone bought it as an antique.

He would not have a car. It's not that it was a sin. Father simply thought it was not the way for him to get from one place to another. He had his horses and that was good enough. Horses didn't make all that noise. Horses listened, and you could talk to them. You had to feed them, and they had a familiar smell.

Towards the end, when he wasn't strong anymore, we worried about him going to town with the wagon. He moved to town then. He was already not very well, and so he didn't last long.

MEDICAL RECORD

NAME John Neufeld

ADDRESS Sundown Lodge PH. NO. 29-1-2

RELIGION Mennonite Protestant RACE Canadian (German)

NEXT OF KIN Ruth Neufeld RELATIONSHIP Wife

ADDRESS Sundown Lodge

FAMILY PHYSICIAN

INFECTIOUS DISEASES None

ILLNESSES, ACCIDENTS, OPERATIONS Scars from burns (forearms); seizure disorder. Admitted under staff. Fatigue. Frequent shortness of breath. Indications of cyanosis tachycardia, edema of the feet. Hb. 16.7% W.B.C. 9 x .0^3 c. mm. Urinalysis - normal. X-rays indicate pulmonary congestion and cardiac enlargement. EKG - L.V. enlargement. Medication - Digoxin 0.25 mg. daily, mersalyl 2 cc. i.m. daily -

AJ

Anna brought me here. She and Aaron were visiting. They said I didn't look good. I told them they didn't need to tell me. I've known that since I was a boy when I first looked in a mirror. They said I couldn't take care of myself anymore. Anything might happen they said I might fall and break a leg and I wouldn't be found for days. Well maybe you should visit oftener I said but of course I was joking because they came often. Sometimes it seemed too often.

So it went. Then the next day a Monday and I was feeding the pigs slop there they were saying I could have a nice room in the old folks home. People would take care of me and I would be closer to Ruth. She was in the hospital because of her circulation. I think they were a bit embarrassed that their old father drove to town twice a week with wagon and horses to visit mother.

They were sure it was for my good. I would never stay at their place that would be too much of a burden besides Anna would always make sure I ate the right things so I packed one suitcase and went with them. They said they would pack everything else later. That's how fast it went. One minute feeding the pigs and the next in their '55 Chev looking back at that old grey barn leaning into the wind the tires bumping over the loose planks on Swallow Bridge.

It wasn't just a room. There were three little rooms. Ruth would soon be out of the hospital to live with me. But before she came Anna took me away again this time to the hospital. I guess I was a little weak. Anyway a doctor came to see me and said I should be in the hospital for a little while at least. The funny thing is that I had been in only one day when Ruth was sent to our new rooms. I never even saw her in the hospital.

Maybe I'll be better soon so I can live with Ruth in those rooms. Maybe I'll have to stay here. I don't know. One thing I know that farm is finished for me. Already it's sold pigs chickens horses and all. Some things they kept the children. A kerosene lamp some harnesses to hang on the basement wall and other junk.

I don't know how the world works anymore. How I got here so fast. And not even sick really. I wanted to fight them but that wouldn't do any good. They're younger probably know better than me what to do. Anyways that's the least I could do for them. Let them do what they think is best. I don't want to be on their conscience even if I don't understand what they're thinking.

Time happens. That's what. I wonder about Barney and Prince. No one uses horses for work anymore and that's all those two know. I wonder who bought them and for what. Anna says they're being looked after. About everything else well I don't think about it much anymore. The creek was pretty well dried up and the buildings falling so there's not much there. Just some things to remember. That's how it goes. You live a while and then time happens.

there's so much I could say about the old man his knobby hands lying on the white sheet blue almost grey ridges of blood running across his hand's map his thin arms the pale blue top nurses tied in bows at his back his brown eyes you could see through if you weren't afraid.

he had nothing to say most of the time.

I rubbed his feet as if I could bring them warmth. I wanted to. he smiled looked through venetian blinds. the room was hot tight. near the window a water glass and the sun revealing his fingerprints.

what time he asked.

6:15.

I mean what year he said. then turned on his side still looking out the window.

tomorrow gives rain.

the ground he chose   to kneel
where he kneeled in mud
where he began to untie his boots
shivering   his hands shaking
and the sun settling in the grass

I know him   not well enough
I know his overalls were wet from knees to cuffs
his eyes were blue
I know he carried a poplar branch to goad the trigger

soft eyes   I think
soft eyes and blue as if the sky bled them

what he smelled at last
water rotting in the reeds
or air sweet with clover

what he saw at dusk
light walking away across fields
the hole a sky can be
what he saw   water rippling in a ring

brummer barking in the trees somewhere

the man johann
who fished here with a crooked nail   he said
who splashed in this creek with his woman
when the sun was high and work could wait
johann   who told how they ducked each other
how they swam underwater and exploded through the surface near
    drinking cows
the cattle lurching   front legs in water
backing up the bank   their large heads swaying

the flames he endured   the iron in him

johann   I remember   leaning against a fence
his bony hands gesturing as he spoke

around us the wreckage of his farm
a rusting harrow   bone buildings careening
grass surging against the barn

johann remembered his brother
who tore the curtain and went blind
who taught johann fear   and not fear
that the child dies no matter what
and a man carries his funeral with him
you never know how many people you bury with a man
nor how many are born again

come   said johann   let's go back to the house
ruth bakes bread today
it's good when it's still warm and the butter melts

listen   he whispered

that rasping sound   that's a yellowhead[31]
see it   over there   near the creek

and I saw
a blackbird with a sun for its head

O dass ich tausend Zungen hätte[32]

---

1. Reprinted from *The Shunning* (Winnipeg: Turnstone Press, 1980). An excerpt of the very early work-in-progress entitled "Tomorrow It Gives Rain" appeared in the *Mennonite Mirror* of October 1979. "The Shunning" was produced as a play by the Prairie Theatre Exchange in Winnipeg in 1985. It is published as such in *New Works I*, ed. Winston Smith and David Carley (Toronto: Playwrights Canada, 1987). An excerpt of the play in prose form appeared in *Border Crossings* (Winter 1985).

In the Turnstone publication, the following note preceded the text proper:

This story concerns two brothers, Peter and Johannes Neufeld, and their families; Peter's wife Helena, Johann's wives Carolina and Ruth, and Johann's daughter Anna.

All diary entries are either those of Mrs. Hiebert, midwife, or of Dr. Blanchard, recently arrived from Orange County, Ontario.

There are numerous other characters, grandfathers and deacons and such, who do not say a word to us. A historian, who keeps time, has a thing or two to say.

All characters in this book are surely fictional.

Patrick Friesen was born in 1946 and grew up in the largely Mennonite community of Steinbach, Manitoba. He now lives in Winnipeg where he produces videos for the Manitoba Department of Education.

2. See *Revelations*.

3. Luke XV: 11-32.

4. This is a line from an old country/gospel song sung in the American South. The title and the remainder of the song are lost to Friesen's memory.

5. *Der blaue Engel* is German for "the blue angel."

6. Matthew XVI: 19.

7. I Corinthians V: 6-7.

8. Hebrews X: 31.

9. *Tsocka boum* is Low German for "maple tree," literally "sugar tree."

10. The Mennonite Church used banning or shunning to encourage solidarity. It is a form of discipline and exclusion designed to bring the "heretic" back to the community. It can be perceived as mental violence or as a type of love. Peter's story emerges from Friesen's investigation of the stories about shunning within the Mennonite tradition.

11. La Broquerie is a Francophone town located southeast of Steinbach.

12. *Vaspa* is a Low German word for the light, late-afternoon lunch, replacing supper on Sundays.

13. During their sojourn in the Low Countries the Anabaptists were named Mennonites.

14. In *On Liberty* (1859), John Stuart Mill (1806-73) championed individual liberty against the "collective mediocrity" often produced by institutions.

15. Blumenort is a town between Winnipeg and Steinbach. The name is German for "the place of flowers." Flowers play a large part in Mennonite domestic culture and in the naming of towns.

16. Here Friesen is quoting from Chapter IX. Using a clothes motif in *Sartor Resartus* (1833), Thomas Carlyle (1795-1881) outlines the belief that the old Christian coverings were threadbare and resolves to tailor a new wardrobe out of the fabric of modern German philosophy. This passage is especially appropriate with respect to Peter.

17. November 11, 1918 is the date of the armistice for W.W.I.

18. This is an obvious reference to the beautiful step-mother queen in *Snow White and the Seven Dwarfs*.

19. "The new city street" is the name of the street in Zurich on which a group of many more than six, mostly young, people broke away from the state church on January 21, 1525 and began the Anabaptist congregation to which the Mennonites trace their source. Certainly present were Conrad Grebel (c. 1498-1526), George Blaurock (c. 1492-martyred 1529), Felix Mans (1498-martyred 1527). The scene is rendered effectively in the recent film *The Radicals*, produced by Michael Hoftettler for Sisters and Brothers Inc. This group rejected infant baptism. They retained only two ordinances, adult baptism and the Lord's Supper, saw the Bible as the sole source of faith and dedicated themselves to a Church as close as possible to that of Apostolic times. They underwent severe persecution, as did the Mennonites who wandered—vaguely on the run—throughout Eastern Europe until well after the Russian Revolution. The name Mennonite arose in the Low Countries when a former priest, Menno Simons (1496-1561), organized and vitalized the diverse groups that took their origin from the Swiss Brethren.

Emigration of groups of Mennonites to Manitoba began in 1894 in response to the promise by the Canadian government to allow them freedom of worship, their own church schools and an exemption from military service, the latter of which had been recently threatened in Russia. At first they settled on reserves north and east of the Rat River and in 1876 west of the Red River along the U.S. border. By 1879 their numbers were near 6000. Although they have not lived in colonies in Manitoba for some time and have integrated extensively into the mainstream of modern secular life, the civic legislation, lifestyle and ethnic make-up of towns such as Altona and Steinbach clearly reveal the influence of their hard-working, family-oriented, pacific German culture that evolved along with their quietest Anabaptist faith. Three publishing houses in Manitoba have especially voiced the Mennonite experience there: Hyperion Press, Kindred Press and Turnstone Press. The latter has published Mennonite writers in significantly looser union with the church. See *My Harp Is Turned to Mourning* (1985) by Al Reimer and *The Salvation of Yasch Siemens* (1984) by Armin Wiebe for two very different views of Mennonite life.

20. The full text of the song is:

Amazing Grace! how sweet the sound
That saved a wretch like me!
I once was lost, but now am found,
Was blind, but now I see.

Twas Grace that taught my heart to fear,
And Grace my fears relieved;
How precious did that Grace appear
The hour I first believed!

The Lord has promised good to me,
His word my hope secures;
He will my shield and portion be
As long as life endures.

Through many dangers, toils and snares,
I have already come;
'Tis Grace has brought me safe thus far,
And Grace will lead me home.

When we've been there ten thousand years,
Bright shining as the sun,
We've no less days to sing God's praise
Than when we'd first begun.

21. Sundogs are dazzling crosses of orange and/or white light that often bracket the sun against a cold, clear prairie sky in winter.

22. Baseball was not only a popular game in Mennonite communities, but also has been a popular summer activity on the prairies, going back to before the days when the original of W.P. Kinsella's Shoeless Joe Jackson, banned from organized baseball in the U.S., came to southern Manitoba to play semi-pro ball. Rudy Wiebe makes a baseball game an important part of *Peace Shall Destroy Many* (1962). Friesen reveals his affection for baseball in "Backstop," *bluebottle* (1978). Both Dennis Cooley and his mentor Robert Kroetsch use baseball allusions in their long poems, as does Helen Hawley.

23. Giroux is three to four miles north of Steinbach. It was where the railway depot was located.

24. John XIV: 2.

25. Eberle and Denck are Lorenz Eberli (?-martyred 1579), Hans Denck (c. 1500-1527). Pastor Philips is either Dirk Philips (1504-1568) or his brother who later left the movement, Obbe Philips (1500-1568).

26. The Rat and Red are rivers in southern Manitoba that have both nourished and threatened Mennonites.

27. The Molotszhna is a river in the Ukraine; the Rhine separates Germany and France. The Limat is a Swiss river which was often used for executing Mennonites.

28. "Simlins" was a word used for sod huts constructed by the Mennonites when they first arrived in Manitoba.

29. Danzig is the Old German for Gdansk in Poland. The marsh was attractive because it defended the Mennonites from large groups of horsemen.

30. Poltava is a town in the Ukraine.

31. The yellowhead is a yellow-headed blackbird.

32. "O that I had a thousand tongues" is the title of a German hymn written by Johann Mentzer and Johann Balthasar König in the eighteenth century.

Grasshopper[1]

Helen Hawley

> A wise man may grasp how ghastly it shall be
> when all this world's wealth standeth waste,
> even as now, in many places, over the earth
> walls stand, wind beaten
> hung with hoar-frost; ruined habitations.
>
> (from *The Wanderer)*

Part One

Prairie floods out on all sides
wind billows grass . . . . and that's all
between Moose Jaw and Medicine Hat
no trees not even (maybe) farms just surge of grass
and the inevitable telephonepole line alongside it
rolls up one inclination
and down into a trough
up towards the next crest and down again
an endless sequence of beginnings

Hop
beginnings or movements suggest hope
and I am immobilized behind green-tinted glass
belting down the Trans Can in a Greyhound bus
a ninety-miles-an-hour wonder bus
that bisects all that grass

I wanted to stand in long grass
watch it flow from my centred feet out
in all directions

or walk through grass and take the centre with me

not by myself not before or after Jennifer[2]
my best friend in high school or Steve my cousin Pat
who used to sit on drifts with me
in crystal winter nights and hear how
Knox church bells could slice the coldest stars
four miles away
hear midges shrill through wild wheat
through the listening ears of Ken
when I had found the half-drowned pup in the creek
promised he'd help me bring it up Aunt Joan
not by myself but with she used to like to walk with me
and talk about the family
and show how meadowlarks leap out of prairie roses not by myself
not bold but bent in the same direction
when a sudden grass wind makes patterns on our skins
but everyone owns cars these days
hoping to embrace my people again I can only drive through them

I was born near here Swift Current why now
do I speed/split my birthright hills/hope
in this bus enthralled?   why did I go away so
for so long: "that's all" is everything!   to go
so far   for so long means   I may never return again
may never again bear blood
through all that waiting grass
                                        out there

Seas of grass   that
run in such questing winds
to round horizons out of sight

Forfeit
forfeit of birthright   for such long absences
Why go?

The old woman loved to sing   every morning
from the balcony of her Saskatoon apartment   she
joined the dawn chorus of birds
                but the chirrup, chirrup
of her voice was too much for the neighbours
they called the cops   took her to court   "It's like
she was mourning the dead"   they said   "we . . .
can't stand it"

Too long away though my bones still rock near Anteloup
Bull Skull is my signpost and I hop
a bit west or east of here for home

Tourist now I am among the names of Muskrat Creek and Balmalea
feet chatter near the Rush Lake[3] detour but I cross
behind the green glass with no fields or face

Beat of my blood is all around me as I am driven through
grass just out of reach along the bus route
and the juice and airs of home removed from me

        Grasshopper
you tour the prairie around
bearing no fields and no footprints with you
to record your various names.

not even as Tourist can be birthplace touched
the glass is always between   death's dark green intervention
deceives the bounding fields
out there . . . . . or maybe   not as tourist
but as sole Survivor
visited this place?

how we long to talk to each other   how we
reach out and we slip
past each other on a different track   you
locked in your bus and I locked in mine
passing each other on empty prairie roads

Hop

hoping to embrace my people again I can only
drive past them
maybe it's not Grasshopper's business
to be there anyway

It's an earthstepper's werth[4]
to wander all over is fixed

Birth-place marks the start
but from then on   birth-space is denied
and today time doesn't matter
since there's no longer home
office to come home from
or deadline to catch

Maybe through wandering I have even pawned my name

Nameless I am   a non-person now
in my own eyes   as in the eyes
of my former families

Freak.   Earthstepper.

A friend tried to help   showed me the Other Regina
the City behind the City   one-storey-frame-houses   cheap
peeled paint   the dog who
barked down silence   the Street-
With- No- Name   empty warehouses
flanked the origins of railway tracks
that sank into weeds not sixty yards away
grain elevator under a spell as junk depot
deserted now   about to crumble
prairie crowded the edges of yards
crept along tracks
took over vacant lots   it was wild and flowing
and the sun blazed all around the ruins
but no people walked there   my friend said
beware of anyone
we might be lucky enough to see "They're only ghosts in here"
he explained

Grasshopper
you will not find your old footprints in that
little prairie city nearly on the roads lost
in the middle of those running plains

How can you   Earthstepper   survive those signs?
wind hits the glass from the other side and
you will not find your old footsteps on this nameless road

Part Two

through holes in the road smell smell the sour earth

through cracks in walls of apartment blocks see see the
incandescent desires orange shivers in
a drear dun room when the door was shut
finally against all expectation[5]

when blocks were first set up people didn't realize
that there would be no transfer

if we shattered them to bits then could we not
rebuild them in a way that moulded them more closely
to our wanting skins?

leaking ceiling rain falls through roof onto the rented tv set
newspapers cover it to try to keep it dry

nobody ever turns up when the emergency service is called

look at Mr Livingstone his body lay
on his bathroom floor for five months and a day
before it was discovered

in the eyes of the man who lives across the landing
also alone in four small rooms the same
questions crease his dreams and desecrate his name

his door's the same
as door next door and miles of corridors repeat
each terror's vandalism just outside identical
but separated rooms

staircases cannot
lead upwards or downwards
or inside
no sirens nothing

"if I ever had a real job you'd see my dust!"
"I've worked hard for more than forty years and
what's it got me?   nothing"
"We loved the kid from his first marriage just like
our own   what went wrong?   i   just
                                                        don't
                                                            understand"
"maybe at six a m they'll kick down my door
haul me out of bed well   it's a deliverance of sorts"
"not much fun being on the dole   no place to go
no one to be   no name   nothing
i'm waiting"   "but Ron went
from his bungalow and carefully planned garden straight
through U of H to study how koalas mate   why
did he try to kill himself?   all I remember is
his wistful eyes that stared and stared month after day all day
out of its big front window"
"I remember too how buffalo blacked plains
just here near Swift Current not more than ninety years ago
and how we had to sell the bones for food"
"I farmed here since I emigrated if I had to do it again
not worth the sweat"

Burnt wrecks of many cars dead   whenever homes
                                                wrecked
vacated become
                  complete destruction might be just the thing
                        bring sanity
                            to all these emptied spaces?
                                No.

No Emergency Service.

I came back to be with you again
Cheryl in your yellow clapboard house
beside the railway tracks
Mike we used to play baseball together in grade five
but now you boss the Last Chance Cafe
I came back to briefly be with you   brother
who seeks gold gophers beyond Eleventh Avenue
I came back to walk on the prairie with you Ann
to recall how we were defined on that country road
the one that turned past the last houses
                    near Smith's Market Garden
out to cryptic fields as wide as continents
under the whine of wind in the ditch grass
listen together to our pivotal voices seeping across the plains
Aunt Fox   Maggy who still whirled through suns

All around the switchgrass blows
and fields flow along the way
as far out as the edge of day
we roll the roads up before us   caught
by the promises of dawn
in this year's sun-caper   dance[6]
                                        whoop for a title

Great Plains: how did we call you?
what will we call you?   you slide
from your one name to the next
like coyote[7] slips from skins
            up in coulees
            or down along streets
from one self to the next . . . . Saskatchewan
Fort Laramie   Mahopa   Burdett[8]
The West   Dakota   Land of Hope and Next Year Country[9]
most of North America
what are your other names?

We moved in that first brave step
across the Bering Straits[10] or
over the Atlantic and the East
bearing a new word
a new round of remembered words

Across what bridges
into which kindling plains
speaking whose tongues?

The West: you are not all of our darknesses

Alone I am
there is no laughter to greet
a returning grasshopper
but it's not from nuclear disaster

There are so many faces that green glass distorts
child images once focussed I moved
gapless
between gripped hands and the revolving grass
touched merry-go-round plains and knew
there could not be a break now freak
grasshopper
I am not even once removed
my cupped flesh rushed up by this bus but not
beyond its dark green windows so the whole round
dissolves and my own walked-memory
heard-memory
heart-memory
holds apart hello! Hello! the greeting smiles not
not! not!! so terrible a break
between grins such a reaching out
out that could mean only just beyond dark glass or spin
like flywheel out to orbit

to close it all again?

Idea of a Desecrated City as a Deserted Threshold

Not even rubble mars the utter desolation of this country road
no stone shifts   no grain of dust breathes
implications of greening earth
across this hollowed sky   the storm clouds blown
Sun switches on
a lintel leaps from a scream and the rectangle beneath it
once door or window   frames a withered field
  Out through such tottering pledges were all people led
  into such absences of leaf
  that business deals rescinded   grains roared fire   governments
  winced of course   firms aimed over the winds
  and fell into Nevada   dust
  we nearly on the roads grew shadows   and our shadows
  struck us back   so in the end
  only our silhouettes held gentian clamours
  on a burnt-out threshold   once there was Mr Bates
  who left to thresh that time   here were his daughters and his son
  playing hop-scotch in such ordinary porches
  Mrs Thomas once
  belonged to say she would be home
  after she'd had her apprehensions drawn
  at the Regina clinic

Fallen bones
will not mar this step to undone roads or fields
nor will any absence of a cry
beat down into these silences

but it's not from nuclear disaster

Idea of a Desecrated City as an Empty Road

Shout
the empty road is as fugitive
as your inability
                    Grasshopper
to account for your passage through

there are no names to show it

"hello hello   I've been expecting you
for a hundred years or more"

there are no sounds of screeching tires
no urgent knocking on doors   replies
to calls   No Emergency Service

"We are concerned about the violations
                    and the rage and rape
directed against us"   "All decisions
have to be objective probably not submitted
to the majority of watchers wanderers
               aren't we all wanderers   all of us . . .

Fragments From the Song of Fools[11]

After Empedocles[12] had named the wonders
Earth and Water, Fire and Air
and told how Strife would knock asunder
all that from each mixing Weather
Love had glued together
he threw himself into the crater too
there are no Afterspeakers there

* * *

The greater the Power, the greater the Folly
the Songs of the Strivers are mighty and jolly
Who listens to each Vow or Lay
Lives like a Fool 'til Earth blows away

* * *

Isolation does not bring relief from the Absurd
a Tourist in a Ruined Home is seldom heard

* * *

That the machines had taken over was insignificant
I am still not afraid of those greenglass buses
boundering these quiet fields
I could walk right up to the reddest combine fears
digital remains will never impress me

the absence of the children is the worst terror

"But we must maintain that terror. It is the deterrent
that has kept the peace for thirty-nine years."[13]

In the middle of that silence
is a deeper silence   fields settle
earth-forming reverses   dust drops
next is the un-leafing of the world
the un-extending of the world
the un-solidifying of the world
the un-quaking of the world
the un-taking-form of the world
          only the void of the world
          which the Source-of-Night has fled[14]

the West is no more

The Sun Beat Down

The field is a memory of a round horizon
bisected by a road
full of locked buses
the city is a road
full of locked buses with green-darkened windows
full of the echoes of our fury
FULL OF THE ECHOES OF OUR FURY
and the latest broadcast winding down
on transistor radios

And we go
past fields no longer newsworthy
beyond split thresholds
on roads that broke the circle

where there is no circle any more around us

The Sun Beat Down

dissolving circles

the sun beat down   honey   over all
the sun beat down
the suns   Oh the sun   Oh the suns is
a brighter blast of black or white could not outlive
such emptiness of road   the road
the rubble   no road
all roads gone
all is gone   honey
                    all is nothing

Idea of a Desecrated City as a Withered Field

It's not a bare field
that will keep us from falling in
rather our reason inverts what we really know
so that we forget what we were looking for
rounds of families in seasoned plains
reduce to metaphors   or search for rings
                                        we're reminded
whenever mist encircles field
that we're named at the centre of that circle
we in the centre of it all
the completed meaning of that growing field
grass sprouting from us all round towards the mist
through mist
to an unbroken circle just beyond the mist[15]
hint of pure white elders
or other faces
withered field
may only contain an intention
is not whole in itself
an intention that flickers like a half-glimpsed path
from one edge of a misunderstanding
across
to the other edge

I will describe my grass faces
how they contour the plains   make the earth round
hold fast from wrecked thresholds
complete the circle again

seas of grass
bend in the winds of our urgent leaps
trace where we long to reach to horizons out of sight

Part Three

Prairie Haiku[16]

They didn't need to kill my Jack when they took the money
he would have given it to them
he wasn't any hero

The house costs ninety thousand and it's only three years old
but there are gaps between the windows and the walls
the basement's sinking

So what if sulphur wastes from my factory run into the lake
nobody lives in these parts at all
only a few Indians

The bracket clock's just darling and it's only four hundred dollars
I must have the enamelled candlesticks as well
to go with my Mauch vase[17]

I'm scared to walk those three blocks from the bus stop to your
    house
after dark   men in cars cruise right beside me
they get out and chase me

We've got two cars and two phones and three television sets
and a computerized purple dishwasher that sings
but it's not as good as Blain's

Catfish Joe's in jail again but he didn't do anything
he got eighteen months for sassing a cop
he wasn't even drunk

I have been too long away my prairie is not so old
but older than this
mindweary
from hesitating alone elsewhere in too-old-too-
cramped-streets; surrounded again by these
dimmed fields hinting rounds now i have
come back only to pass through again though
a grasshopper may jump seas I may never
encompass Earthstepper I
I could have walked for years over these surging
plains because there i was born believing that
I was once more contained in the centre of their
charmed horizons between Moose Jaw and
Medicine Hat I could have
talked I cannot even hear I
could have talked to
all those voices still concerned
behind thin telephone wires
but there was only time to say how
are you what
are the children doing?

The earthworks crumble   their titles lie[18]
stripped of laughter   held sere[19]
beside locked doors   wars shook off several
most honourable names   some victims of car crashes slid
over the highway   one was smothered as a babe
by his mother who could not stand his screams   one by
cancer forced to die and by hollow-eyed brother Bob
buried   everyone is not
felled by nuclear terror   some holocausts are found
every day among our common thresholds

A city in normal times is always so blasted

where is Suzanne these days? Why doesn't Eddy ever write?
you'd think he didn't care

Barry has his nose forever in his work   no time
for anybody else   look at his family wife left him
fled to Alagoinhas[20] in Brazil two sons in jail for larceny and Sue
who walks the streets   for nights   who
and who cares

the deaths of all my families
arrived at different times with different hungers help
        Winyanketehca[21]
        Shoveller
        or Jane MacVie or Tom Hunt or other help
help   and no one comes   nor cares
flat circle could be moonplain not seed not god
good for anything (but synonymous with greed)

We wanted fair land a delight of plain
where blossoms of every colour lifted
to brighten the air where lasting song
was season's rondel of praise there would be
gold cloth of cattle mantling earth
silver cloth of geese embroidering skies
there would not be any greed treachery
or harsh voices would not turn us from each other
no one would stand higher to make smaller
we would all dance together in the best of sweet grass
circled by pure white elders
across the shining prairie
this is what we thought we were looking for

West desecrated
Grasshopper roams
the several deaths of those dear at home shunt
Grasshopper away

it's an old flight across seas to call cares
among unheeding ears meanwhile back on the plains
things go on much as they did before

when the wanderer
longing to rediscover round memories of Jim and Mom
and Sarah Jane and Avonlea[22] or fields a once-remembered
wholeness returns to flicker momentarily
on that same prairie only can
be rushed through landscape as a tourist on a bus

highly sophisticated technology does not lead to
any jubilee
Big Time machines do not run to Better Bonding

Oh that bare prairie![23]
Oh the smallness of our moments   the hugeness of its plains
it mocks us on our roads   then swears to let us free
its sense of past and now   of tears and ecstasy
pours from the promised fields and recalls each transient name

First in that radiant sweep there's a sense of daze and dread
vast isolation swells   divides me from my fellow souls
then from a racking haze deep compassion wells and rolls
for faces not yet born and for faces long since dead

Then there's a lightness in my head and a losing sense of pain
then prairie resolves outward and I see the coyotes pass
and mirrored in my meagre years like images on glass
flying fragments of my people that will not whoop again

And I'm a speck in dust in that outward rushing will
a grasshopper who's weirded[24] to call the roads alone
yet even as I'm driven through my broken prairie home
held at the storm's round eye   that being eye of still

I gambolled across the continental field
the surrendered metaphors of sea
I called from a clue of wholeness
whenever mists rolled the horizon nearer
or when its eye chose to jump through masks

And I carried the nub of that round grass

through Ed who waited underneath the streetlight
through Joe who could not go
because he did not have a home to come from
through Winiford who had not dawdled but had gone straight
          on through school

through Darlene   the darling of the town . . . whose smiles
were as wide as the canyons she had to walk through
her eyes were as deep   (they were as deep)
as the discarded pledge of big bluestem
that once had brought them all to light

through Gene who was the neatest   shelving stray thirsts
through Abe who was first to raise his pigs here back in ninety-three
through Jinny who loved her aunt the best

through Jake who was the toughest   loudest   quickest
because he was so small inside his fist

and Little Mo the most forgotten of them all

through Missus Preiss once a middling bloom
but wilted since her thousand days
bent over the stove to feed nine mouths
on half a forkful of grit

through Mister Bradshaw who was once a soldier
until a brighter flower struck his gut
now he is watchman at the Purley Works

through Beverley who fought back
and her sister Mae who didn't

through Dan who would not leave his Mom
wet his bed at nights but dreamed
in colours no one else had ever seen

through Gibbs who made nothing but money

through the baby nobody knew

through Eileen eight and frightened to look at Mister Dix
next door in case she saw his tawny eyes
begin to whizz again his yellow thumbs
reach out to grab her

through Pete and Lupe and Once a Minute Ben
and old hawk warrior Jeanette
on the sunporch of her Crane Hills shack
surrounded by the sweating grass and singing about rain

through each dear asking face
wherever I went from there
and even my return behind dark glass
could not alter that
place circles
face circles
can be recalled in transit even across the disguised grass
even the lost postulations for the Last Best West[25]
can be called back again[26]

---

1. Reprinted from *Grasshopper* (Winnipeg: Turnstone Press, 1984). The Turnstone publication is 58 pages in length. Because of space constraints the vertical spacing has been compressed considerably here. Hawley disclaims any direct influence from Richard Lovelace's poem "The Grasshopper" (1649).

Writer and artist Helen Hawley was born in Swift Current, Saskatchewan in 1937 and now lives in London, England.

2. Although some of the characters in "Grasshopper" are based on friends and family, many aren't. Hawley says she "slides between realities." Aunt Fox and Maggy, who appear later, have literal sources, but at the same time take on characteristics Hawley describes as "archetypal." They are not her family ancestors, but her prairie ancestors.

3. As Hawley explores the meaning of the prairie experience the names change. Bull Skull is another older name for Moose Jaw, Anteloup another form of Antelope, Muskrat Creek a synonym of Maple Creek; Balmalea is the alter ego of Beverly. Rush Lake is located on the Trans-Canada Highway between Moose Jaw and Swift Current. We seem to be proceeding east on the Trans-Canada towards Swift

Current and Rush Lake. Maple Creek is east of Medicine Hat, Alberta, close to the junction of the Trans-Canada and Highway 21; Beverly is just west of Swift Current.

4. Here the links between "Grasshopper" and *The Wanderer* (c. late nineteenth century) established by the epigraph become much closer. Earthstepper is a translation of the Anglo-Saxon word "eardstapa": wanderer. Like her namesake, this wanderer returns to a fragmented and decaying world, accompanied by a gilded past with which she has difficulty maintaining communion. Hawley uses the Anglo-Saxon word "werth" here because of its rich connotations of honour, preciousness and splendour. The *O.E.D.* reveals that "Wertherian" means "morbidly sentimental." The hero of Goethe's romance *Leiden des Jungen Werther* (1774) is called Werther.

5. Hawley's description of ruined dwellings recalls that of the wind-blown, frost-bitten wine-halls and walls in the section that occupies the same structural place in *The Wanderer*. In both cases the ruined secular world mirrors a more fundamental and less tangible devastation.

6. The Sun Dance is the popular name for the Thirst Dance, perhaps the major religious ceremony of Plains Indians such as the Cree, Blackfoot, Assiniboine and Sioux. The dancers, who could include people from all segments of society, experienced varying degrees of self-abnegation in a search for a vision and for the regeneration of the community. It virtually disappeared among the Canadian Sioux by 1910, but is still performed infrequently by other Native groups, although not quite in the manner of the nineteenth century. See Andrew Suknaski's poem "The Sun Dance at Wood Mountain" in *Wood Mountain Poems* (1976).

7. Coyotes are often portrayed as trickster figures in the folklore of the Plains Indians. Robert Kroetsch speaks of them as such (see "The Fascinating Place Between: the Fiction of Robert Kroetsch" by R. Sullivan in *Mosaic* XI, 3 [1978], 167). So do Sid Marty in *Men For the Mountains* (1978) and Rudy Wiebe in *The Temptations of Big Bear* (1973).

8. Fort Laramie is in Wyoming. Burdett is southwest of Medicine Hat in Alberta. With Mahopa, Hawley is probably thinking of the Mahope Indian Reserve in British Columbia.

9. These are all (un)popular names for the prairie space. In his "Preface" to *Next Year Country* (Toronto: McClelland and Stewart, 1988), Barry Broadfoot defines the term: "he is probably the best grain farmer in the world. . . . The prairie farmer can handle the cyclic nature of recessions and natural disasters. He pulls in his belt another notch. Fair crop last year, bad this year, maybe it will get better come next spring. . . . Next-year country."

10. Most historians now believe that North American Indians originally came across the once-existent land-bridge over Bering Strait.

11. This section is a pastiche of *The Ship of Fools* (1944) by Sebastian Brant.

12. Empedocles (c. 495-c. 435 B.C.) was a Greek philosopher and ardent advocate of democracy. He saw the four basic elements of earth, air, fire and water as

indestructible and fundamental to reality. He also believed life was composed of two opposing forces—harmony and discord—which in their interaction produced diversity in the world. In the best rendering of his experience, "Empedocles on Etna" (1852) by Matthew Arnold, a disillusioned and cynical Empedocles commits suicide by hurling himself into the volcano.

13. Hawley is quoting Margaret Thatcher rationalizing Britain's nuclear arsenal.

14. This verse paragraph contains a reversal of a creation song from the Tuamotu Islands (near the Marquesas Islands).

15. One of the central symbols of both *The Wanderer* and "Grasshopper" is the circle, here making its appearance as a field surrounded by mist, an image of a lost, although findable, unity, a hope involving land and people, but also—considering the open ending of the poem—an image of the structure of the poem itself. The more natural image of the circle has priority in this poem over the artificial geometric construction, the straight line.

16. Haiku is a Japanese lyric form of seventeen syllables. In the English language tradition it is a form that we usually associate with the Imagist Movement.

17. The name of this much prized antique German vase may have been derived from a style established by Johann Michael Maucher (1645-1700), a German baroque ivory-carver who specialized in carving elaborate cups and urns.

18. Compare with *The Wanderer* lines 78-80: "The wine halls crumble: rulers lie lifeless / Deprived of Joy, all the weary warriors / Dead by the wall, destroyed by some war. . . ."

19. Sere is an archaic word meaning dry or withered.

20. Alagoinhas is a place many people associate with escape.

21. This is a Dakota word meaning woman. Shoveller is perhaps the English translation of another Native word. Such names link the prairie to pre-European experience.

22. Avonlea is located southwest of Regina near the junction of Highways 334 and 339.

23. These four stages are a vague pastiche of Emily Bronte's poem "Julian M. and A.G. Rochelle" (1844?).

24. "Grasshopper" contains a good deal of verbal play. Here Hawley seems to be using the modern "worded," the adjective "weird" (i.e. strange), and the Middle English verb "weird" (i.e. to be destined or fated).

25. "The Last Best West" is a pioneer name for the prairies, especially for the area around Saskatoon.

26. While *The Wanderer* ends by placing its faith in heaven, here hope for a return to fulfilment, community and home focusses on the experience of ordinary people.

Fielding[1]

(for my father)[2]

Dennis Cooley

silent (sī/lent) adj. [L. *silens* < prp. of *silēre*, to be silent, still, prop. < IE. base *sei-, *si-, to rest, to let the hand fall, whence SEED, SIDE, Goth. *(ana)silan*, to cease (of the wind)]

What is spoken is never, and in no language, what is said.

—Martin Heidegger[3]

I.

Thanks for everything you quietly tell us
boldly for you who never knew quite how
to say such things with any ease
as we load our girls and luggage
into the car heading once more back to Winnipeg
and you pack your coffee and science fiction
into the cardboard box that is to see you
through the day watching alone
over a monstrous claw[4] that needs
only the iron bones to rise
rigid behind it
to rip off the overburden
sandy earth in abandoned fields
sealing the darkness sown
40 feet beneath us

where driven by thistles and dust
you spent your prime
stood knee deep in water
steeping in those strange long holes
punched coal from layers of packed clay
picking fire out of gleaming black seams[5]

no place for any man
certainly no place for a young man like you
tempered to life by a thin white disc
that scraped inside your lungs
                                        gently
with its sharp metal breathing

that was no place for you to be father
far below the wasted prairie slamming its way
above you
the baseball diamonds you told me about
where Clarey Weir ran 5 miles
from his father's dairy farm every game
to catch pop-ups in his hip pocket
and Barney Krivel swung under liners
in centre field with his back to the plate[6]
and where you yourself pasted baseballs
through the Thirties / your twenties
using that ridiculous stubby glove i found
on the farm one day
you a sunburned farmer
born to the prairies
held hard to the place
holding in the peak of your strength
those smooth wooden bats
the angular picks
as they all did

the men who stayed on
stood swinging at the blurs
firing past them
knelt digging in lignite
pockets of brown carbon
crumbling

I remember you
years later
bent in the white heat
on our 55 Massey
dragging the discer
over Evendon's[7] section 7 miles north of town
its plates glinting on the rub of dirt
and the loud scrape of rocks
grinding off sparks
your engineer's cap ruling the red
across your forehead
and the startling white softness of your body
underneath the gray cotton shirt you always wore
and the smell of soap and cream
you pulled through the zipper of
your leather shaving kit
on Saturday nights and how
the heat losing its dirt edges fast
we rolled down the gravel road
over the big hill under
the orange slant of sun
with Hank Snow[8] blowing us down into Estevan
from CHAB in Moose Jaw yellow
on the radio of our '53 green Ford

Just to think it could be
Time has opened the door
And at last I am free
I don't hurt anymore

and how the mercury-vapour street lights
would take us in their blueness past
the forkclinks and the lemonhalibut smells
fanning from the Canada Cafe
direct to the onoffonoffon incandescence
drawing us
dreaming down into
the violet of the Orpheum[9] theatre
where for 15 cents we witnessed
Gene Autry[10] *the singing cowboy*
rescuing flickering women
in black and white shadows

now the sunburn has
almost gone from your neck
and the blackness from your hair
but your hardened wrists
still thicken and move
after all these years
and we see again
the light that has always sat/
sits now
in the brown of your eyes
the slight halt that
rests in your words

II.

now
David[11] drops me off
Winnipeg International Airport
gate 8 600 pm AC 179
sit here on the runway humid
10 minutes to fix the plane
iced up
mild for Feb 13
what's on their minds these people
newspapers & magazines men in
3-piece suits & wire-rim glasses
coughing
women in loose sweaters & smoke

anaeurysm
a permanent abnormal blood-filled dilation
of a blood vessel resulting from disease of
the vessel wall

out of surgery
long ago
mom not well herself calling her family
excited stewardesses talk loud
in the front
luminous blue lights pulse
bleaching as an incoming plane
washes the landing strip

blacked out
in the ndp[12] committee rooms
spasm in your back
Barry[13] killed/ young
by the tangle of cells in his back
overnight in Estevan hospital suspect
a leakage
somewhere drugged
telling Lynn[14]
to phone about the special
Lignite Louis[15] night
you won't be able to make it
the ambulance angling
north to Regina
in the clean morning air
great day isn't it
Bill[16]
in the doorway

bottom of winter
waiting for repairs &
where are you father
spun thru
the thin wall of linen sun
frayed into
hospital whiteness laid upon you
i remember
the alarm that would climb
into your eyes
all those years of your sickness
once a man with sunstained arms sustained in
sweat not small never small like Andy's
dad Andy[17] telling me torn
in his father's death

but paler
more uncertain than you'd been
We certify that[18]

the plane lurches back thinking of Walter[19]
dead in July
mom there with you
the years you may never have
may never have had
braided in dirt & coal dust &
school kids' mud

molecules boil and
push us
bubbles jutting
up the prairie nightsky
vaporous lights
wintered below
probe into
delicate
black membrane stretches deep
around us stewardesses steeping us
full of coffee & rye

& already the engines cut back
& we begin our slide into Regina
heavy black gumbo[20] frigid beneath the radiant
tissue of snow
use seat cushion for flotation the bronze
sticker says &
a red sticker tells us not to smoke
ratios of travel
seat belt (1E) fastened all the way
quotients of sense

the overriding
words
as they fall
out into
freighted
over the silent wheatfields
fractions of truth
on the 18th day of February 1980
350 miles angry
for you frightened
for us all
who will be there
for the passengers going on to Vancouver
there will be a hot meal after Regina.

730 the captain good news tailwind
pick up 5 minutes
we'll get you there in 25 minutes. weather
in Regina tonight is broken
clouds and minus 12 degrees Celsius.

fractured sounds lining my skull
will they bounce in
your retina's
curve of light

i'm coming father to see you
in your pain still living still
did you wonder at all where we were
when we would

the jet hisses & quivers slightly
as it comes into
Regina dumbly rising
in yellow gas[21]
our records show
don't know what to
fearing your death
have always feared
knowing always
never knowing

plane pumps us
freezing
onto the runway
Plains Hospital i tell the driver

III.

Feb. 15 915 a.m.

P.M. Joe Clarke told a Toronto audience yesterday that Canadians should think hard before going to the polls on Monday.

Liberal leader Pierre Trudeau said the Liberal party if elected would negotiate a better deal on Autopac with the U.S.

The condition of President Marshal Tito of Yugoslavia is improving his doctors said this morning.

Gold prices fell on the Zurich bullion market today in anticipation of the release of the American hostages held in Tehran.

15 years ago today the maple leaf flag was first flown in Ottawa.

huddle down in these annealing words
where is there anything to feed your hunger mother
click the locks on the cardoors
drifting as we head home on 39 to Estevan
107.2 KPA   Hum 85%   Temp -18°C   Wind NW 22 kph
ice crystals suspended in the air   reduce visibility
can't get the heat back there Lorne[22] says
blustery sky   wind gusts   shoves us south
loosen your shoes
so your
feet won't freeze

the 125 miles we drove
how many times together
died with the sounds congealed
like phlegm in your throat
nothing for your healing
We certify
stubble jabs above the matting of snow
words to ward off what we know
don't know
the cold eating you
machines stuffed in your failing body
flailing weakly at the tubes that caught
your voice   now gone
snapped like barb wire

and this is not my voice
                                        father
you would see that
these words that fall
filling the page
taking over
your arms to pull
the plastic from your throat
to release
what blessing

cheated of even that
you who so seldom
spoke the
shaking inside you
at last wanting
                  (to say)
what wanting
                 (out)
now you are dead   more silent than ever
past Corinne[23]   the old coffeeshop where we'd always stop
whenever you took us
                              everytime
                                          like Christmasevekids into Regina

snarl of thoughts
   will reduce them soon
have contracted them now in   this spelling
only our bodies' cramp could show

drifting thickens to smoke
hardened arteries
renal failure they thought
& no chance for you
spinning slower
& slower inside yourself
to draw out your swift last love

hot in the waiting room
Mr. Wheeler:[24] *sorry*
CBC: -45 Celsius in 1936
Yellow Grass where the Souris River once began
what was it like

curled on the verge of
a long white absence
the prairie that rustles   silently
around us
sundogs[25]
sprung open low on the sky
sun a sunken period   hung in their parentheses
(gone now on a second take)
leaks its chilled light
bleakly
even now   hauling its way
back to life

Funeral Directors

STATEMENT OF DEATH

We certify that *Mr. Orin Cooley* died at *Regina, Saskatchewan* on the *15th* day of *February 1980.*
The funeral of the above named deceased person was conducted by this Funeral Home on the *18th* day of *February 1980* with burial at *City Cemetery, Estevan, Saskatchewan.*
Our records show the next-of-kin to be:
NAME: *Mrs. Irene Cooley*
ADDRESS: *Estevan, Saskatchewan*
RELATIONSHIP: *wife*
We certify the above to be a true statement from our records.
Dated in *Estevan, Saskatchewan,* this *20* day of *February 1980*
City Prov. Orsted Funeral Home Ltd.
Estevan-Oxbow-Carlyle-Arcola
Per ____________________
Funeral Director

but you are dead
& the Honda bumps over the ice
snow cabling then dusting to wisps
yellow stripe holds on the right
oncoming headlights thrown at us
now & then
the punctual nurses delaying the final stop

a blue & white ambulance erupts out of the haze
just as we catch the fringe of Weyburn
city of old rivalries
before your
unspeaking / unspeakable pride
as i curved
baseballs singing thru the
sudden singe of summers (*I don't care what train i'm on*
as long as it keeps rolling on[26]
(13 & bewildered
by the cotton girls[27]
swelling around me

frost resists the heater's fan
& our wet breath blurs
across the glass
as it threaded our windows with ice once
always thru the bright cold of our farm
winters years ago
breath going in long white
whips on our way to the barn

winter moon/

was a grape

laid

on our barn

not now

the far sun
a tumour burred in our brains
is it

it is
there & you are
nowhere father

we are here
under this white shell
burnt
on the 15th day of February 1980
Ralph
can see better now
banks of monitors
red jerk of numbers
tightening in our shoulders
gauging your life
strung with tubes
they shaved you
back in the drifting
/slowmotion/
snow almost stopped
whorls on the road
Don Harron CBC[28]
something about
black ice
3 feet thick
you can see right through it
icefishing
someone says
your unsaid
love & grief

Halbrite

an 83 yr. old woman ice-fishing
& you just retired
working off & on
to arrange those years
filling holes with annuities
always a plain man
farmer miner farmer janitor
oil wells on the sides closing in

Dear Kathy Feb 15, 1980

Kathy, grandpa Cooley isn't feeling well, he had an operation on wednesday and isn't doing to well on recovering. This is why he had the operation, the tube connected to his heart is blocked so they took that tube out and replaced it with another one so he might die. How are things down there? Its fine down here, except granpa. For assembly this week our class does it this is what I have to memorize,

turn over the paper.

La voyageur employé de la campagnie du Nord Ouest faissait la traite des fourrures. C'etait un homme, robuste, joueux et incouciant. Il était court, ne dépassent pas cinq pieds et six pousse accose du manque d'espace dans les canots. Il avait cepantdent la force d'un géant. Il pouvait nager out avirneur de quinze à dix-huite heures dans une journé et porter de très lourd fardeaux.

Love
Megan
Cooley[29]

the CPR spur to Moose Jaw[30] alongside us
the Thirties drying air you breathed
young then riding
steel dreams to Alberta crops
Midale a storage battery[31]

not far now
to a house
emptied of your ills & teasing

mom with her cold
could hardly talk
kissed you
hard

it was Feb 14 & you were dying
he never had a chance
all the voice she could find

no chance at all
hardly ever
in your life
shut down
syphon nothing from your body
no words no wastes
cold as bottled methane

Galloway's farm[32]
nearly home

books here that i lug everywhere
with me
& you
wanting to say
wrapped wordless in those
sheets by our love
lie still dad we told you
believing
you're looking strong it's
just a tube to help you breathe *but you*
can't move *with the needles*
just yet
ending
your life like that
what sounds
can there be

in the end we didn't even let you speak

Kathy, Feb 16

Did you hear about grandpa Cooley? He had an operation and didn't recover. He died friday at 10 after six. The Thompsons just arrived today. Tara has grown a lot. Darcy and the other boys haven't changed. How is everybody?

Love,

Megan

IV.

Friday morning
(Feb 23)
in your down-filled parka
lined boots softened to your foot's shape
the house emptying now
relatives gone
Diane and the girls gone
Sharon & Laurel leaving soon[33]
mom in tears
someone else cut out of her house
you could write sometimes

all the letters i never wrote
listen Irene, Irene, if anybody needs a bed
i have a big room, yes[34]

Pat's car rolls east to Winnipeg[35]
300 miles
windows clear returning
coarse snowflakes
slope across road
slow roil sun/hole
punched in
aluminum sky

in my dream
/one winter/
we were dreaming
you & i

cattails
broken back
on themselves
clumps of fireweed rusting thru
clover
almost oily
glows
& ridges in banks fluting
down & in
on themselves
stress lines
like lesions in a giant brain
wooden wind
breaks along north side

sloughs clogged with reeds like
broken sticks

pass an oil well
deformed birdhead
pecking at the crude oil
gushing spasmodically up from the casing
oncoming grader
blade scrapes the shoulder
& snow peels off
clouding
another well chopping   slower shorter strokes
and straggles of trees
hang black
onto the low spots
bunch & we move east
trunks strangled with winter
priming now with
light

stand in strange
relief against the sky
no depth total depth
no this is

not what i wanted to say
nothing i should be writing

road bare sun
sands ice away
more wells they voted conservative here
Diane's mom on the short wave
hoarse in her chest & throat
can't make out what
she's saying
the car's shadow
running
steadily
beside us
beside ourselves
snowdrift stalling behind

turbulence decreases with viscosity, as the measure of the internal function of the stream, the ability of the stream to stick together, to withstand shear.[36]

hit the abrupt
drop into the valley
ice & snow
built up
Pat rides the ruts worn into the highway
like a crosscountry ski course
ravine at bottom
ragged with brush

Moose Mountain Creek
a stiff black twist
a sliver of land
pitted with trucks &
halftons
ripping by with snowmobiles in the backs
silver fuel tanks
Rosco bins[37]
bound side by side
hard scars in the snow
only the rush & rap of wind
one thing you can always count on
in this country Gordon[38] said when we
looked for the graveside on the hill north of town
the thrum of car eating
fossil fire

what is the use of talking[39]

ruined yards & barns
)our yellow brick house that burnt down
after we left the farm(
& they have broken my house[40]
2 brown horses
feeding on bales
in one corner of a pasture
shaggy winter coats
)soft muzzles
water snorting
ice on long hair

)& the cows
their breaths
stifflegged run
the frozen trough
puffing jets of vapour
orange cat her back warm
& tea-bag smell of hay
breathing into barn
sweet breath
squashed one night flat in the stall
frost growing out of the nails

a true statement from our records[41]

not empty this space is not empty
where is the poem in this
locked in this
calm

& earth turns
under us

#18 east &
houses knotting regularly
every 7 or 8 miles
elevators like columns of dried blood
snaring
names / numbers
Bienfait[42] Steelman Hirsch Frobisher Oxbow
Glen Ewen Carnduff Carievale Gainsborough

wires tracks roads
twining
our doubtful lives over
this stunning plain

Oxbow
Ralph Allen[43] Memorial Museum
a converted railway station
2 pigeons slap
fast from the side of the road
595 the red metal stencil reads in the ditch
at Glen Ewen a homemade sign
YE MUST BE BORN AGAIN
red letters

the black railline tracks
us on the right
telephone posts trail
/pencils/
on the other side
virgules that measure
our passing
sinking to periods
out of sight
their brittle braille
stipples the prairie
wires that hum &
sigh in the heat &
the cold
& loudly shed the wind in storm

Carnduff
Dale's[44] hometown
ice puttied on the road

Carievale 12 km
highway a gash
sometimes black / sometimes brown
in the fresh snow
barbwire fences
splicing them with pliers
in spring
cracked dry
stitching
the endless seam between
earth & sky
bright white bleeding to
uncertain white
sky packed granular like
crushed salt
dissolving
strong whiff of the coffee i drink/
you drank/
splashing in our nostrils
your death turning
father in
my head / this poem
Bob saying *we silence words by*
writing them down[45]
from our records
sharp scent of your cigarettes in the parka i wear
im sorry to hear about your father dennis
saltsour sweat i always liked
wet in
shift cramped in the seats
where we are strapped
windslap against car
billions of new flakes ground
off sun

eyes hurt
in the reflection
frost folded fibrous
in the air
grains of light
fogging the sky

but where are you my father
what trace of you in this
country you farmed & dug
this dirt
the wind erases

inside glass feel warm
yellow rub
against back of neck arm
barely awake
nap over the drowsing fields
& under crust
muffled grouse crouch hidden
in gauze pockets

will flash
when sun touches them
off
sun will wipe
off dazzle
so March inks in
like broken veins
raw scraggle of crows
coalblue bruises
on wet snow
aaaaaawwwwww *aaw*[46]
damp earthsmell[47]

April scrawl of frogs
slippery green
days drawn darkly thru
smother of frost
that he eat of the barley corn
and move with the seed's breath[48]

now there is only
the freeze of wind
sawing the drifts
opening furrows
inside our
dozing
wind & a
blunt sun

& we are skinbags of heated water dreaming
brains grayly
balloon in our heads
nerves skein blind
albino seaweed blown
in our bodies' pools
listening

carbon phases / your phrases
strung between us father
your breath tumbles
shining quiet
inside my ribs
find your hand hard in mine
your lines wound in
the stretch of my muscles
still living

but you are dead
& we float like lost birds
over this frozen
land reading
these things
that we know
the long silence slanting past
now in the mind[49]

riding

edges of sound

simply past metaphor[50]

sun wind snow sky

these lines/

letters/

my words for i loved you

thinking of you

David saying

it is always better to be alive[51]

epilogue

in the dream
another dream
a year & a half later

arriving late
at the cabin[52]
hauling my things into
the living room
dark & cold
out then into the front yard
red
sun rising in the northwest
warm wind
warm like water
a friend
out of the guest cabin
i didnt hear you come
you didnt make a sound
& then a loud shout from the cabin
my father
not at all my father
in that remote hard voice
no father
yes you did where have you been

& in i in
to the chilled cabin
shaken
with my fathers rage

finally going into
the bed room
my father there
in the bed
my father &
an old man
beside him
in a round tight face
my fathers face
swollen & bruised
left side

whats wrong
whats wrong dad
& he
nothing
looks/ quickly
at the old man
me shaking
son of a bitch
son of a bitch
screaming & slapping the old man i

wake shivering
into the night
into the cold
tightness in my chest
the same room
Diane
in my fathers place
coughing
Sept 2 / 81

---

1. Reprinted from *Fielding* (Saskatoon: Thistledown Press, 1983). Part I of the poem was published in *Leaving* (Winnipeg: Turnstone Press, 1980) and most of Parts II, III and the last part of Part IV were published in *Grain* of May 1980. The Thistledown Press publication is 82 pages in length. Because of space constraints the vertical spacing has been compressed considerably here, but the original layout has been simulated as closely as possible.

Dennis Cooley was born in Estevan, Saskatchewan in 1944. He now teaches Canadian Literature at the University of Manitoba.

2. The poem is written in the tradition of the elegy. Seen as such, Cooley's omission of any obvious consolation is significant.

3. "The Thinker as Poet," trans. Albert Hofstadter (New York: Harper and Row, 1975), p. 11.

4. The "monstrous claw" is a reference to the great drag-lines presently used in strip mining near Estevan.

5. Cooley's father was both a miner and a farmer for a time. Cooley is working on a long poem called *1931*, dealing with the issues surrounding the Estevan Miners' Strike of 1931. It is an event rarely far from his mind.

6. Clarey Weir and Barney Krivel (a cousin of Eli Mandel) were local Estevan baseball players whose abilities were legendary. Here Cooley focusses on their fielding abilities. The author too was an outfielder known for his fielding rather than his hitting in the Saskatchewan Senior Baseball League. Here the author is also fielding—as his father did as a farmer—in that he is well aware of Charles Olson's conception of the poem as a field of play.

7. Dennis Cooley's father farmed a section of land he rented from a Mr. Evendon.

8. Hank Snow is a popular Country and Western singer born in the Maritimes but now living in Nashville. CHAB is a Moose Jaw radio station.

9. A hero in Greek mythology renowned for the beauty and power of his singing, Orpheus descended to the underworld to retrieve his dead wife Eurydice. Apparently successful, he turned back to look at Eurydice as she followed him, thereby breaking his promise to Hades and Persephone, and they retrieved her. Disconsolate, he died. The manner of his death varies according to the telling. In some versions his severed head continued its enchanting music. Cooley, his father, and perhaps Gene Autry, Hank Snow and later in the poem Ferlin Husky, with their grassroots subject matter, are types of underground singers.

10. Gene Autry was a grade B movie star in the '40s and the '50s. He is now the owner of the Los Angeles Angels baseball team.

11. David Arnason is a colleague, friend, and former neighbour of Dennis

Cooley. Part I is documented by memory. The next three parts are travelling sections. Here we fly from Winnipeg to Regina, as well as through memory time.

12. The New Democratic Party is a social democratic political party. It has never formed the government on the federal level. Nevertheless, the provinces of Manitoba, Saskatchewan and British Columbia have had N.D.P. governments. Dennis Cooley and his father have been active supporters of the party.

13. Barry Allison, Cooley's cousin, died of a malignancy in his back. He figures in another poem, "Walter," Cooley's uncle and Barry Allison's father.

14. Cooley has a sister named Lynn.

15. Louis Lignite is a comic/mythic symbol of the miner.

16. Bill Kniskern was a visitor to Cooley's office that morning.

17. Cooley is referring to Andrew Suknaski, the Wood Mountain poet.

18. See the Statement of Death, p. 235.

19. Walter Allison was Dennis Cooley's uncle. *Leaving* (1980) contains a poem called "Walter."

20. Gumbo is a particularly malicious prairie mud.

21. The street lights in Regina have a yellow luminosity, especially when viewed from an airplane.

22. Lorne Duczek is Dennis Cooley's brother-in-law.

23. We are now travelling south from Regina to Estevan past Corinne, Yellow Grass, Weyburn, Ralph, Halbrite and Midale.

24. Mr. Wheeler is a friend of the Cooley family in Estevan.

25. Sundogs are brilliant crosses of orange or white light that often bracket the sun against a cold, clear, blue prairie sky in winter.

26. These lines are from the popular Country song "Freight Train, Freight Train goin' so fast . . ." often sung by Ferlin Husky.

27. Does Cooley mean girls dressed in cotton???

28. Don Harron, the Toronto actor, had been the host of CBC's radio program "Morningside" since 1978.

29. Dennis Cooley has two daughters, Megan and Dana, aged nine and eleven respectively in 1980. The editor's translation cannot adequately reproduce the charm and naïveté of the rather rough French of the nine-year-old child: "The voyageur employed in the Northwest Company was involved in the fur trade. This was a sturdy man, full of joy and carefree. He was short, not over five feet six inches tall, because of the lack of space in the canoes. However, he had the strength of a giant. He could swim or paddle(???) from fifteen to eighteen hours per day and carry very heavy loads."

30. Moose Jaw is northwest of Estevan.

31. Midale is a small town in the oil fields around Estevan. Crude oil is temporarily stored there in storage batteries.

32. Galloway's farm is just north of Estevan on Highway 39.

33. Dennis Cooley's wife is named Diane. Sharon, Lynn and Laurel are his sisters.

34. Cooley's mother's name is Irene. This interjection is probably the voice of a friend or neighbour.

35. Pat Sanderson is Dennis Cooley's sister-in-law. We are proceeding east on Saskatchewan Highway No. 18. The place names that follow occur on the way to Winnipeg.

36. Cooley is quoting from Peter Stevens' *Patterns in Nature* (Boston: Little, Brown, 1974), p. 56.

37. Rosco bins are round, metal grain bins.

38. Cooley has an uncle Gordon Wilson who lives at Melville, Saskatchewan.

39. The allusion here is to Ezra Pound, "Exile's Letter." The remainder of the sentence is: "and there is no end of talking / There is no end of things in the heart."

40. See Ezra Pound, *The Pisan Cantos*, LXXVI.

41. See the Statement of Death on p. 235.

42. Bienfait is pronounced Beanfate. Three of the miners killed in the 1931 strike in Estevan are buried here.

43. Ralph Allen was a journalist from Oxbow.

44. Dale Thompson is Cooley's brother-in-law.

45. "Bob" is Robert Kroetsch in "Seed Catalogue." See p. 124.

46. This sound is the cry of a crow or a person. In *Line* 7/8 (Spring/Fall 1986), Cooley calls the crow "anti-establishment . . . noisy and rambunctious . . . a symbol of the rebel, of the margins . . . [a] muse symbol . . . for Cooley, Krafchenko, or Kroetsch" (p. 177).

47. Here the clipped, economical diction and syntax are broken slightly by the long unorthodox sound and by the keening that follows. Such verbal play looks forward to much more elaborate verbal variety and delight in language in poems such as "cunning linguist" and "vulva jig" in *Bloody Jack* (1984), as well as *Soul Searching* (1987), *Perishable Light* (1988), *Dedications* (1988) and even Cooley's book of criticism *The Vernacular Muse* (1987).

48. See Ezra Pound, *The Pisan Cantos,* LXXXIII.

49. The line is "now in the mind indestructible," in Ezra Pound's *The Pisan Cantos*, LXXIV.

50. Cooley has misquoted Pound slightly, leaving out the comma. The lines from *The Pisan Cantos*, LXXXII, are: "Wisdom lies next thee / simply, past metaphor."

51. Cooley's reference is to David Arnason quoting Paul B. Taylor and W.H. Auden's translation of *The Elder Edda* (London: Faber, 1969), a long Old Norse poem. The next line is "The living man can [at least] keep a cow . . ." p. 69.

52. Cooley bought his Winnipeg Beach cabin from Dorothy Livesay.

Marsh Burning[1]

David Arnason

Section I

1

driving through New Brunswick
the sifting rain steady
on the windshield of my Chev
you spoke to me Thor[2]
saying

Baldur[3] is dead / slain
Baldur
who was white as the snows on Hecla[4]
Loki is free[5]
Fenrir[6] prowls just beyond the horizon
somewhere over Fundy[7]

the world ash is rotting
you said *eaten from without and within*
Nidhogg gnaws at the roots of Yggdrasil[8]
the reindeer in the branches paw and fret[9]

rain was heavy on the windshield
that night I remember
as it is now
on the window near my bed

I wait for you to speak again Thor
and hear you rumbling and threatening in the distance
there beyond the Naashwaak
over Oman's creek[10]

Freya has come twice since that day[11]
weeping tears of gold
once to warn me that Odin[12]
had been nine days hanging
and had lost an eye

saying *answer his questions quickly*
and do not lie
whatever he should ask

Odin did not come
but Freya came again
the first warm day of summer

saying *do not ride the reindeer*
in the trees behind the house

I have not seen them there
but hear them every night
rutting and fighting at the foot of the hill

the dog has heard them and is afraid
and will not leave the house

if I get a chance I will ride them

2

this morning making bread
my wife found a toad in the dough
just as it had begun to rise

it is perhaps an omen
and I shall have to watch for others

the children complain that there are worms
in the flour
but there are none

still they watch their food
and have begun to worry

speak to me Thor
there are things I must know
if I am to protect my family

today is cloudy
and the drizzling rain that merges with the fog
makes it impossible to see
into the valley behind the house

I know you are there

3

the reindeer are becoming braver
I have not seen them yet
but hear them every night
outside my window locking horns

the dog cowers under the bed and will not move

today I will walk through the thickets by the creek
yesterday I saw their tracks
their trails crushed in the undergrowth

a small man came to my door
in an old blue overcoat
that hung around his neck like a cloak

he had one good eye only
and said he was a Jehovah's Witness
I bought a *Watchtower* from him
and he went away

saying *This is the God's Truth*

4

the weather is unsettled
rain and haze and sunshine
and always there are rainbows in the sky

never have I seen so many rainbows
and so much traffic in the heavens
they curve and bridge in all directions
but mostly to the north
and always seem to touch down on the earth
just at the power station
on the way to Marysville

twice it was struck by lightning this past week
but Hydro crews were out
and we had light again within an hour

this morning there were dwarves
on my front lawn[13]
(hitch-hiking on the road to Newcastle)[14]
one stood with his thumb out
while the others laughed
and tumbled on the lawn
I watched them through the curtains
they had too much luggage for dwarves
and could not expect a ride
but a half-ton Ford stopped near them
they leaped into the box and it was gone

there are ravens in the ash tree in my yard
I have not seen ravens here before

5

my neighbour is troubled by the reindeer
he hears them in the night
and wonders what they are

he too has lost an eye
but has replaced it with an eye of glass
a jewelled eye
with a clock in the centre

the numbers on the dial are backward
and the hands go counterclockwise

he says that this is so
that he can read it in a mirror
(the clock is always wrong)

he says that he was born in Bognor Regis[15]
and sets the clock so that the time it shows
is right in Sussex

he wants his death to be exact
recorded in the numbers of his birth
(sometimes the clock is fast
and sometimes slow
but never is it right)

6

this is the route to Gimli[16]
up the transcanada highway
past Woodstock
down to Rivière du Loup
then left to Montreal
through the Louis Lafontaine tunnel
right at Toronto
to Sudbury Sault Ste. Marie
around Superior
through Wawa   Nipigon
past Thunder Bay   Kenora   bursting free
at last into the open prairie
right at Winnipeg   then north
and I am
home

if anything is to happen before I leave
then it must happen soon

there are more dwarves on the road
they travel openly
walking, hitching rides
they laugh and play
tumbling and rolling
and calling out
in their strange sing-song language
in every group there is one greybeard
who does not laugh or play

why are they going to Newcastle

there has been a great thunderstorm Thor
and I hear you

great Mjollnir[17] must have hit the power station
one more time
the Hydro men have not been able
to repair the damage
though a semi-trailer just came by
a large transformer on the trailer
and they may repair it soon

the man who lives beside me is a saint
he told me so himself showing me
a five-leafed clover on his lawn
at eight he died from whooping cough
was taken to heaven
visited with the lord
and was sent back to lead his life
as a model to men
and it was then he lost his eye
twice since he has seen the lord

once
when his brother died

and once again
at his mother-in-law's passing

he says the lord is balder than a plate
and has no beard

7

in South Dakota it began
five hundred dead and others missing
rain swept down   flash floods
the Rapid Creek became a mighty river for a day

did the bodies sweep past Mt. Rushmore
arms and legs
tumbling and rolling
swept on the surging flood
rising and falling
while Washington and Lincoln gazed benevolently down

the Rockies have flash floods
and no one knows where
the next one will strike

hurricane Agnes[18]
has turned the east coast of the states into a giant pond

television shows it all
homeless weeping folk
water swirling in the streets
bodies of the dead

the camera is a knowing eye   prescient

behind my house Oman's Creek has overflowed its banks
and the reindeer have moved into the thickets
higher up the slope
I shall ride them soon

8

five thousand died
this week
in Bangla Desh
there is a famine and no end in sight
we have rushed them wheat which they will not touch
preferring famine

scientists discovered a tribe not previously known
in the jungles of the upper Amazon near Peru
untouched they were starving
eating a strange bark
that gave them diarrhea

twelve miles of tape were made before the last one died
at least their language will be saved

perhaps there will be only cries for food

I am hungry
the house is filled with food
but nothing
satisfies
my senseless craving

9

cancer is in the air

four men have died this week
and all from cancer

small details

men are repairing the bridge across the river
we have to use the Princess Margaret bridge
near Lincoln

men are working there too
and the traffic is impossible
the bridge across the Naashwaak needs repairs
cracks in the iron form a rainbow

something is wrong with the telephone
people call but cannot hear my voice
they shout hello hello hello
and I shout back hello
the company sent out a man
to do repairs
but there was nothing wrong
perhaps it is only my voice that cannot be heard

I get no mail
or at least no letters
I would like to have
not even bills
advertisements for seat covers
invitations to send money
to charities I have not heard of
a company that wants to sell me new stick-free frying pans
has begun to threaten
Dear sir:
This is your third and final notice . . .

the man who brings the mail has no uniform
he wears a red plaid shirt
and carries mail in a gunny sack

old Mrs. Carter
does not trust him
and aims a rifle at him
as he does our street

channel 13 has become unstuck
it always shows a man seated at a desk
bored and gazing from the screen

sometimes he reads but only for a moment
it seems that he is waiting
there is no one else
except that once a dwarf
came by with coffee
and once a hand appeared and gave him papers
he read and burned
the neighbours say
it is an advertising stunt for cigarettes
he does smoke a lot
but never shows his package to the screen

radio signals are strong
stations from as far away as Texas
crowd and jostle so
that nothing can be heard

10

I have ridden the reindeer out behind the house

last night when they came
trampling through the bush
snorting and grunting
bellowing in rage
I hid in the lowest branches of the cherry tree
and when the biggest buck
came by I leaped
I landed true
one arm around his neck
and one hand clutching to his horns

he bellowed once with rage
then ran
a whirlwind sweeping through the trees
my face was brushed by branches and by stars
we burst into the moonlit field

plunged into the Naashwaak
swam to the hydro lines
then up the hill
to gallop into mist
and holes in the wind
I clung exhausted as we moved
through regions of cold
swam through thin fire
and finally fell exhausted
on the slope of hill
behind my house
tumbling into the bush below

this was not a dream

I think I remember
two ravens

11

the men from the hydro company came by today
to prune the ash tree in my yard
the branches tangling with the wires

a young man came to my door
to apologize
telling me

you should call a tree surgeon
that ash you have is rotting from within

a grey squirrel sits in the branches
and scolds at all who pass
the children call him Rat-tooth

mirrors in my house have begun to warp
it is so dry
their frames twist
and the reflections they give
are crazy and askew

lunatic faces grimace
and weep
bodies are bent and humped
arms and legs thicken and strain

the house is filled with dust
and fine volcanic ash[19]

12

I was born under Gemini
and I should have been twins
my twinned soul wars in my single body
Frey and Freya have been here
                                        Baldur is dead
they say
newly slain
always he is newly slain
his death a catastrophe so near
that every second he is newly slain
the grief so fresh
that even knowing he will rise again
cannot soften the suffering
                                        Baldur is dead
they tell me
bursting with the news

they cannot help me
having no future
and no past

I must make plans
and the intense moments they inhabit
have no room for plans
always they burst into being
born and dying
all events are one to them
except that Baldur's death
is under everything

christmas is coming and I must get mistletoe

13

snow has fallen
and the crows have gathered in the spruces
for their winter dance
I have seen no dwarves
but the clock in my kitchen
is reflected in the mirror in the hall
so that time is backward
and I must look into my eye
to see the reflection
reflected true

14

Heimaey has cracked in two
and Vestmanaeyjar buried under ash[20]

it has begun
the rainbows of the summer
were no lie

I thought it would be faster
the boiling of the sea
the sun and moon swallowed at the start

it is not so

15

it has been an unusual winter
since the day that Helgafell exploded
the snow has gone
when there should be snow
flowers have begun to bud
and birds come back
before their time

perhaps this is the final spring
and must be rushed

16

today my son brought home from school
a bracelet he had found

he had worn it all day
and already seemed to glow
he had become beautiful
wearing the metal ring
before I took it from him

metal cannot be that heavy
nor can it shine so brightly
the bracelet is scarred
as though by fire

I must get rid of it

I must make plans

17

others have heard the promptings

madness is abroad
or else Mike knows something that I don't

one day
a perfect day of sunshine
he hanged himself in his garage

he was found and saved
(if
really
he was saved)

the other day I saw him at the ward
                    a wolf
he says   *is living in my head*
                    eating my brain
                    it wants my death
                    orders my death
electric shocks have stunned the wolf
still it is not dead

Mike lives before us
and must come back in time
to speak to me
                    volcanic ash is over everything
he says   *and I remember all*
                    even this meeting

                    words
he says   *are what the world is made from*
                    and when I learned this
                    I could move in time
                    backwards and forwards
                    until I met the wolf
                    and was made prisoner

the psychiatrist is frightened
and will not talk to Mike

he says a locksmith
is what Mike needs

18

today I will leave
the car is packed and gassed
the movers came last night
and so the house is empty
except for voices
barely audible inside the walls
speaking a language that I know
but can't quite understand

my wife and children are waiting in the car

paint is peeling from the wall in the kitchen

the power is off and so there are no lights

I have never noticed
that pattern in the tiles before
those broken circles

they are waiting

I must go

Section II

1

after the long rolling hills of Ontario
lake and river
hill and river
lake
we swept over Manitoba's border
down the undulating road
past the burned out forest deadfall
now greening again

and only a few skeletal trees
to remind us of fire
memory singing now
we slid into
fields
green and yellow
barley wheat and oats
flax the colour a lake should be
poles that vee'd to the horizon
a high sky with clouds
massed and turbulent
past the elevator at Dufresne[21]
we slid faster and faster
the road becoming flatter as we moved
as if the car no longer needed power
but could glide
did glide
into the heart of that prairie
into Winnipeg
into home

2

and again that year the world failed to end

the randomness of order
bud leaf stalk and branch
circling the seasons

the liquid harmonics of waves
eroding a shore
sidewalks going where no one walks
geese navigating the arctic skies
elaborate maps in the neural traceways
of their narrow heads
sun moon and stars
leading them to a hunter's gun
days heavy with portent
when nothing happens
death by traffic
stellar accidents
that change the colour
of lichen and moss
intricate patterns on the wing of a moth
stunning itself against the light bulb
above my cottage door

leaning against the balcony
on the fourteenth floor of the Regency Towers[22]
Winnipeg spread out before us this night
an electric map of irrational ganglia
I am tempted to jump
to hurl myself into the centre of this space
and never land
but we are drinking Tequila
and making plans
our desires sharpened by alcohol

the room loses focus
but next year is hard and clear
Greece Turkey the Isle of Crete
the Parthenon the hot Mediterranean sun
all stronger than the tang of lemons
the soft bland taste of salt

3

the circumambulations of desire
ventricle auricle artery vein
blood surging
the heart awash with it
the brain soaked
steeped in it
all the intricate tracery
of artery and vein
filled with the traffic of blood
all the crackling electricity of the body
the delicate wiring of nerves
fueled by the fire of blood
the pump and the pulse of it

we met at the blood donor clinic
lying on cots next to each other
our blood threading its separate ways into bottles
as we gazed at the ceiling
trying to unscramble the hidden messages
a code of geography
in the signs above us
takosonas medtonon rovecavun[23]

afterwards we drank coffee and ate doughnuts
talking about the destination of our blood
and wondering whether it might meet
in some other body
and we were tired from the loss of blood
tired as though we had just made love
as if our giving blood were a conspiracy
tied somehow to pain and to loss
and we parted
having given just enough clues
that we might accidentally meet again

4

the urgency of sap:
stamen sepal petal leaf
the surge of chlorophyll
bleeding into green
capillaries deep in earth
each cell swamped in sap
the leaves steeped in it
underground messages translated
into blossom and nectar
perfume become a siren alarm
to fumbling bees
trees vulnerable to air
suck at earth   suck at air
leaves map and multiply

driving down Notre Dame
northward   westward
leaving the city
knowing why we are here
not where we are going
I picked you up at the church
the church behind us ringing yet with your voice

then after the guise of it
the trick of the register
the clerk tired
tossing the key on the desk with an empty ring
our reflection
whorls in the square scarred mirror
above the fire alarm

after that the white sunwashed room
your green dress slipped lightly
our unpeeling
the casual urgency of
our fumblings/my rising
cool flesh mouths tongues
the sweet sour taste of you
words spilled in embrace
the suck of that sunshine
stunned/stung
we are falling
I am drawn into you
lost in you
          it is October
                    we flower into winter

5

red light/green light:
the binary static of poles
ion electron neutron proton
caught in their web of electrical dance
the casual symmetry
of instantaneous flow
this into that
time is mutation
attraction/repulsion
shape is a gesture
now into then
(a scar on the cosmos
no more)

in my house we come and go
orbit the empty living room
awaiting its rug and drapes

independent as stars
our children touch us at edges
tangents to our circling
we meet in the mornings
stains on the red table cloth
shift us farther apart

then
and it might have been yesterday
we waltzed until four in the morning
Tommy Edwards scratching on the phonograph
please love me forever[24]
until we were covered
with sweat and perfume
our clothes sticking to us
so that we slowly peeled them off
slowly made love
slowly

now
the static of your comb
crackles in the brittle air

6

systems

the neutral distillations of decay
slow fire in the heart of rocks
wet burning in the trunks of dying trees
each to its elements
phosphorous nitrogen carbon from clay
split/shattered
one tick
of the entropy clock
the dying of desire
when everything is on fire

your voice across the table in the bar
is flat and hard
this is the way it ends
you say
going on forever
and I hear my own voice rising
hollow in its practised
rhythms of regret
my hand butting a cigarette
waving to the waitress
for another double scotch
my daughter's letter in my pocket
Daddy please come home
like acid working on the hardest stone

7

free fall
the heart's trajectory
random coordinates
describe
the mind's parabolas of intent
the angle of descent
the half-
life of loss

I say too much
more than I need
and the rental agent's blank sympathy
tarnishes my despair
sometimes it's for the best
the apartment's polar emptiness
the blank waste of rugs
the barren sweep of wall
are like the pain that hangs
an odour in the hall

the view is fine
a frozen river
circling through the frozen city
in a prairie winter

8

all the permutations of despair
along the axis of event
death by drowning
death by traffic accident
death by gunshot
death by disease
death by deception
death by decay
death by the slow
inertial circling of the clock

here from my bed
on the fourth floor of the Lakeshore Towers
I can see the lights of cars
circling the perimeter highway
appearing out of nowhere
and vanishing into night
my life half over
poised on the fulcrum of descent
I lie on my mattress
on the floor
in a room without furniture
paintings haphazard
on the hooks of former tenants
my books in boxes
filled with lies
about beginnings and endings

Section III

1

It isn't the shape:
strawberries on a bed of clay
poplar roots against an eroding shore.
Or even the texture: bark
peeling from a birch
women weeping at a funeral
a hawk circling in the high
sky over a marsh.
It isn't the colour: dun horses
against a stubble field
wet stones at the edge of a lake.
Or even the scent of hay
rotting in a field flooded
by June rains.

It is the hold the mind takes
on these things:
the green of July   yellow of August
ochre of a September day.
Not rain but the slope of rain
not snow but the curve of drifting fields
fluttering whiteness of December
like the unexpected sharpness
of mint   childhood
and a fire when it's
much too late.

2

It isn't the shape:
strawberries yellowing into red
against a bed of clay
in my grandmother's garden
between the spruces and the lilac bush.
Not poplar roots white and naked
swirling in the spring flood on Willow Creek.[25]
Or even the texture: bark
peeling from the birch
beside the chicken house
women wailing at Tony's mother's funeral
laughter and drinking in the yard
and three old women in the parlour
framing our grief in one communal cry.
It's not a hawk circling in the high
sky over the marsh
that stretched behind our house
all the way to the south point.
It isn't the colour: Minnie and Betty
dappled grey against a stubble field
as I raked the flax straw
on a misty October morning.
Or even the musty smell of hay
rotting in the north pasture flooded
by June rains.

It is the hold the mind takes
on these things:
the green of July   yellow of August
ochre of a September day.
Not rain but the slope of rain
not snow but the curve of drifting fields
fluttering whiteness of December
like the unexpected sharpness
of mint   childhood
and a fire when it's
much too late.

3

Strawberries are yellowing into red
in a bed of clay in my grandmother's garden
between the spruces by the railway fence
and the row of lilacs
at the edge of the lawn.
My grandmother is watering her peonies.
I want a strawberry
but they are not ripe.
I know how they will taste
warm and sweet
with a hint of bitterness
but they are not ripe.
My grandmother reaches into her apron
and gives me a mint   brown
because it was in her apron pocket.
My mouth
which should have been warm and sweet from strawberries
is clean and cold.
Later
when my grandmother has gone
I eat a strawberry but it is not ripe.

4

In 1950
the year my cousin Brett was born
the spring thaw crested on the sixth of May.
Then Willow Creek became a river
and the muddy water from the ridge five miles away
tumbled and swept out bridges.
The fish are running
Charley[26] said
and so we made a scoop from chicken wire
poising it over the culvert
that remained although the road was gone.
A poplar on the far bank of the creek
leaned to the centre
its white and naked roots dangling in the water
creatures from underground   angling
for Jackfish and Suckers.[27]
We caught three hundred pounds of fish that day
and people came from miles around
wondering at our scoop
and the green and silver Jacks
and Dr. Johnson came
to tell my uncle that he had another son
and stayed to try the scoop
flipping the fish up on the melting bank
until the nurse came
and he had to go.

5

It was my cousin Len who killed the chickens.
Jerry[28] and I caught them
diving into the squawking mass
grabbing the rough and horny legs
folding the heads under their wings

so that they didn't flop and get away.
We put them into empty short sacks
three chickens to a sack
and Len swung the sack   beating
it on the concrete door stoop.
Then the next sack
and the next
until the mound of white bodies
chilled us and we ran.
I hid behind the birch
in the bush behind the chickenhouse
running my cheek against the smooth white bark
thinking of the dead white chickens
thinking of mother and her pails of grain.

6

The yard around the old grey farmhouse
is full of people. In the kitchen
there is homebrew and government whiskey.
The cases of Blue are piled by the door
and a washtub with water and ice
is under the ash beside the summer house.
In the parlour
Tony's mother lies in her coffin.
I have parked the Pontiac
next to the priest's red and black Impala.
I am led by Billy
to the door of the parlour.
Inside three women rage and mourn
framing their grief in one communal cry.
Tony's mother lies stiffly in her coffin.
Her flesh has turned to paraffin
and she is not anyone I know.
Outside
I take a Blue from the washtub.

The label is slimy in my hands.
I pull it off and throw it on the grass.
Now the priest is singing the litany
his voice curving and rising
dipping and falling   merging
with the laughter in the yard.
Tony stands beside me under the ash
and says *It isn't grief.*
It isn't anything.

Later
the priest and the women from the parlour
stand beside the Impala.
They are laughing
and the priest strokes the youngest woman's arm
strokes the smooth body of his car.
In the house there are new mourners
and their wailing rises
and falls between the laughter on the lawn.
Tony's mother is in her coffin.
She is made of wax.

7

Behind our house on highway nine
the marshes stretch all the way to the south point.
The muskrat house on which I sit is at the far edge
near the lagoon. Our house
white against the dark
line of trees
is the only human thing in sight.
I am in love
so I have unloaded my twenty gauge
and the small tight flocks of teals
the heavier mallards
are safe from me.

A hawk is circling in the high
sky above me.
The girl I love is in Sam's cafe in town
serving chips and gravy to my friends
putting her quarters in the jukebox
to hear Elvis' Love Me Tender one more time.
I want to be there
but I am in the marshes
sitting on a muskrat house.
A hawk is circling overhead.

8

I am raking flax on an October morning
heavy with mist.
The wheels rattle and clang
the tines ring like bells when they hit stones.
The flax straw is thicker than any hay
and I have hit the trip lever
till my leg is sore.
Minnie plods on
the sweat around her collar
turning her grey to yellow. She stops to piss
and the yellow shower is hot
and acrid in the damp October air.
It splashes off the singletree
and onto my rubber boots.
Jerry is on the good rake
following down the windrows
bucking the straw into piles for the sweep.
Beyond him
the Farmall[29] drones bright red
against the yellow ochre poplar leaves
the black and white of trunks.

9

The day you left was far too fine
for such a parting.
We sat at the edge of the water
out at Black Rock bay
the sun hot on our bodies.
The water was high that summer
and the fishing skiffs cut through the passage
on the near side of the buoy.
We were in the willows
leaning against the twisted roots.
You explained your leaving
but I don't remember the words
only that your voice and the lapping of the water
were the same. The wet stones red and yellow
blue and grey are all the reason I remember.
I went back there this summer with my camera.
The water was high again
so I took a picture of the stones.
It is an abstract painting.

10

When I was twelve
I fetched the cattle every morning
walking out to the north pasture
to bring them in for milking.
We had cut the hay early that year
but every day in June
rain slanted from the east
and so we gave up on the hay
turning the cattle loose.
All those still mornings
I walked through Paul's bush to the pasture
in an ecstasy of fear.

I was there when they found the body.
For three days the skiffs had circled the dock
trailing their hooks   fishermen
hoping for no catch.
I was on my way to a movie.
I stopped at the dock only to watch them drag.
When Red Walker[30] pulled Rollie from the water
and threw him on the dock
bloated and stiff   I couldn't run
but had to stay and memorize
the curve of his back
the angle of his arms and legs.

When I got beyond Paul's bush
the smell of rotting hay
meant the safety of the cattle
and I drove them home.

11

At the end of April
when the ice breaks from the lake
my grandfather burns the marshes.
With a can of gasoline and his torch
he walks the edge of the lagoon
touching the dried reeds and rushes into life.
He starts late in the afternoon
so that when he is done
the horizon is a line of fire
against the darkness of the night.
Each year
the fires dwindle
and go out before it's dawn.
One year the fire did not stop
but circled our house
so we had to go out with wet sacks

beating at the flames.
We saved the house
then looked to Old Arni's shack
a half a mile away
where flames still leaped and danced.
We tried to help him
the old man blind and crying
but it was much too late.

It is the hold the mind takes on things
green of July   yellow of August   ochre of September
not rain but the slope of rain
not snow but the curve of drifted fields
whiteness of December
the unexpected sharpness of mint
childhood and a fire
when it's much too late.

Section IV[31]

Out of the mind's turning, the body's loss, time and the objects of desire.

Out of a vision of fields

thornberry   roses by the sides of roads
blackberry
                        a fine finish
chokecherry
pincherry   marsh burning

On the second of May, 1958, I caught my thumb in the door of my father's new Pontiac Parisienne. After about ten days the nail came off, by which time it was badly swollen and blue. When the nail grew back, it wasn't right. There was a bump on it, and there still is.

Out of the moon's perfection

cranberry nectar of the honeysuckle
sandcherry
the blue patina
hawthorn
elderberry grackles nesting in the dead tree

Later that night she came back to the cabin and told me she was sorry. I was still angry, so we walked along the beach up to the point and back. The waves were really big so I rolled up my jeans, but I got soaked anyway. We went back to the cabin and made love. We decided it would be best just not to talk about it anymore. Those were the good times.

Out of the sway, the branching of trees

raspberry marsh marigold
strawberry
reflection on water
gooseberry
hawberry flickers by the barbed-wire fence

We'd spent the whole day dragging a magnet over the bottom of the bay trying to find the guns but it was no use. So Willie took us in his boat over to the island. It was just about dark, and I shot two ducks with one shot, only one of them turned out to be a crow duck and so no use after all. I stepped in a hole and filled up my chestwaders so I could hardly walk. Then we couldn't find Willie with the boat and had to walk all the way back the long way. I've never been so tired.

Out of the crow's call

poplar
oak
ash
spruce

fireweed in the burnt swamp

scales on a goldeye[32]

grebes, dancing

I probably shouldn't tell you this, but I was there in the park and saw you and Inga doing it standing up against a tree. Me and big Ed had bought a mickey from the taxidriver and were drinking it out behind the swings. Inga was crying, I think. That was a long time ago and I guess it doesn't matter no more.

Out of the green curl of leaves

elm
maple
cottonwood
birch

cabbage butterflies on a white stalk

a sense of loss

spears of willow leaf

Jerry and me found an old duckboat by the edge of the lagoon. We stole one of Dad's old fishnets from the basement and poled the boat out to the edge of the ice. We set it and next day when we came back we had a batch of pickerel, but what was horrible, about half way down the net we'd caught a merganser. It was all tangled up and could barely get its head out of water. I tried to untangle it but it bit me, and so I killed it with the two by four we were using as an oar. A little further along I saw the biggest fish I've ever seen, caught by only one strand. I reached over and grabbed it under the belly and heaved it into the boat. It was a big Jackfish, fourteen pounds when Grandpa weighed it afterward and it nearly upset the boat, thrashing around. I was really excited, and I've never forgotten it since. Funny though, that merganser somehow ruined everything. It would've been perfect if it wasn't for that goddam merganser.

Out of the crescent moon

green willow wild ferns in the marshy bush
red willow
a growing desire
plum tree
crabapple caterpillars on the underside of leaves

We were just leaving the pavilion, Marilyn and me, when the fight started. Marilyn was mad because I'd left her there alone and gone and had a beer out in the car with Charley. Anyway, this little guy was trying to start a fight with a big guy. The big guy didn't want any of it, and he kept backing up, saying, "I don't want to fight." The little guy kept calling him a coward, and finally he got so mad he grabbed the big guy and tore his shirt right off him. The big guy just stood there for a minute, then he grabbed the little guy and hit him about six times in the face. The little guy just crumpled to the ground with blood all over him and his teeth all broken. Then the big guy leaned over him and tore his shirt off and walked back into the dance. They were both airmen I think. Marilyn said it was a horrible thing, but she was really excited and couldn't talk about anything else for the rest of the night. I guess maybe she'd have stayed with me if I'd fought somebody, but there never seemed to be any chance, and I never liked fighting, not even with my brothers.

Out of fire, late fall

cat fish ladybugs on the boat's deck
pickerel
looking through cracked glass
sauger
perch broken reeds in still water

About a week after the accident she was still crying. She told me that she'd been seeing Jim when I was away. I told her she could get the hell out and go cry on his grave. That was kind of cruel I guess.

Out of the north wind, high water

bullhead
ladyslippers
carp
seen through a heavy mist
sucker
jack
spruceneedles

We'd blocked all the holes in the centre section of the chickenhouse and me, Jerry and Charley each had a pitchfork. We pulled over the grainbin, and suddenly the place was swarming with rats, big ones, about a foot long. Jerry screamed and stabbed himself in the foot trying to kill a rat that ran up his leg. I used my fork like a golf club and smashed them into walls. Charley stabbed them. After, we counted them and there were ninety-six dead rats.

Out of drifting snow

sunfish
sprucegum, yellow and cracked
goldeye
falling, falling
mooneye
pike
gold eyes in the headlights

I never told this story before. Me and Jerry had gone looking for crayfish along Willow Creek. About a mile west of highway eight where the creek makes that hairpin bend we saw an old lady sitting in the mud by the edge of the water. She had no shoes on, and her face and hair were all covered with blood. She was crying with loud bawling moans, just screaming, there in the middle of nowhere. I guess we should have asked her what was wrong, but we were so scared we just ran home. I guess she must have been o.k. though. I never heard of no old lady dying on Willow Creek.

Out of the islands

burdock green ferns in the north bush
chickweed
as if under water
mustard
mint wolfwillow

One time I met this girl named Angela at a dance at Crabby Steve's barn.[33] That was the time the police caught me and Tony with illegal liquor in the car, and Tony's brother Billy said it was his and paid the fine. I danced a couple of times with her, then asked her if I could drive her home. We made love about three times in the back seat of the car right in the driveway to her Dad's farm. It was getting bright already when she said she had to go in. I asked her if I could take her out on Saturday. She said no, cause she was getting married on Saturday. I think about that quite a lot.

Out of the cry of geese

sowthistle dragonflies in the hot field
foxtail
all along the edge
dandelion
dock bats in the early dark

I've been there, and I wouldn't go back if you paid me.

Out of waking, dreaming

sumac
cedar
balsam
fir

white band of a marsh hawk

scum on swamp water

bees on the rotting plums

I just turned over an old sheet of plywood out east of the farm and there were these tiny red ants fighting with great big white maggots. The ants were trying to pick up the maggots and carry them off. The maggots squirmed and rolled around, and funny, ugly, blind and white as they were, they kept breaking the ants' backs as they flipped. I watched for about two hours, and when it was all over the ants were dead and most of the maggots too. But the maggots won. Think about that.

Out of sheet lightning, east of home

juniper
hazelnut
lamb's quarter
mustard

the calf's carcass, rotting on the manure pile

a quick glance

slippery timbers of the old dock

I was about eight and Jerry was six when we found the old yellow dog in the spruce bush. We followed her and found a brush pile with eight puppies. We went there every day and played with them but we didn't tell anybody because we already had two dogs and we thought Dad would kill them. One day though when they got bigger they all followed us home, eight puppies and the yellow bitch. We were pretty worried, but Dad just gave them away to farmers. I don't think I was ever happier.

Out of the breaking waves, late afternoon

hollyhock   wrens in the maple
goldenrod
                    sweet as the new mown hay
sweet pea
sowthistle   killdeers, their morning cry

I was inside reading when Jerry came running in white as a sheet and told me I'd have to go out and kill the rabbit. He shot it with his slingshot, he said, and it was crying just like a baby. It was too when I got to the other side of the south bush where it was lying. It was spring and everything brown but the rabbit was still white. I grabbed it by the back feet and whapped its head against a birch. It wouldn't die, but just kept crying. I must have hit it fifty times against that tree till it was covered with blood and I was covered with blood, and the rabbit didn't have a head anymore. Jerry was always a better shot than me, but I was better at killing things.

Out of the hawk's flight

fishflies   yellowheads on the fenceposts
bullflies
                    putting an end to it
deerflies
blackflies   green slime on the drainage ditch

You remember Carla old Joe Wilson's daughter the one that married the airman. I used to sit behind her in school. She got killed in a car crash out at the coast. I was really sorry to hear that because I liked her a lot. Once we got stuck out near Fraserwood in a bad storm and had to spend the whole night in the car. I hardly even knew her then but we had to neck all night just to keep warm. That's true.

Out of the drifting clouds, slanting rain

wheat — terns intent in their concentrated flight
barley
— at a distance
rapeseed
rye — cobwebs thick in the sweltering bush

Dad was firing before I was even out of the car. I saw the doe collapse in sections falling first to her front knees then the back and finally toppling sideways. The buck broke fast and I missed with the first two shots. The third caught him in the heart, low behind the front legs. He spun forward, pinwheeling, slowly circling in the frozen air. They were both dead when we got there and I gutted them quickly. Children from a school bus waved to us.

Out of the black spruce

sweet pea — sheen of silver on wet morning grass
pansy
— holding back
iris
phlox — redwing blackbird on a cattail stalk

Of course he was o.k., he was always o.k. But that one night when he was caught out on the lake in a storm Mom was really worried. It turned out that his outboard had broken down and he'd had to row back and I guess he just about did drown fishing all those years and never able to swim. Anyway, what I remember is that Mom kept the back door open and we all looked out into the pitch black, waiting for him. The crazy thing is, we weren't even on the lake, we were looking out over the field to the bush. There was nothing there to see.

Out of the grass road

clover   swarm of bees on the tarpaper shack
alfalfa
                hands grasped, holding
timothy
brome   milkweed out by devil's curve

I waited for her by the highway all afternoon in the blazing sun, then all evening by myself, not knowing what to do. Now I don't wait for nobody any more.

Out of the black sheen of a crow's wings, purple on the head of a grackle, low mist over October fields, out of the mind's bent, the twisted shapes of memory and desire. Out of the word's glow, the word's flowering, the word taking on the world's shape the mind's shape, out of desire and loss, out of entry and withdrawal, out of the surfaces of things, out of the surrounding air, out of the brightening, the fading, the collapsing words

name them
marsh hawk
marigold
winter
crow
raspberry
willow
elm oak ash
every word a world

every world a gathering of words, out of the neural traceways of the brain, out of the banks of memory, out of cliff swallows gathering by the water's edge, out of gulls shrieking, the hawk's tearing, the ripped entrails, out of all the lost worlds the lost words

say it and make it happen

we were walking in the water, knee deep, our jeans rolled up
it just fell and lay there at our feet
the sun that morning
later, when I thought it was all over
the birch trees by the chicken house
Tony's mother's coffin
the first candle
claws

a thousand stories wound around
the coil of letters in a single word

the word angling for desire, drawing
memory out of the brain's random electricity, out of the blood's plasma, the heart's erratic pump, out of white chickens dead on the chickenhouse floor, out of horses plowing in October, out of fire, out of the named things, the lettered words, the alphabet of need

abcdefghijklmnopqrstuvwxyz

all that is required
for the invention, the making, the doing, all that is required for ecstasy and loss, all that was ever there, all that will be there, out of elm tree bark, out of willow roots in the swollen creek, out of the drifting snow, the slanting rain, out of the pregnant words heavy with desire

say them

Section V

Out of the mysteries, dreams

Out of an empty sky, thunder without a godhead, lightning that strikes although it isn't thrown. The ash beside my house rots, three years now without leaves. Trees die. Their slow decay is home to insects, home to birds, fuel for the whirling world. Roots huddle underground holding the spark that flowers forth in spring or else dies deep under frozen earth. We bury too deep, denying each corpse its vegetable renewal until it is leached by groundwater and seeks the surface.

Dreaming of smallpox

My darling Pheobe[34]

I am going to fulful my promis. That was as soon as I got back to Winnipeg. I was to write and tell you all I did during the winter. I left this Sunday the 26 of November—I got up to Gimli the next day—in the evening. Next Morning, I went over with Dr. Lynch—to visit the Hospital. It was full of patients, of course all with small pox. They were to be seen in every stage, some dieing—and some convalescents. The next day I went to visit several houses and such a sight you never saw—Every house had somebody down with the disease—The settlement extends about forty five Miles. And the houses were of the worst description. I had to stoop to go into nearly every house—There were some doors so low, that I had to go on my hands and knees to get in—And such filth. I cannot describe it—And fancy, I had to sleep in these wretched houses. I always slept with my clothes on so that I would not get lice on me. I wore a leather coat. The houses are all one room. And in some there would be 18 or 19 in them. they would all be huddled together like so many pigs—And then those houses that had room. they would have their cows in them—I had to sleep several times in the same house in which they had their cows at the other end of the room—in which I was sleeping—You can imagin that it would not smell very sweet—And one of the cows were neigh her accouchement—And the way she would grunt and groan. She would not let me sleep very much.

The baby is dead. Asdis is weeping and the cousins are huddled in the corner. Their scabs drip and they scratch and moan. I tell them not to scratch or they will leave scars. They tell me a corpse may have scars. The scent of death is everywhere, and now it is in my house. The baby is dead and now we know that we may die too. Asdis holds it to her breast and weeps. Let her weep. There is little enough left. Tomorrow I will put its body on the roof, out of the reach of wolves. I will make it a coffin with my own hands though there is little enough wood for the fire. A man may bury his dead.

Govt. House
Fort Garry, Manitoba
18th December 1876

Sir:

I have the honour to inform you that in consequence of the disease of smallpox being greatly and virulently prevalent in the Icelandic and Indian settlements on the west side of Lake Winnipeg it has been found expedient in order as much as possible to isolate and repress the spread of the pestilence to prohibit traffic southward eastward and westward of the line of demarcation shown in the accompanying map as well as communication with the area from northern posts.

It is also necessary that every effort should be made to suppress traffic and intercourse as much as is possible between the various bands of Indians and others who are within the limits therein described.

A copy of the proclamation of his Excellency, the Lieut. Governor and the act of the council of Kee-wa-tin relative to smallpox is herewith enclosed.

I am further to inform you that you have been appointed a Justice of the Peace for the district of Kee-wa-tin.

I have the honour to be
Sir
Your obedient servant

Frank G. Beechen
L.C.R.

We are coming back from a journey so horrible I cannot begin to tell you of it. Yesterday a police came to Gimli to get some men to help him go to an Indian settlement on the other side of the lake. Hannes and I said we would go with him. There are not many others well enough to travel. We left right away walking across the lake pulling some supplies on a small sleigh. It was dark when we got to the other side and the Indian settlement still some miles to the north. I thought we would be lost when the snow came in the afternoon but Hannes is always right for direction and we passed just to the north of Elk Island. We spent the night in a small tent and next morning early we got to the Indian settlement. There was no smoke from the shacks and nobody around. We went from shack to shack and in every one they were all dead. Dead women hugged dead children to their dead breasts. Men were dead sitting up holding dead children. Old women were dead with small scraps of food in their hands. There are some bodies tied in a tree near the camp. Except for that it looks as if everybody died at the same time. Sixty-five I think, though there may be more. We did not look under blankets after the first house. We lit a torch and one by one we burned all the shacks with the bodies in them. Now the police is ill and we must pull him back to Gimli on the sleigh. Hannes wants to stay another night, but I will go myself if he does. The police will be dead when we get there anyway.

Siri Bjarni came to preach this Sunday. He is a brave man, they say, risking the pestilence to bring us the word. My wife dead, my daughter dead, I asked him to leave his lord and pray for us to the god of smallpox.

For three months I did nothing but treat for small pox — so you can imagin that I have seen enough of it — When I went to some of the houses, I would find perhaps some six or eight sick, some that had only a few hours to live — You would see Old Men and woman, Young men and girls, and poor little infants that would make the hardest heart ache for them, and to see them at their Mother's breast and perhaps the next time I came around their little bodies would be put out side till they had time to make a rough box to bury them in. On my second trip I heard that there was a family on Big Black Island. So I went to see them. And such a sight. The Mother had just got over the small pox and her infant at her brest, dieing and they had not a thing to cover the poor thing — The house was so small that I could not stand up in it. I was compeled to sit down. I brought my tea and pemacan and me and my Indian guide had to have our dinner on that a lone — after a whole days travel — They had no flour infact, had nothing but fish — I left what medicine and nurishment I had — which I brought for the sick — and to see their eyes brighten up, to hopes that it came in time to save their little one can never be forgoten — But alas, the little thing only nine months old, died next day. And then they had to put the little thing on top of the house till they could get some boards to make a box for the little one — I had a pretty hard time myself, but when I looked at the poor Icelanders I faired like a King — Though I had to sleep on a bed made of hay — No body, but one that has a strong stomach could have eaten what I did this winter, unless they were the Icelanders themselves — In one house a woman asked me if I would have a cup of coffee. I said yes, as the day was cold, so while I was making up some medicine for a poor sick boy — What do you think I saw the woman do — She no doubt thought that the cup was not clean enough for me, so she licked the cup all around with her tongue and then took a towel as black as it could be — without it being a bit of black cloth and dryed with it, and then gave it to me to drink. A nice sight to see for a man that wanted a drink to warm him. I could tell you worse than this.

I could tell you worse. I could tell you of the first swelling on the child you love. I could tell you of a trip across the ocean, across miles of land by train, a trip down a river, and through a lake larger than a sea, a dream journey to a land of pestilence. I could tell you of nights so cold that nothing could make you warm, of insects and lice and illness. I could tell you all this and more.

Dreaming of boats

Sails sharp against the grey horizon. The whip of wind on my own sails, blur of rope grazing my cheek as the boat rolls and bucks in the surge and swell of waves. Then the dropped sails, sag of canvas wet and dark draped in the bow as I bend to the oars, finding the buoy. And the filigree of net, water stretched and dripping from the seines. The clatter of corks striking the gunwales as I draw the net across the boat. The luminescent green of pickerel, rainbows in the silver scales of goldeye, dark weight of suckers and catfish, the soft tumescent squeeze of marias, tulibees silver smallness, bump and protuberance of sturgeon, sticky yellowness and spines of bullheads, the silver platter flatness of sunfish, jackfish with their prehistoric heads, my net draws them up aghast in the open air where I catch them, twist them free and flip them into the fishbox on the floor.

The Goldfield heaves and plows in a heavy rolling sea, the Hecla reef off to our left and the Narrows straight ahead. The steady throb of the motors enters through my bones, charges the air around me. We plunge under crests of waves, shattering the shape of the lake, laying a furrow of tamed turbulence in our wake. Rounding Anderson point and Kristjanson's camp we wave to the tiny figures reeling the nets to dry on the shore at the edge of Grindstone, the water calmer now as we enter the mouth of Washow Bay in the lee of Beaver point. The Goldfield's motors cough like a missed heartbeat and that second's hesitation releases my body's panic. At the Narrows the current surges the wrong way, fueled by a three-day blow from the north. The Goldfield pitches and fights, flounders and recovers. Forty-five gallon drums bump together like thunder under the deck. The smell of bluestone is sharp and sour in the sodden air. Ahead, Black Island lies like a low menace on the lake. We nuzzle the pier and the Goldfield chokes and dies. Three days' journey in a single day.

Dreams of drowning

Always the water parting as I enter, the ease of moving downward into it. Always the struggle, the gasping for breath. Always the sense of peace, the drifting like seaweed, moving through a green world, the bob and surge of death deep under weather, the listless languid dancing of the drowned.

In my dreams I am pitched from my boat. I lean too far over, grasping for my nets or my foot slips as I walk on the gunwale of my boat. Sometimes the swell of waves rolls the boat so it is swamped and I am swept away.

Sometimes I fall from the dock, or a board gives way and I tumble through. Sometimes a rope twists around my foot and I am hauled away by a boat, nobody noticing.

Sometimes the water comes to claim me. I am camped on a beach, but the lake rises quickly, the land disappears. I clamber for higher ground, but it is too late, too late.

Sometimes I walk into the water, deeper and deeper, till I can no longer touch, and I am whirled away.

Sometimes the ice fails. I am walking over spring ice and suddenly it gives way. The water shocks me, chills and numbs.

Sometimes there is no event. I am only in the water, drowning.

Description of a body found by Edward Smith in Lake Winnipeg south of Willow Harbour on the 1th of July, 1878.

The body is of a man about 5 feet 6 inches. It was very much disfigured and swollen; the hair and beard, which seem to have been light or red was almost entirely fallen off. The body was dressed in a suit of fine black cloth, cotton undershirt & drawers and striped flannel overshirt; white woolen socks and moccasins: black silk necktie and striped linen collar. In the breast pocket of his coat was found a passbook with some writing in, a Map of the North West Territory and a letter, showing that the name of the deceased had been Charles Funck. In the inside vestpocket were $56.00, in four dollar bills: in the pantspocket a purse containing $1.75 in Canadian silver and a ring with stone in.

The body was examined by twelve persons and the verdict given by them was: Found dead in Lake Winnipeg.

E. Fridricksson

foreman of the examiners

Gimli July 3th 1878

Dreaming of birds

September 11. A fine day, warm and sunny with a wind from the south. Towards evening a few clouds. The women have cleaned the last of the birds and will do them tomorrow. They came toward evening, darkening the sky, thousands and thousands of wild chickens. They landed in the trees so thick that they broke branches and tumbled down. At dark, we went out with sticks and killed the birds sleeping in the lower branches. The children ran behind with sacks, collecting the birds and taking them to the women who skinned and cleaned them. At first they tried to pluck them, but the skin is too fine. It breaks when you tug at the feathers. We will have eight barrels for the winter. If the birds are here again tomorrow, we will have more. Still no word from Charley who should have brought word of the inheritance. Perhaps it is all a dream.

white geese rising from a field of summer snow
leaving it fallow   their crazed crackling
lingers after they have flown   mad blackbirds
flash red chevrons crying *kyrie eleison*[35]
a sloughpump gurgles in a shallow swamp
overhead sandpipers whimper and wheel
snipes whistle in their sudden dives
ducks croak and call   splashing in stagnant
sloughs smoke hovers on the spare horizon
sparrows twitter in the reeds   flit
from willows to weeds   a hawk drifts
silent in the sullen sky   above the margins
of the marsh   the raucous cry of crows
that follow   black in their rising

Dreaming of rainbows

I am not myself today. Children are playing near the boats that have to be unloaded, and there is always the chance that one of them will drown. The fishermen are annoyed because I have ordered that the boats may not be unloaded while the children are near the loading dock. I am swimming with the children, the water cool and green on my naked skin, the rough planking on the dock warm to my feet. From my office window, I can see Dori and Haldur chasing after the children, their oilskins oddly dull in the bright sunshine. I have boats to unload, and the children are like a burr in my stockings, standing between me and my work and cold beer. My oilskins squeak as I chase after the squealing boys. From the gutting shed next to my office, I can hear the singsong rhythm of women's voices, the click and scrape of their knives as they fillet. My knife touches the soft belly, finds the spot below the two bottom fins and slides in to the bone. Then a sharp snap and twist of the knife and the pickerel is headless. I slide it down the table, and my left hand has already picked the next fish. The cracked glass in my office window casts a rainbow on the white paper of the orders pinned to the door. Perhaps I will leave the work to Siggi and go home to the house of my dead wife and my vanished children and lie in the cool of my white sheets. I am not myself.

out of a black sky
the rainbow touches down
just beyond the ash tree
where the ravens gather
the sun low in the west
slants gold on every
tree leaf blade of grass
rain in a fine mist
blurs the edges
so that I blink
and rub my eyes
startled by thunder
the dog is frightened
but I rub his head

and pretend there are sheep
sending him in excited circles
a beetle glistens on the potatoes
in the garden where I stand
we need this rain
today every living thing
may live   tomorrow
I will tend my garden

Dreaming of love

Dear Tommi

We've been a month at the camp now. Halli goes to Gimli with the dogs for more supplies and takes our letters with him. Twenty years in this country and still I can't believe it. Who in Reykjavik could believe this winter? When I tell Rikka that it is fifty below she writes back and asks me if that is cold. The snow is right over the top of the camp and we must shovel it off the roof nearly every day or water drips over everything then freezes at night.

Could you send me some mitts? The Indians had no mitts so I had to give them mine and now I have only one pair. Give them to Halli before he goes back.

The new cook is wonderful. Even an Icelander gets sick of fish sometime but somehow she makes it always good. This might be the first season I come back fatter than when I left. Her name is Runa and she was married to Steini boatbuilder from Big Island before she left him three years ago to be a cook. Now she won't go back. He was a pig and used to beat her.

Anyway, Einar and me had a fight and don't talk anymore. He grabbed Runa and when I made him stop he fought me. I think my nose is broken so I am not so pretty anymore. Its not so bad not talking but I miss the chess.

Anyway, Runa will come to live in my house when we come back in the spring, so if you could make the twins ready for it, that would help me. Maybe Sybil could talk to them.

Valdi[36]

these are my fields
from where the black
spruces stretch to where
the marsh begins   this
is my house built
out of last years crop
those rafters will be a barn
this year or next
here there is room for a garden
I have two horses
three cows and seven sheep
and a skiff for the fishing
what I have is mine
I am a gentle man
drunk only twice a year
and stronger than most
a woman could do worse

Dreaming of objects

A wooden wheel, its spokes dried or decayed, half buried in the rotting leaves.

A tiny china cup and saucer, fat hand-painted children playing in a riot of roses, the glaze exquisitely cracked.

The remains of a Rumley tractor sunk halfway into earth behind the manure pile.

A wooden box with a glass front. Inside a white flower made from cloth. Perhaps a rose.

A broken gate, the hinges still working though the wooden bars are now broken, the latch gone. The fence it commanded gone too. Nothing to indicate the size and shape of the field it defended.

An iron dipper, rusted through.

Metal bars, their use beyond guessing.

A stuffed deer head, the skin rotted away leaving a mat of straw, a rough wooden block, antlers and two glass eyes.

A pile of rocks beside a field that is now so overgrown with poplar and spruce it is impossible to tell what was field, what bush.

Pressed flowers without colour, now like the dusty wings of dead moths.

Shards, fragments, detritus.

this has happened before
it will happen again
smallpox   death by drowning
death by fire
all the crackling static
of x-rays and electric
impulse   the shaggy
magnetic coating
of planets and stars
it has happened before
the courtly minuet of molecular motion
ecstatic electrons
bowing and swaying
their brownian ballet
turning and turning
and always returning to this
it will happen again
smallpox   love   death and decay

ways of ending

this is the end
the final tie
the line broken
the circle closed

invoke

all the miraculous molecules
knitting and un-
ravelling electricity
bathed in a sea of amino acids
nucleotides bending with the moon
blood and sap mingled on a cross
Fenrir
with the sun and the moon
in his belly
Odin and Thor
jostled by the random vectors of entropy
(a hard journey over snow
smallpox
scarring the moon
death by drowning
death by fire)

an ash tree rotting from within
a private place
waves
crashing on a sandy shore
(the quantum energy of love
its pulse)
down the dark stairs

(rain slanting from the east
the fabric torn)
fragments
of a vision
fragments of a life

---

1. Reprinted from *Marsh Burning* (Winnipeg: Turnstone Press, 1980).

David Arnason was born in 1940 at Gimli, Manitoba. He now teaches Canadian Literature and Creative Writing at the University of Manitoba.

2. Section I of "Marsh Burning" reveals the major protagonist viewing an entropic world in terms of Norse myth. The name "Thor" means roaring. Thor was the Norse god of thunder, of fertility and of the peasants. He was the rival of his father Odin.

3. The half-brother of Thor, Baldur was the god of sunlight, of life, of innocence and virtue. He was "The Good." In fact, Odin his father made all creation promise not to harm him. Only the mistletoe was not asked because of its insignificance.

4. Hecla is an island in Lake Winnipeg where Icelanders settled in the nineteenth century. It is also a volcano in Iceland often frequented by gods.

5. Loki was the brother of Odin and Hoener, with whom he made the world and the first people. He was a fire-demon and a thunder and lightning god, a Protean figure, and a trickster god. When you answer the telephone at 3:00 a.m. and there is silence on the other end, that is Loki. By directing blind Hoder's (dark winter's) hand holding the mistletoe-tipped arrow, he engineered the death of Baldur at the Winter Solstice and evil, darkness and winter overcame their contraries.

6. When the World Ash that supports heaven, hell and earth collapsed, Fenrir, the son of Loki and an enormous wolf and storm creature, swallowed the sun to bring about Ragnarök, the end of the world.

7. The Bay of Fundy separates Nova Scotia from New Brunswick.

8. Nidhogg was a dragon-like underworld symbol of decay. It fed on corpses and the roots of Yggdrasil, the World Ash, the Norse Tree of Life.

9. Four reindeer and Ratatosk (Rat-tooth) the squirrel gnawed at the branches of Yggdrasil as part of its inevitable tragic condition.

10. The Naashwaak is a river in Fredericton, New Brunswick, where Arnason lived for several years. Oman's Creek is located near Fredericton. It is *not* Omand's Creek in West Winnipeg.

11. Freya and her brother Frey are fertility divinities.

12. Odin was chief of all the gods. A Protean figure, he was a god of wisdom, fertility, love, poetry and even war. In return for wisdom he threw his eye into Memir's well. Accordingly, he was often depicted with one eye and a slouch hat. Nevertheless, he possessed insight into the past and future. He was also a messiah figure who hung for nine days annually on Yggdrasil.

13. In Norse myth, after Fenrir eats the rainbow bridge between the four kingdoms—those of humanity, of the gods, of the dwarves and of the Frost Giants—Ragnarök occurs. Here the rainbow bridge has collapsed and the four worlds are in chaos together.

14. Marysville is a suburb of Fredericton and Newcastle is a New Brunswick town close to the Atlantic.

15. Bognor Regis is a seaside town in the south of England.

16. After Ragnarök occurs, out of the final chaos arises an island with a great hall called Gimli where the best of the four other worlds and the best of those in hell will live. Only two of the gods will be good enough to live here. Gimli is also a town on Lake Winnipeg where Icelandic emigrants first settled.

17. Myollnir is Thor's hammer.

18. In June 1972 Hurricane Agnes devastated the east coast of North America, killing 134 people and causing three billion dollars in damage. Robert Kroetsch also speaks of Agnes in his journal entry for Friday, June 23, 1972. See "Towards an Essay: My Upstate New York Journals," *The Lovely Treachery of Words* (Toronto: Oxford University Press, 1989), p. 143.

19. In January of 1973, Helgafell, a volcano on the island of Heimaey, erupted and places as far away as New Brunswick were peppered with ash.

20. Vestmanaeyjar is a town on the island of Heimaey.

21. Dufresne is east of Winnipeg. We are proceeding west on Highway 1.

22. The Regency Towers was an apartment block in Winnipeg.

23. These anagrams for Saskatoon, Edmonton and Vancouver still exist on the ceiling of the Red Cross Blood Clinic at 226 Osborne Street North in Winnipeg. Section II clearly works with a much more natural system rather than with imported European myth.

24. During the 1960s Edwards' songs were waltz favourites at week-end dances in Manitoba, especially "Please Love Me Forever," "It's All in the Game" and "The Morning Side of the Mountain." Elvis Presley's "Love Me Tender" (p. 288) was another favourite.

25. Willow Creek is close to Gimli, Manitoba.

26. All the characters in the poem are fictitious, but some are clearly based on Arnason's relatives or friends. He does have an Uncle Charley. Here Arnason's persona attempts to impose meaning on reality by creating a system out of a personal past that is similar to that of the author himself.

27. Arnason is careful to use the Manitoba names for these fish. Americans and Europeans call jackfish "pike." When he does use the word pike later, he is referring to walleye pike.

28. Arnason has a brother Jerry and a cousin Len.

29. A Farmall is a type of tractor.

30. Red Walker was a well-known policeman in Gimli.

31. Section IV adds a strong geographical component to the personal mythology of Section III. Arnason is also attempting to voice the space near Gimli.

32. The goldeye is a small fish native to Manitoba and Saskatchewan and sometimes used as a Manitoba symbol. It is delicious smoked.

33. Crabby Steve's Barn is a dance hall near Fraserwood, west of Gimli.

34. In 1873 Mt. Hecla erupted in Iceland and covered miles of pastureland, driving Icelandic settlers to the Muskoka area of southern Ontario. However, by 1875, 285 members of this group moved to the western shore of Lake Winnipeg and in the following year the colony expanded to 1226. Without adequate capital to begin with, the Icelanders endured severe hardships, to say the least, particularly in the winter of 1876-77 when smallpox ravaged communities on the lake. The journey over the Atlantic, across Canada and up the Red River on flat-bottom boats, and the Icelanders' problems in adapting to the severe environment, are brilliantly and sensitively dealt with in Kristjana Gunnars' *Settlement Poems 1* (1980) and 2 (1980). Also see Arnason's and Michael Olito's *The Icelanders* (1981) and *People of the Interlake* (1986) by Andrew Blicq and Ken Gigliotti.

This letter (the remainder of which is on p. 305) and the next two can be found in the Manitoba Provincial Archives. Both refer to the smallpox epidemic on the lake during the winter of 1876-77. Here, in his attempt at mythmaking, the protagonist includes the past of his people, the Icelanders.

35. "Lord have mercy" is from the Roman Catholic Latin mass.

36. This letter is probably fictional rather than found. Voyaging along postmodern frontiers, the author is perhaps trying to blur fiction and history.

Calgary, this growing graveyard[1]

Aritha van Herk

QUADRANT ONE—STONES

From within the grave you can only leave into light

burst through dark soil

arrival the admission of belonging: here/there/within.

Or coming from.

Where is the world?

"If everybody stayed at home, they would be good people."
(Saint Joan via Shaw)[2]

So would she. You too.

And helicopters remind you of the ground they settle on,

the gerund they choose arriving or belonging, even leaving.

Leaving becomes an active grace, how it's done that is;

belonging only a question of luck, ladies in high slippers doling out cards.

Why go away when everything is here? decremental:

Canada, the west, prairie, Alberta, the south, Calgary
a house northwest, room, chair within the room, the molecules of breath
(an address)

Hemispheres and crumbling shores of rock

name us a place to stay and hope it's there when we turn around,
hope we're there when it turns around.

You learned one thing—settle under an escarpment, the omen of its
shoulder nudging up the sky,

you can afford to sleep
at night, in the day sit tight under its shadow

safety in that wedge of neck.

Found yourselves a Jericho, have you?

And the rest of the world has a sore throat.

Lucky for you Joshua's[3] moved east, he's whoring after strange
places too,
(the temptations of exile)

Keeps calling his travel agent and demanding another ticket.

You don't know how he gets through customs. *You* can't, not
without them tearing everything apart, accusing you of buying
new shoes. Your theory is they don't have enough to do,
they're so bored that even one planeload is a diversion.
"Let's see how these guys pack."
(On arrival)

Hermetics: the chambers of arrival.

And when you finally hit the air, no choice but to be drunk on the
altitude, that clichéd cerulean sky,
P.K. Page's rarified crystalline air.[4]
(She says it better than you do, but she doesn't have to live here)

Well, airports are graves
sounding chambers for the city as a unit of civilization.

Despite the coyote chasing a rabbit across runways
dodging jetstreams.

Hah.

It's been said before:
archeologies are (in)formed by those who (in)vent them.

Graves are for their visitors. Residents beware.

And stones will work their way to the surface, no matter how buried and buried again. Rocks clattered onto the stoneboat hot August afternoons out in the summerfallow behind your father's and brothers' overalled legs, the little ones were yours while they levered the heavy ones with a crowbar.

When you get old you get to carry the crowbar.
(You've got one now, in your garage, because it's a crowbar)

You carry stones home with you, the flutes of pebbles ground soft by tide, knife stones from the Indian quarry, you lay on your back to chip them from the roof. A small coffin that. The house is full of rocks shining in corners. Enough to cover a grave, and heaped up too.

Well yes, it's death that makes a place its own.

A city is counted for the people who die there and who stay, are buried. There aren't enough graveyards here, people go away to die, their bones too go elsewhere.

Calgary is a silent freight train carrying away long rows of boxcars neatly stacked with coffins.

Box cars? How do bodies move?

Plastic over a solemn grey coffin in the back of a Dan Dy Delivery pickup.[5]

A refrigerator car you suppose, but the CPR,
CPR, that's who does it, this is a CPR town, would've died otherwise.
"The greatest transportation company the world has ever known."
(E.A. Victor, Architect and Surveyor)

The CPR rails reached the east banks of the Bow River on August 9, 1883.

Forget freight rates,[6] that's another story.
(Don't get involved)

But yes, a place is counted for the people buried there. Joyce (James) in Zurich perched neatly in brass, so much himself between the sorted and arranged, that formational Swiss cemetery. Giving the lie to Dublin, to Trieste. Waiting for pilgrims.

No, not enough cemeteries here.

Although there are G/R/A/V/E/S on the first map, 1883, right beside the RC Mission.
(Section 10 just west of the Elbow, though later maps move the RCs east)

Graves elbowing each other awake, saying "move over." Marked on the maps an odd tinted green: Queens Park Cemetery, Burnsland Cemetery, Union Cemetery.

Cementery.[7] *Koimētērion.*[8]

Queens Park remote and placid above the city, high-sticking its way through Cambrian Heights. Heights for the depths, crematoriumed over the spread city. More a field than a cemetery, those acres of rough prairie grass cut into hay mows, grass edging over the stones flattened against the ground, ears back, names disappearing into the foxtail and broom. Taken over, named effacement—gophers and rabbits alert and unrestricted, the acres and acres of henges stoning themselves up the hills.
(no, coulees)

Acres yes, fields, even sections: you got lost in the rows of upright
headstones, thought you were going north when you were
really going east, gravity does that to you, loss of orientation in
the acres and acres rolling against Nose Creek[9] there in the
middle of split-level bungalows the cemetery partakes of
several coulees and a poplar bluff[10] creek, acres and acres of
prairie hay. Recorded history not in the austere and polite
markers (granite, sandstone, marble, fieldstone) but the
promise of names held and used and recorded:

Tickler/Jealous/Kwong/Dearness/Chan
Nowogrodski/Reizevoort/Kiss
Bitonti/de Champlain/Stipic
Taylor/Evans/Fuchs/Zwir/Koo
Lightbody

And the others, sliced by Macleod Trail[11] pushing itself souther and
souther, the rattle of motels and car-wash gaseries, car lots and
windowed food souther and souther even to the Ranchman's
Bar[12] smoky and rumbling pretending to cowboys
("Where the hell are we going?"),
souther and souther.
("Are we in Lethbridge yet?")

But yes, the city gets flatter and faster the souther and souther you
go. You're driving over graves, that's when you know you're
on the right trail,
graves.

And the Chinese graveyard delicate and moving, its enigmatic
calligraphy, Lee Yip (from Coaldale) all the homesick Chinese
gathered into this bird's nest of eternal poise, all the homesick
Chinese of southern Alberta buried high. And at night the
tombstones
(tablets)
lean against each other in the eerie spool of headlights
searching through their maze.
(Templecular)

But acres and acres, there are not enough cemeteries here. In the phone book they are discreet, public and private, a short listing with numbers to call for information who will have numbers to call for a list of names, alphabetical probably and with location. (Section One, Row M, plot eighteen)

They are under the auspices of City Parks and Recreation, no pun intended. The private ones offer comforting names
(Garden of Peace) (Memorial Gardens)
As if it wasn't gardens that got you into trouble in the first place.
Rows and rows, a garden.
(a place for growing)

And no mention of graveyards, that repository of the poor, a blank space between gravel and greenhouse, though both might be appropriate, connected. Columbarium[13] vaulting into heaven.

Of course, this is the sky of heaven, where it's kept in the meantime.

And the wind makes this a dusty city, your archeological longings flung into your eyes, induced tears.

Engravement then. The home of the spirit? To dare to stay here to die, to dare to stay after death, to implant yourself firmly and say, "Here I stay, let those who would look for a record come here." You want a death more exotic than it is, would choose repose in the arms of foreign grass, odd moles rather than gophers.

But the lengths of darkness measured metre for metre are shorter here and the pin-hole photography of death as immobilizing as east or west. The graveyards of Calgary are your grottos and even ashes scattered and unburied settle here with the mosquitoes and the rippled gusts of wind off the foothills.

To belong then. Leaving not here but
from here. Return implied.

Sounding chambers for the city as a unit of civilization.
Enclosured, focussed, a possible fortress in walls and tombs.

Choosing one or the other you stay. And in that staying you decide
that home is here and death too is allowed.

You dare to be buried here,
this Jericho revisited.

QUADRANT TWO—SOLVENCY

The declension of Calgary insists on money, although money rejects
declension.
(Banking on itself, receivable)

Abbatoirs and railway yards, oil offices.
(of course)

Not derricks and pipelines but the bureaus, departments of and
sections and divisions glued together in a scraper of intention,
the crooked teeth of tilted buildings harbouring ambition, short-
sightedness.

(Frac/tions)

And money's occupations live their own short-lived lives.

Abbatoirs have become Meatpackers and their offshoots, although
Slaughter Houses are delicately mentioned and re-named. Beef
Packers always specialists now generalized but the stockyards,
their high leathery smell all through the south east.
(Burns Avenue, of course the first millionaire)[14]

Effaced into the Stock Exchange, small as it is. Still,
despite unlisting, the stock yards retain their labyrinth, sprawl
over their own railway mesh bawling and dusty, a swarm of
hereford backs on weekdays, buyers and auctioneers
(many, many, as always)
converging on the high-slatted trucks that roll in from the south
and the east and the west.

Shoe leather. Tanneries have given way to tanning salons
(despite 2207 hours of shine per year)
and the hides of all the slaughtered animals are shipped away,
east. Their bones ground fertilizer. A different
coming to the garden, underground.

Ho, although undertakers have become funeral directors (and a good
many too) embalmers lost between elocution and embassies
(not one). Shall we presume there are none, that there is no
money in the business?
(of death)

But ah, blacksmiths there were (many) now only three, specializing
in jackhammer points, then in horses.

Horse Dealers then too (many) and still a few, but without the
personality, the checked jacket and rakish cap, the
trick with a foreleg and a burr.

Who hung around the shooting gallery (one), now obscured behind
some other muffled sound, distant thunder still hangs in quiet
evenings, despite the range, despite the earphones and the
cardboard men.

And Gun Shops thrive, their wares behind fly-blown windows.
(All Stories End)[15]

Galleries are otherwise, under art, the two artists proudly listed in
1910 are commercial and designer now, and follow
artificial limbs.

Scenic artists vanished utterly, scenes too.

And those cynical suspect a loss of purity, how barbers have become
hair stylists and boot blacks shoe shine agencies, haberdashers
lost themselves in department stores and hat reblockers (many)
become one hat renovator, who presumably rebuilds from the
skull up.

Dressmakers have altered themselves to designers, clothiers, tailors and fashion consultants. And somehow you are certain that this is no longer the safe occupation of mildewing maidens who stitch behind the safely drawn curtains waiting for spinsterhood to pass. Although gloves and mittens are the same. So much for everyday.

So much for everyday. Money talks.

What about the coffee roasters
(machines instead of persons)
the fire escape makers
(completely gone)

Bible depots
(proselytized)
the mince meat manufacturers, the oyster dealers
(prairie and pacific)
piano polishers
(with a soft cloth and a gleaming eye)
turkish baths, milk dealers???

Dealers in—an interrupted need, the needing service changed. Who can say which comes first, money or the source.

There will, it seems always be a call for billiards and dentists and collection agencies.

For interpreters and translators.
(although the one German translator in 1910 could hardly have credited the tongues unleashed now, would have opened an agency—gone crazy with delight in one word's inability to understand another)

There's money to be made. The new languages of the world call.

And laundries do their best to keep you clean; nurses keep you well; wedding cakes persist.

The quarries
(two, of sandstone, long used up and closed)
of money continue; and the once six surveyors have expanded all categories:
Aerial, Alberta, Construction, Inertial, Marine, Offshore, Seismic.
Surveyors and purveyors, a measuring and a counting, a weighing out.

As for pleasure, beyond the lost Turkish baths, the restaurants have always been Chinese; the theatres
(the Dreamland, the Empire, the Lyric, the Orpheum, the Princess, the Starland)
amalgamated filmic frames; the Orchestras and Bands
(the Calgary Coloured Quartette)
play on. Pleasure domes increase.

The boarding houses have all closed.

In this iconography of money, you are sharply divided. There are those who collect and those who will not, those who scorn to stoop for the quarter on the sidewalk and those who hoard, stuff mattresses.
(remember winter)

There are seasons of money, houses bought and sold and never lived in, land surveyed into inches, buildings flooring themselves into Babel.

Even when the cranes were abandoned and the vacant lots blew dust, the hoarding gaping and permanent, there was a season on money, that season when the secret hand writes a well-concealed cheque buying speculation and aspiration, banking on ugly phrases:

real estate market
retail space
oil and gas futures
for lease
the property of mercy

Like death, money leaves, pretends it never lived here, and the rusty
cranes and empty buildings fold and whisper on themselves, in
the rustling silence of Calgary's own seduction and
abandonment.

What's to be expected whoring after strange futures?

Still, beautiful enough for the next one to be caught, to hesitate and
wager this or that against the lure of profit.

Despite the office owners camped out on their unrented carpets,
the bath shops out of gold-plated faucets.

The declension of money is measurement.

How much/how long/how old/how big?

Your love of money is a frisson of pleasure to large-numbered years.
The celebration of invented anniversaries.

Economic intention signed sealed and delivered. Struck a deal.

All those Americans. Peter Prince and the Eau Claire and Bow River
Lumber Company.[16]
(1886)
American hill.

Obsessed with profession and ambition and not enough low-brow
back-sliding pleasure-taking pleasure.

Longing for Golden Fridays and the complimentary car, an in-car
phone, a pull-out couch. Eternal happy hours.

Grit-blown monoliths bounce measured hours of sunlight from
their golden glass and stand for death, another Stonehenge[17] in
haphazard phalanx between Bow River and CPR tracks
(compressed)
between two insoluble immovable configurations.

Hanging there, in their moments of aspiration, the cranes wait for
another boom to announce itself, another graveyard to rear
headstones.

QUADRANT THREE—DENIZEN

Habitué, hooked, a citizen of.

Within this enclosure
(Calgary)
the city a centre of spokes, empenned.

(What does home mean?)

(Where is it?)

Frequential, inhabiting.

Spearpoints found in plowed fields east of the city.
(12,000 years old)

Teepee rings, medicine wheels, effigies:[18]

Blackfoot
Sarcee
Stoney

Boucher de Niverville:[19] may have gone as far as Calgary
may have seen—
(1751)

David Thompson and Peter Fidler.[20] Then only the glacial valleys
and the foreland thrust sheets
(foothills)
predicating the Rockies.

Palliser.[21] Come and gone.

NWMP. Of course. Calgary no fur-trader's post but a mountie set-up.
(1875, F-troop)
And Brisebois with no leg to stand on and only Brisebois Drive left[22]
(not even a trail)
before Macleod and Hardisty.[23]

Desert nomads, transient denizens. Arriving and leaving,
citizens of their own rules:

Ex-mounties
Ex-speculators
Ex-Metis buffalo hunters
Ex-arrivals

Nomadic ranchers converging from the wide cattle-sweeping country around.

Not so smart either: in 1890 *everybody* failed the territorial university entrance exam.

And the first police chief
(couldn't compete with the NWMP)
rigged dice games and pocketed fines.[24]

Always boostermen, the ever proliferating real-estate outriders.

And someone is waiting to write a story about Calgary quarrymen, a particular quarryman covered in sandstone dust as the lead in this romantic sound *et lumière*.

Brothels to the east, up past Nose Creek.

Some Germans and Italians, more Chinese:
"the mongolians in our midst."
(an unspecified citizen)

Anglo-Saxon, English-speaking, Protestant.

Nobody famous.

But angular and affronted frame houses jutting roofs into the acrid sky.

And everywhere picket fences fencing out the prairie, fencing houses from themselves and each other, the neat divisions of denizens.

Home of chinooks.[25]
("disarming winter of its severity")
Erotic in intent.

("Blizzards are unknown.")
A lie, but there are always those who lie, continue to lie. Believe it, you say, blizzards are known and not only in the passive sense. The great snow of May, 1986, there were no tracks.

And yes, the denizens of this city, huddled in basement suites, climbing to apartments in the upper stories of large frame houses.

Declarations: bumper stickers and license plates.
(*I'd rather push this car a mile than buy from Petro Can*)[26]
(*You're ugly and your mother dresses you funny*)
You too.

ZZZAP. MBA.[27] The denizens of automobiles, grinding their teeth, whistling, moving their lips drive up and down the trails, back and forth from quadrant to quadrant, restless and moving, moving, the natives are restless, up over the coulees and down, west, west west west, to Banff and the mountains.

(Where does home mean?)

Begun by the oldest occupation, the nomadic herding of grazing animals. Ranchers unsettled, the cattle themselves moving, always moving, their cattle kingdom a transported and elegiac shuffle.

With the endless arrival of the CPR, a movement established and
ingrained. Restlessness, an historic restlessness, following the
backs of beasts. Sleep on the ground, move again in the
morning. This companion of settlement. Here, this place.

And the Sarcee woman in the Co-op store turning over running shoes
(related to Deerfoot)[28]
her hair knifing over her face. You edge past her, but
always want to touch that encarved posture:

She knows home better than you do, she knows where it is.

And the lanky man slouched down on his backbone in the Plaza,
sitting through the still ads for cultural artefacts, alone at the
end of an aisle and still there the next week, the next month,
endlessly watching moving movies of the world.

And the denizen who cannot help
(her) (him)
self, cannot resist rushing under the swift silence of the lrt
train,[29] surprised by the impact, that it can be so silent and still
so solid. Between platforms all movement is insubstantial, like
the river below bridges sitting still it is despite eroded banks.

And some cowboy singers wailing against clinked glasses, trying to
earn themselves another checkered shirt, and the best boots
made anywhere in the world.

(this is the truth):
boots.

"This is Ernest C. Manning and the Prophetic Bible Institute's Back
to the Bible Hour[30] coming to you from Calgary, Alberta, in the
foothills of the Canadian Rockies."
(You could hear his Capitals)

The horse on Eighth Avenue, paint flaking and chipped, a dead horse,
a dry wind, a quiet hockey player.

You fail to believe that others can see the passion within you.

You pretend not to see theirs.

Who dares to confess to feeling, to anger, to rage, to joy.
Not here.
Stay calm, keep moving, don't look up.

Above you hang the boomtown ghosts, half-finished buildings, struts and ceilings between gaping floors. The skeletons within your skins. You are those ghosts, construction and destruction, shareholders and mortgagees, full of sites and demolition.

Drink up.

"Picturesquely situated so as to be within easy reach of the brewery, Calgary extends right and left, north and south, up and down, in and out, expanding as she goes, swelling in her pride, puffing in her might, blowing in her majesty and revolving in eccentric orbits around a couple of dozen large bars which close promptly at 11:30 right or wrong."
(Bob Edwards)[31]

The York. The King Edward. The Alberta Hotel, the longest bar.[32]

Wait.

Brewing and malting.

Exporting dead meat.

Quarrying sandstone.

Right or wrong.

Transient: the nomadic legacy of the ranchers, east of the main north/south route of prehistoric man, balloons drift overhead.

Denizen: to live here you must move, although the stones command stillness, and the grass demands its own growing.

Home is a movement, a quick tug at itself and it packs up.

Call yourself a taxi and consult a map.

A blur.

And these discreet entities of movement are Calgary's denizens.

You do live here.

Habitants of a glass sky and cardboard mountains shining off stage, checking Nose Hill for the moisture levels and never daring to kiss. You may dance Electric Avenue, eat on the Stephen Avenue Mall, grow cabbages in your back yards, rent out your basements, buy kitchen slicers and suitcases.

Afraid to hang your masks on your walls, choose not to recognize moments of iconography: that you will probably stay here, die here, and perhaps even have yourselves buried.

QUADRANT FOUR—OUTSKIRTS OF OUTSKIRTS

Calgary as quadrant, the sweep of a long-armed compass quartering the city NW NE SE SW, segmented.[33]

Each quadrant leaks outward up the hills, along the coulees in a sprawl of roofs.

But the north side accidental, begun by squatters/the first wave immigrants, Germans and Italians, brothels to the east.

The REAL city south, inched its way southward, money and business moving down from the low and gravelled Bow. No designations needed there, neither SW or SE until years later, it was the north that needed division and indication, North beyond, over the river, squatters and whores.

The divisions/labyrinthine begun.

And when they talked "annex" NW kept at arm's length, safely out there.

Offered the streets names:

Aaron/Jacob/Joshua/
(him again)
Matthew/Mark/Luke/John/
Esther/Sarah/Moses/Mark/
Jeremiah

proper names of biblical intention, but subsumed
(1912)
by numbers, the sweet anonymity of 6th. Only Kensington left unnumbered and itself.

An acroustic[34] of place, 4th St. S.E. far away from 4th St. N.W. divided into quarters and beyond the quarters suburbs themselves divided and names picked up from the subdivisions.

There has to be a minotaur somewhere.

How to find yourself: see map.

A majority of roads are named by number.

Within the quadrantic network 14th Ave. N.W. will run east-west in the north west quadrant.

Where is home?

But from the outside, as early wo
(man)
a nomad wandering the prairie?

From Nightingale east, moving west toward only a cleft in the hills, no evidence of city. And the pretence of buildings a slight inflection that swells as the body moves. The mountains overweigh all and only when you dip south into the valley of the Bow the gaunt buildings appear, innocuous from this angle buried in themselves. And black. Unless you are at exactly the right hillcrest at dawn enigmatic and unreflective, none of the golden flash that you expect.

From High River south, the old 2A leading itself north into
appropriation, and the curve of double road that splits the
collective huddled suburbicarian purlieus, outskirts of outskirts
outskirted by those same foothills
(are we in Lethbridge yet?)
the overflung devouring edges stitching themselves into the
ground.

The ground, that yellow and black prairie ground between the
fingers crumbling and soft. The foothills/foreland thrust sheets.

And in your swing up through Millarville, Priddis, Bragg Creek and
Morley[35] the fortress begins to tower and sway, sown dragon's
teeth that have grown themselves into monoliths without the
sacred sites at their bases, without pictographs and secret
springs, and *Uluru*
(that red nose in the Australian desert)[36]
complete in their unscalability.

Except for the window washers
(of course)
Except for the falling accountants, except for the clefts and
ledges of hurt that have all been smoothed down, polished over
into a flat blank surface, refracting only itself. You too can
jump.

And from the
(north)
bush and parkland, Bashaw, Tees, Lacombe,
(who taught you to forget Siksika)
Olds and Didsbury and Carstairs a descent.[37]

That snaky arrival between the sexual clefts of the hills again
surprised at the arrogance of those other coulees brooding in on
themselves in a pretence at centre, an underground that repels.

Calgary is a place to run away from, although you claim to have run to it. And everyone claims to be from somewhere else, not here, no babies born in this city except reluctantly, extracted from their mothers' bodies in a storm of protest. Most children born in moving vehicles:

the C-train
buses
pickup trucks
(inevitable gun racks)
moving vans

An acroustic of place: If there were time to count muffler shops and Sleepeazy motels, faster and faster food and the secret motives of car dealerships
(pricing themselves on windshields)
you would never bc found. Again.

But there are labyrinths in the shopping malls, bubbles of light and air that claim closure, insist on wholeness and order, and you wandering, lost, cannot find the door you came in or any door at all and behind the shop window mannequins there is nothing: darkness, a bed, a small room full of stifled
whispers that pretend to be obscene.

Strip malls too: a dry cleaners, a Chinese restaurant, an uncrashed bank pasting themselves onto the crossword puzzle of street.

And behind their plate glass only darkness, a winnowed square of space that offers sleep and dreams, a queer fishbowl silence from the shrieking air outside.

You begin to look for lovers in these labyrinths of solar light.
In the secret floors of hotel rooms, hotels interlocked by Plus 15s,[38] ghostly vaginas:

In one green room you bathe together, splash each other.
In another you lie side by side, breathing gently.
You are seldom locked together, sex is too playful for Jericho
and two pieces of the puzzle might connect.

What would happen then—all the interlocking bridges
(Louise and Langevin)
(Louise should really be buried)
unnecessary
—all the trails
(Crowchild, Marquis de Lorne, Shaganappi, Deerfoot)[39]
overruled, all 3000 kilometres of paved road bypassed in a
flyover of lust, for once lust.

You need practice in the geography of lust.

You need to find lovers in used bookstores
take someone else's clothes from the cleaners
invade the bushes of Spruce Cliff.[40]

There are incipient connections between lonely watchers at the
Plaza and in the playgrounds bodies lying on their backs in the
grass. Snow bodies.

Freeways stop abruptly, refuse to handle themselves into the hills
farther than they are, abandonment in a fringe of crumbling
asphalt.

Plus 15s drop into space and connect nothing.

Paths lead a darkness of wooded coulee impossible to return from.

Mud rooms front the marble foyers of post-modern buildings,
log houses hewn into modern pretence a visceral cry against
glass.

Who can find you here, a clumsy bawling beast in the centre of a
web of thread, a cat's cradle of encapturement?

Located by confluence, the Bow and Elbow jointing themselves in
an impassable lock. Without their deliberated quadrant you
scramble in hollow streets and scanty hills, looking to the
escarpment above, the sharp edge of Shaganappi coulee cutting
off the mountains.

In the squats and dry electricity of basement flats where printmakers
select inks and artists draw faces
(faces of women looking sidelong at one another)
in the quarrels of the colleges and schools students foundering
into a sadly chosen ritual, there is still the labyrinth of stone.

The fossils of lost centuries embedded in walls, an
architect's drawing of place. Brachiopods shine through their
sealed surface, erypsids genuflect.[41]

You too sheathed in prehistoric stone, the gravestones of Jericho
before the walls tumble down.

Shout Calgary.

---

1. "Calgary, this growing graveyard" originally appeared in slightly different form in *NeWest Review*, Vol. 13, No. 4 (Dec. 1987), 5-11.

Aritha van Herk was born in 1954 in central Alberta and grew up on a farm near the village of Edberg. She currently teaches English and Creative Writing at the University of Calgary.

2. Van Herk is providing a précis of the passage in *Saint Joan* (1924) in which Joan, speaking of the English, says:

> God will be merciful to them; and they will act like His good children when they go back to the country He made for them, and made them for. I have heard the tales of the Black Prince. The moment he touched the soil of our country the devil entered into him and made him a black fiend. But at home, in the place made for him by God, he was good. It is always so. If I went into England against the will of God to conquer England, and tried to live there and speak its language, the devil would enter into me; and when I was old I should shudder to remember the wickednesses I did.

This allusion suggests that van Herk, like Robert Kroetsch and possibly Dennis Cooley, is playfully engaging in cultural warfare.

3. The children of Israel were promised by God that, under Joshua's leadership, they would overthrow the land of Jordan. Jericho was an impermeable city fortress, key citadel of the Jordan Valley. The children of Israel camped outside Jericho and every morning at dawn, for six days, led by priests blowing trumpets of rams' horns and the ark of the covenant, they circled the city. On the seventh day, they compassed the city seven times and when the priests blew the trumpets, they shouted a great shout, and the walls of the city fell down flat. See the Old Testament, Joshua VI. Calgary with its boom-and-bust pattern obviously resembles Jericho.

4. P.K. Page's poetry, especially her earlier work, is cerebral, cool, and possesses a peculiar purity. See for example "Photos of a Salt Mine" and "Images of Angels."

5. Dan Dy Delivery is the name of a delivery service.

6. Western farmers have always felt discriminated against by Ontario and Quebec because of the freight rate structure that makes them pay excessively—in their view—for transporting their grain.

7. Van Herk is engaging in verbal gymnastics here. Cementery is probably a combination of cemetery and cement.

8. The word cemetery comes from the Latin word *coemeterium* and the Greek word *koimētērion*. Both are probably derived from the Greek word *koimaein* which means "to put to sleep."

9. Nose Creek is a tributary of the Bow River. It still exists, but has been largely covered over and redirected.

10. Van Herk uses "bluff" in the prairie sense, to mean a clump of trees, not a promontory.

11. The Macleod Trail was an old cattle trail that is now a modern expressway.

12. The Ranchman's is a famous cowboy bar that is almost a Calgary landmark. It regularly brings in famous Country and Western singers, and it is especially active during the Calgary Stampede. It is not to be confused with the Ranchman's Club, which is the rich Calgary businessman's club.

13. A columbarium is both a pigeon house and a subterranean sepulchre with a niche in the wall for burial urns.

14. Arriving poor from Minnesota via Winnipeg in 1890, by 1902 Pat Burns had built a Calgary-based operation that dominated the meat industry in Western Canada.

15. All Stories End is the name of a gun store.

16. Peter Prince was one of the Canadian directors of this American-owned company, by 1891 the largest producer of lumber in the Northwest. He was also the founder of Calgary Water Power Company, the unreliable but dominant producer of power until 1905.

17. Stonehenge is a roughly circular series of stone monoliths, the origin and significance of which scholars are uncertain. They may have been contemporaneous with the Druids. They are often associated with sun-worship.

18. Teepee rings were formed by the stones used to anchor the flaps of a teepee. Medicine wheels were formed by a series of boulders placed in the shape of a spoked wheel. They appear to have had religious significance for the Plains Indians. Plains Indians such as the Blackfoot, Sarcee and Stoney often made effigies of animal spirits and even of people.

19. Joseph Claude Boucher, Chevalier de Niverville, was a soldier and explorer who co-led an expedition to the upper Saskatchewan River in 1750.

20. David Thompson was an explorer, fur trader and geographer who probably wintered near Calgary in 1787-88. Peter Fidler was chief surveyor and map-maker of the Hudson's Bay Company between 1796 and 1821. He mapped, in a general way, the Canadian West.

21. John Palliser was an explorer who visited the prairies and the Rockies between 1857 and 1860 to investigate the feasibility of farming the land and of building a trans-Canadian railway. The Palliser Hotel is named after him.

22. In September of 1875 a new N.W.M.P. post was established at the junction of the Bow and Elbow Rivers. The officer in charge, Inspector Ephrem A. Brisebois, named it Fort Brisebois. His superiors countermanded his indiscreet suggestion, the first in a series of events that resulted in his being removed from command of F. Troop by the following spring. The new post then became Fort Calgary, a name suggested by Colonel J.F. Macleod.

23. Richard Hardisty was appointed chief factor of the Hudson's Bay Company in 1875. He became the first Canadian Senator from the district of Alberta.

24. John Ingram was appointed the town's first chief constable in 1885. Such charges against both the city police and the N.W.M.P. were not uncommon during this period.

25. The chinook is a warm wind that comes off the Rocky Mountains in the winter. Within an hour it can produce a temperature change of as much as 20 to 30 degrees.

26. Petro-Can is a crown corporation established in 1975 by the Liberal government of Pierre Trudeau in an attempt to counter the rise in world oil prices and protect Canadian interests such as the security of supply and price. Of course, the interests of the federal government were not always perceived in Conservative Alberta as synonymous with its own, which were somewhat less defensive, to say the least, towards multi-national oil corporations. Many in the province of Alberta have bitterly opposed Petro-Can, as well as the National Energy Program, which was announced on October 28, 1980 and which expanded Petro-Can's role.

27. ZZZAP and MBA are personalized license plates.

28. Deerfoot was the name of an Indian who was particularly fleet of foot and who used to win all the foot races. Calgary has named the main freeway, an artery that goes right through the city, after him.

29. LRT train refers to the light rapid transit in Calgary.

30. Ernest C. Manning was Social Credit premier of Alberta from 1943 to 1968. A Baptist minister, he often spoke on the "Back to the Bible Hour" on the radio on Sunday mornings.

31. Bob Edwards was editor of the *Eyeopener* (1904-1922) and a social reformer. In often hilarious satire he railed against institutional insensitivity and arrogance, especially as manifested in brewers.

32. The Alberta Hotel was said to have the longest bar in Calgary. The Alberta Hotel Building, a beautiful sandstone structure, still stands, but it is no longer a hotel. It now contains commercial outlets.

33. In 1912 street names were changed and the grid system was adopted in all but a few cases.

34. Acroustic is probably a combination of acrostic and acoustic.

35. We are within 100 kilometres southwest of Calgary.

36. This is the aboriginal name for what was formerly called Ayer's Rock. Sacred to the aboriginal people, it was recently returned to them by the Australian government.

37. These places are all located near Highway 21 southeast of Edmonton on the way to Calgary.

38. Plus 15s are glass walkways connecting buildings in downtown Calgary. They are traditionally 15 feet above the street so they span the traffic below. It is said that one can walk 20 blocks downtown without going outside, by using the plus 15s.

39. These "trails" are now all expressways in Calgary.

40. Spruce Cliff is the name of a wooded cliff on the south side of the Bow River. It is famous as a place for misadventures, roaming kids and sexual encounters.

41. Brachiopods and erypsids are both mollusc fossils.